OH JOEY, JOEY!

MY LIFE IN FOOTBALL, BY JOEY JONES

OH JOEY, JOEY!

MY LIFE IN FOOTBALL, BY JOEY JONES

FOREWORD BY IAN RUSH

JOHN BLAKE

Published by John Blake Publishing Ltd,
3 Bramber Court, 2 Bramber Road,
London W14 9PB, England

www.johnblakepublishing.co.uk

First published in paperback in 2009

ISBN: 978 1 84454 835 4

British Library Cataloguing-in-Publication Data:

A catalogue record for this book is available from the British Library.

Design by www.envydesign.co.uk

Printed in Great Britain by CPI Bookmarque, Croydon, CR0 4TD

1 3 5 7 9 10 8 6 4 2

Papers used by John Blake Publishing are natural, recyclable products made
from wood grown in sustainable forests. The manufacturing processes conform
to the environmental regulations of the country of origin.

Every attempt has been made to contact the relevant copyright-holders,
but some were unobtainable. We would be grateful if the appropriate
people could contact us.

I would like to dedicate this book to my late mam and dad, who supported me at all times; good and bad; Also my wife Janice, who has been the biggest influence that I could have asked for, and Darren, Renay, and my grand daughters Mia and Maisie, who have given me much happiness.

ACKNOWLEDGEMENTS

To all the managers that I played under, thank you for your patience. To all the supporters who have supported me over the years. All my mates who I grew up with from Llandudno. My sisters Sue and Kath, my brother Frank, and my nephews and nieces. My sister-in-law Denise, and especially my mother-in-law 'Ag' (Margaret). A big thank you to Rob McCaffrey and Peter Jones for all their help in pushing me to complete my autobiography. I would also like to give a big thank you to all my footballing mates, but especially Mickey Thomas and Eddie Niedzwiecki for laughing at all my jokes; Brian Flynn and Kevin Reeves for giving me the chance of staying in football when my playing days ended; And Cliff Sear for passing on his coaching skills. Finally, the people of Wrexham for accepting me as one of their own.

Also thanks to *Wrexham Evening Leader* and *Liverpool Daily Post* for kind permission to reproduce photos.

CONTENTS

FOREWORD BY IAN RUSH MBE

I feel privileged to have been asked to write the foreword to the autobiography of a man whom I cannot bring to mind without a smile being brought to my face.

I first met Joey when I was called up for the Welsh squad for the first time in May 1980 for the Home internationals. When I arrived at the Bryn Howell Hotel in Llangollen, Mike England informed me that he had roomed me with Joey.

However, I went to bed without having met him, but at about one o'clock in the morning I was woken by a knock on the door, and when I opened it, in barged Joey full of the joys of spring! He had been playing in a testimonial match at Liverpool for Ray Clemence.

I soon found out why Mike England had roomed me with Joey. He was to relax and settle me into the squad as quickly as possible, which was a fantastic help, as I was really shy at that time. There's just no edge to him at all, he was just one of the lads and soon made me feel welcome.

I know from my time at Liverpool how much the fans adored him. The kop had idolised him when he was at Anfield, which was very rare for a left back at any club. I know Joey took immense pleasure every time he'd walked out at Anfield as he had supported the club since a boy.

He was a player who grew in stature when he played for Wales. He epitomised the team spirit of the Welsh side in the mid-1980s, and I'm sure no other international team had as many laughs as we did. When you've got characters like Joey and Mickey Thomas around, you know there's bound to be a joke being played on somebody. Joey really is the most irrepressible person I've ever met. Obviously he was as sick as anyone when we were beaten, but even then his sense of humour would come out. Joey was more responsible than anyone else for the spirit that ran through the Welsh squad.

Throughout my career I have kept in touch with Joey and regard him as a close friend. When I went to Juventus, and things weren't going right, I would phone him up for a chat because I knew that, as soon as we'd finish talking, I'd come off the phone with a smile on my face.

Joey was one of the reasons I joined Wrexham in the summer of 1998. I'd done my coaching 'B' licence with him at Aberystwyth and wanted to become involved in coaching, and I knew Joey would be a great help.

As well as playing for the first team, I also worked with him for the reserves. This was a real eye-opener for me, and a great insight into the coaching side of the game. I would sit back and watch to begin with, but Joey soon gave me the confidence to become more involved by giving me the opportunity to give team talks.

As a player I would train and go home, but I soon came to realise that the coaching side of the game was a 24/7 job. We would be out every night watching games, either looking at forthcoming opposition, or looking at players. We would also have to be in early to plan the training sessions for the day, as well as preparing for the games coming up. I soon found out it was a job that needed total commitment.

Joey taught me something I'd never forget: how to coach in the right way. I couldn't work out why the kids at Wrexham weren't doing certain things. These were natural things for the likes of Joey and I, but I soon realised that they needed to be told how to do things first. It was back to my roots. Joey told me to say what I think, as he had always been like that.

Wrexham have been very lucky to have someone as committed and loyal as Joey. Nobody has a bad thing to say about him. Even when I went back to manage Chester he actually spoke to me! Something that was never heard of!

The great thing about Joey is that fame has never affected him in any way. He'd do anything for anyone ... though I wouldn't ask him to put up any shelves!

INTRODUCTION

Joey Jones was the most capped footballer in Welsh history. In a 20-year career, he won almost every major honour in the game including the European Cup and two Football League Championship medals with Liverpool. He's played with and against the world's greatest players. From Russia to Wrexham, Joey Jones has left his mark every inch of the way.

Joey Jones grew up on a council estate in Llandudno, North Wales. As a boy, when he wasn't in trouble with the police or playing football, he'd travel to see the great Shankly side of the late-1960s, featuring stars like Ian St John, Roger Hunt and his idol Tommy Smith. Years later, Joey played alongside Smith as Liverpool took the 1977 European Cup with a win over Borussia Moenchengladbach in Rome.

'Everyone's got a story about Joey,' says former Liverpool supersub David Fairclough. 'He's hilarious.' There's no doubt about that, or the fact that Joey Jones divided the fans – they either loved him or loathed him.

'We were playing Barcelona in Spain,' says Fairclough, 'and were beating them 1-0 with a few minutes to go. Joey was sitting on the subs' bench next to me. As the Spanish fans began hurling cushions down at their players and coaches in disgust, one nearly hit Joey; he thought they were aiming at him and he started flinging them back into the stand

Frisbee-style. We were killing ourselves laughing. When the final whistle went, Bob Paisley grabbed him by the collar and threw him down the steps, muttering something about an international incident.'

Despite several such bust-ups, the great Bob Paisley thought highly of the 'Wild Man of Borneo' as he later nicknamed him. 'He was one of the "clowns" – a real lively character. You need the extroverts in the dressing room alongside the quiet men and the loners. It didn't worry me that Joey might have lacked a little bit of footballing ability when you put him alongside some of the other players on our books like Chris Lawler and Phil Thompson. He more than made up for that with the type of player he was. He wasn't a coward – he was the opposite. If anyone was going around kicking our players, then Joey would be after them. He was a real comedian and sometimes it is good to have that in the side. But don't get me wrong. Joey could play a bit of football.'

As a teenager, Joey ran with the local 'Parrots' gang, who caused havoc up and down the North Wales coast. He was arrested several times and narrowly avoided being locked up soon after breaking into the Wrexham first team at the age of 17.

Amateur and professional youth international caps were followed by Under-23s recognition. As Wrexham embarked on a giant-killing run that took them into the quarter-finals of the FA Cup, the major clubs gradually began taking notice of the skinny full-back from the small town. He was destined for the big time.

In 1975, Joey signed for his beloved Liverpool in what was at that time a record transfer deal for Wrexham. It was what he had always dreamed of. The Kop has had its idols over the years, Billy Liddell, Ian St John, Roger Hunt and Kevin Keegan, but there weren't many who were worshipped by supporters of that period quite like Joey Jones. His clenched-fist salute as he ran from the tunnel would spark the chanting of his name again and again and again.

Full international recognition for Wales followed soon afterwards; the first of a then record 72 international caps was gained against Austria. Joey Jones has played football in 21 different countries and he's got a thousand stories covering events along the way. 'I've kicked the very best,' he says, and who's to argue? Karl-Heinz Rummenigge, Brazil star Socrates and English players from every league have felt the weight of the Jones left boot.

When Wales lost 3-0 to the Soviet Union in Moscow, the legendary striker Oleg Blokhin scored twice while Joey was supposed to be marking him. A journalist asked him afterwards what had gone wrong. 'His mam and dad are Russian Olympic sprinters. My mam's a cleaner and my dad's a porter in a hospital. What chance did I have?'

After leaving Liverpool and returning to Wrexham for a short spell, Joey signed for Chelsea, linking up again with John Neal, his former boss, and his best friend Mickey Thomas. Joey became the club's Player of the Year in his first season, while helping guide the west London club back into the First Division. Both he and Mickey Thomas were unable to sell their houses in North Wales, so they commuted from Wrexham to London every morning. When they had nowhere to stay, they'd remain at Stamford Bridge and sleep overnight in the changing rooms without anyone knowing.

In Soho, they sneaked into a party that was being held by the Wham pop duo, Andrew Ridgley and George Michael, and stayed out until dawn before playing in an FA Cup tie, which they won. The fans loved Joey; but following a couple of run-in's with chairman Ken Bates, Joey decided to leave for Huddersfield, where he continued his international career and finally broke Ivor Allchurch's Welsh record of 68 caps.

Joey Jones overcame a career-threatening broken ankle to finish his career with Wrexham, before finally hanging up his boots up on his 37th birthday in March 1992. However, his enthusiasm and fighting spirit were not lost to the game since he stayed on as first-team coach to Brian Flynn, remaining the life and soul of the dressing room.

A life-threatening heart condition in 2002 saw Joey fight his way back to a full recovery and today, under manager Denis Smith, he remains at his beloved Racecourse Ground as reserve team coach.

CHAPTER ONE

HOME FROM HOME

I first began playing football in the streets of Llandudno and the first team I played for was our street team. Games took place on the field near to my house on the council estate in Llandudno. We'd pick our team in school and then meet up, put bags down for goalposts and play for hours against Joey Kincade's mob from around the corner. There was loads of rivalry with tackles flying in. I'd try to slide them on to the road so it would hurt more!

We had our own trophy which had been found on a nearby tip. It was a toilet seat, and one of the lads had painted 'Charity Shield' on it. The winners were allowed to parade it round the pitch on a lap of honour. We nearly always won and would set off together in front of Kincade's team to spite them. Later on, when the toilet seat went down the pan, as it were, we found an old cup, which took its place. All the time, I'd imagine myself playing for Liverpool, performing yet another lap of honour as we beat them yet again. When Kincade's mob actually won, we wouldn't give them the trophy – all the lads jumped on it and bent it and shouted, 'You're not having it!' I played in these types of games until I was about 17, just after I had broken into Wrexham's first team. The lads would meet up on a Sunday and take on the workers from the local hotels. I loved it, although God knows what Wrexham would have said if they'd found out.

I've always supported Liverpool mainly because my dad supported them. In the early days, I'd be Peter Thompson if I was on the wing and I would get good crosses in. Ian St John was another hero from that 1960s side, though more often than not I was Tommy Smith with another solid tackle. Tommy was the player I admired above all – it's still the same now, but, if I'm brilliant in training and score a couple of goals, these days I'm Rushie.

I was born in Bangor on 4 March 1955, which means I've just passed my 50th birthday (I never thought I would get this far, but more of that later!). Llandudno didn't have a maternity unit as far as I know at that time, so my two older sisters, Kath and Sue, twins incidentally, were also born there, but my younger brother Frank was spared the trip and can honestly say he's Llandudno-born and bred. My dad, Harry, lived there all his life and constitutes the Jones' Welsh link. My mam, Eileen, was a Scouser from the Dingle in Liverpool. She met my dad when she was working in Llandudno for the summer – I'm not exactly sure when and how since I wasn't around at the time but they lived there until they died. By the way, I always referred to my mother as Mam and that's how I refer to her throughout this book.

My dad worked on the production line at the local Hotpoint factory and later became a porter in the local hospital. From a very early age, I can remember him coming home and taking Frank and me on to the estate to kick a ball round. If we were going to the shops, he'd shout, 'Take the ball with you, lad.' His ambition was to have sons who played professional football and he certainly gave us every chance.

When we went to bed, he'd tuck us in and say, 'Right, lads, close your eyes and imagine you're running out at Wembley with the crowd shouting your name.' We thought the old man's lost his marbles.

He'd give us a threepenny bit if we kicked with our weaker foot. I was right-footed when I was little and he'd keep on at us about it: 'Use the left, use the left.' I did and soon I was able to kick just as badly with either foot! However, I became much stronger with my left peg, though I never got to keep the threepenny bits. He'd sneak them back off us and stick them on the sideboard.

Dad was a Liverpool fanatic and would always send Frank or me down for the *Liverpool Echo* on a Saturday evening to get the result and read the reports. I had pictures all over my bedroom wall, though the first big game

I ever saw was at Goodison. The Hotpoint factory ran a trip once a year to see Liverpool or Everton play. It was Everton against Blackpool this one year and Emlyn Hughes was playing for Blackpool. It was a big thrill for me to take in the atmosphere of the game, to see these big stars I'd only read about. My dad said to me that day he thought Hughes was the type of player Liverpool should sign. A few weeks later, I ran back with the *Liverpool Echo* to tell him Hughes had signed. He said, 'I told you so.'

My mam was always a cleaner and I know all their lives they struggled bringing up the four of us. We never had a holiday apart from one day each year just up the road in Rhyl. In fact, my mam and dad had their first proper holiday when they went away for a couple of days to Blackpool for their 40th wedding anniversary. Apart from that, a trip to Wembley in 1977 for the FA Cup Final against Manchester United was the most exotic location they went to. They'd never go abroad – they couldn't afford it!

We never went short though, particularly Frank and I who always had football boots when perhaps the girls missed out on a dress or skirt. I'd always be nagging Mam to buy me a Ben Sherman shirt, which was all the rage at the time. The nearest I got was one that looked like it was from Ben Nevis rather than one from the Lazars shop in the town!

Llandudno is a typical holiday resort – packed in the summer, dead in the winter, with little else in between. I went back to see my mam and dad quite a lot, and by and large it's never really changed from the way I've always known it. The hotels, pubs, bars and amusements are still there. Sure the names have changed, but the tourists still come and go. Overlooking the town itself is the Great Orme, an enormous hill that falls away down to the sea. On the outskirts is our estate, which I suppose the tourists don't see unless they read their maps the wrong way up! Basically, it's just a council estate like any other with houses close together and similar in style. Our house almost backed on to the house where Neville Southall lived, with only a wall to separate us.

When we played our inter-street games on the council pitch nearby, our team would line up in one of the alleyways tucked in between the houses, and Joey Kincade's mob would line up in another one further down. One of the lads would shout, 'Here come the teams,' and we'd all trot across the road on to the pitch as if we'd been waiting nervously in the tunnel before the Cup Final at Wembley.

Before I was old enough to travel to Liverpool to watch the match, I'd nip down to Llandudno's ground, which was only a stone's throw from my house, with the lads. We'd be there at noon kicking a ball in the goalmouth before the teams arrived. As much as anything, we did it to annoy the club committee in the hope of getting them to chase us. They'd go berserk because we were on the pitch and it was always more entertaining than the game. To keep us under control, they asked us to sell programmes outside the ground, but they'd never check how many they gave us, so it would be sixpence for Llandudno, threepence for Joey Jones.

In the end, they tried to ban us, but we'd sneak in and hide under the seats in the main stand when the committee arrived at the ground. They couldn't see us from the pitch, but one of them shouted, 'Who wants to sell programmes today?' All the lads jumped up and ran into the room where they collected the programmes and the door was locked behind us. Next minute a policeman came in and gave us a right bollocking! We never sold programmes again, but I'd still sneak in to watch the games because Llandudno weren't a bad side in those days and my other hero Gareth Davies played.

Having played for Wrexham and Wales together, Gareth and I are great mates now. Back then he was the lad off our estate who was about to hit the big time. I'd get his brother Glyn to take me down to his house to borrow his scrapbooks. I'd spend hours reading the cuttings that Gareth had gathered together and decided to do likewise, even though my own career at that time ran to about two lines and a few crossings-out. These days I've got scrapbooks all over the house with pictures and articles dating back to the age of ten.

It wasn't long after that Wrexham signed Gareth. I'd always look for his report first in the *Football Pink*. When he came home to the estate at weekends, I'd have a chat about how he was doing and what it was like. One time he brought home the shirt he'd worn playing for a Welsh select side against Manchester United at Bangor. I got a thrill just touching it. After all, this was what it was about; this was the big time. Manchester United, Everton and Tranmere would often come to Llandudno for a mid-season break to relax and train. All our lads would hang round their hotel staring at the likes of Best, Law and Charlton, whom we'd only seen on the telly. They were all really helpful and spent time signing autograph after autograph, but one of them told me where to go ... and it's something I've always remembered when people ask me to sign.

Pat Crerand was the player involved, although I have met him since and found him very friendly. I only asked for an autograph and he told me to get out of my way. I was only about ten or 11 and was more embarrassed than anything. It wasn't as if I'd been rude at all. Maybe he had something on his mind. Years later, I always remember Bob Paisley saying, 'It's nice to be important – but it's more important to be nice.' I'd never heard that saying before, but it's advice I've always tried to follow.

Lloyd Street Primary was my first school in Llandudno, but I was only on loan if you like, waiting until the new Stella Maris Catholic School was built. I was happy to go on because the football was going to be good, but not many of my mates were Catholics and it meant leaving them behind. It was very, very strict, or at least I thought it was and, apart from one male teacher Mr Jones, nuns taught us. I don't know what was more of a mystery to me: the Catholic faith or schoolwork. I wasn't the greatest Catholic in the world, although I'm proud of my religion, and I certainly wasn't Einstein.

In fact, I was rubbish at school. I'd try and do the work, but I just couldn't figure it out. My dad would help me when I got home and he could always get the answers, but I needed to know how he got them. If we had homework, I'd just scribble anything down. I wasn't too bad at Welsh and in the secondary school I was all right at woodwork, but the rest you can forget – I just wasn't interested. I got the cane quite a few times and, to be honest, I still believe in the cane as it really frightens you!

The nuns said I was a scallywag. I was never cheeky because I respected them and actually quite liked them. You could tell they liked me because I was never caned as hard as some of the others. I was caned often enough though. If a week went by without a caning it was a miracle – quite apt for a Catholic school! Mr Jones ran the football team and Mother Owen joined in the kickabouts. She'd be there in her habit getting stuck in; she wasn't bad to be honest. All the lads loved her and she loved football. I gave her one of my Welsh youth shirts a few years later. I thought it was the least I could do for all the effort she'd put into teaching and coaching us.

Even now I can't go to sleep unless I've said my prayers, but the religion preached in our school confused me no end. If you missed Mass on Sunday, you got the cane or the slipper on Monday. My parents didn't go to church and neither did I, but it was me who had to face the punishments. The nuns told us that, if you admitted your sins, then you'd be forgiven. One afternoon the whole school was marched out into the playground and made to stand still until someone owned up to breaking a window. We all knew who'd done it, but after waiting for ages I stuck my hand up and pleaded guilty just so we could all get home. The school was dismissed and I was caned. My cries for forgiveness fell on deaf ears. Confusing or what?

I liked three things about school: playtime, football and going home. The school joined the Llandudno and Conwy Primary School League just after it began and we were soon playing regularly against local sides. I was ten when we won the Primary Cup, my first major final against Lloyd Street, the school I'd just left. Everyone was given the afternoon off to come and watch down at Llandudno's ground. Lloyd Street had been bought a lovely new kit for the occasion, powder blue, silky and with a round neck. We still had our maroon-and-white rugby shirts, which didn't even match the nuns' habits. My cousin John Jones captained the Lloyd Street team and they were red-hot favourites. It was a brilliant game because we won 1-0. Peter Alderson scored the winning goal. He was a hotshot in those days and I was called up to pick up the trophy.

My mam and dad had sneaked down to see me play. I didn't like them coming to watch – it put me off – and my dad spent most of my career coming to games without me knowing. Even when I was at Liverpool, I wasn't keen on them watching. I just felt uncomfortable. After our victory, there were pictures in the local press and a medal which I've still got. My mam gave me a few bob to go down to Billy Mac's store to get some Fanta. That was my champagne. It was great!

The Stella Maris Primary was brilliant for football considering it was so small, and that there were so few male teachers. We even went international with a game against St Alfonso College from Manchester, who came down to play us. The nuns got out the Welsh flags and the press came down to take photos of me shaking hands with their captain, James Branagan, who grew up to be Jim Branagan of Oldham, Huddersfield, York and Preston. I played against him a few times in the league and still have the pictures.

My lasting recollection of that game was running out on to the pitch with 'Men of Harlech' blaring from the school record player. I laugh now, but at the time it was brilliant; it was just like being a pro before a proper game. It was the real business.

CHAPTER TWO

PARROTS ON TOUR

All in all, there were about 20 lads off our estate who grew up together, mucked about together and got into trouble together. We were a gang, who fought for each other if need be, and we met up back on the estate as soon as school finished.

We called ourselves the 'Parrots' and even now, if you asked anyone in Llandudno who'd been around at the time, they'd tell you about the trouble we used to get into. We took our name from the comedian Freddie 'Parrot Face' Davies. Remember him? He had a bowler hat pulled down over his ears and blew raspberries with his tongue, slobbering everywhere. We thought he was hilarious and his was the only show on TV I'd stay in for.

The 'Parrots' – who included Robert Hawkins, Bryn Hughes, Mark Prichard, Alan Jones, Brian Limacher (Bell), Dave 'Coffee Spot' Jones, Mark 'Bert Pres' Roberts, Robert Lloyd, Robert Dwyer, Canker Kid, Ian 'Stui' Vale, Ronnie Price, Glyn Davies, Nicky Evans and Bobby Wynn (sorry if I've missed anyone out, but my memory's not too good after all the balls I've headed!) – would roam the estate knocking on people's doors, running away, ducking and diving down the alleys and entries that we all knew so well and getting into fights with lads from other areas.

I was first arrested and taken to court at the age of ten. Sure enough, it brought shame on the family name. No one in our house had been in trouble for anything before and I was very sorry. It was really much ado about nothing. This older lad had told a few of us to get some balls of string from a greenhouse to burn on his bonfire. I don't know whose string it was, but we thought nothing of it and, fair dos, it burned bloody well. So well in fact that we couldn't get rid of the evidence as it was still going three days later!

Quite rightly, the owners complained and, before we knew it, the police were after us. I was hardly on the run, but I was still grabbed by two detectives in the street coming out of the local shop with my *Liverpool Echo*. At first I thought they just wanted to know the results, but I was taken to the local station and told I'd have to appear before a juvenile court.

The older lad had shopped us and the three of us were summonsed. Worst of all, on the day I was due to appear, two policemen came into the classroom to talk to us. Talk about embarrassment in front of the nuns! Three of us stood to hear the magistrate give us a conditional discharge. I went home and got a good hiding from my dad.

I didn't enjoy being in trouble, but I loved being with the 'Parrots'. I've always been the same – anything for a good laugh – and I suppose it was in my nature to mess about. I never hurt anybody, just myself. The nuns, as I've mentioned earlier, said I was a scallywag and that was a pretty fair assessment!

In the winter, the 'Parrots' would wander down to the local youth club for boxing training and at one stage I thought seriously about taking it up full-time. The trainer was one of my dad's mates from the Hotpoint factory and he kept saying I had a real chance of making it. I'm glad he didn't let me know his opinion.

My dad always told Frank and me, 'If you think someone's going to hit you, hit them first and sort it out later,' and I've lived by that rule all my life – sometimes to my cost! All the lads loved the shadow boxing and the skipping. I was good at it, though who knows what weight they would have made me – string weight probably! My nickname was Rembrandt … as I was always on the canvas! In fact, I was the only one who had the sponsor's name on the sole of my boots!

We didn't often fight in the ring – because we never had one – but the coaches would sometimes match you with kids from outside. I was paired up with a Welsh Schoolboy Champion called Alan Roberts and I knocked him down twice in one round. They'd given him a gum shield, but I couldn't wear one and, after he flicked out a couple of jabs, there was blood everywhere from my split lip. That was it. I went mad swinging my arms around like a windmill and I caught him with an absolute peach right on the chin, which knocked him over. Not pretty, but effective ... a bit like my football. After that, I persevered for a while but I just couldn't adjust to wearing a gum shield. Every time I put it in my mouth, I felt sick.

One of the 'Parrots', Alan Jones, or 'Ali Benn' as we called him, qualified for the Welsh Schools Finals down in Cardiff. We couldn't afford to go and see him, but we were waiting on the estate for him to get back. 'How'd you get on?' we asked eagerly. 'Well, I remember the first bell and then waking up in a wheelchair!'

Apparently Ali's opponent had run across the ring and flattened him first punch! We were killing ourselves laughing. Ali never fought again after that, and neither did I.

Sadly, Ali died at an early age, the first of the lads to go. He's buried in the graveyard at the top of the Great Orme. I still sometimes go up there for a walk with my dogs when I go home. I know it sounds a bit morbid, but it's a beautiful place and it's perfectly kept. It's a bit like those graveyards you see in westerns sometimes, Old Boot Hill, fenced off. It's fitting he should be buried there because the graveyard and the Orme were important 'Parrots' playgrounds.

In the summer the 'Parrots' would go up the Orme to play football against the lads who lived up there. It was only 25 minutes' walk, but we always told everyone it was the 'Parrots' on tour.

We'd probably been thrown out of the amusement arcades in town for kicking the machines to make pennies fall, or for just causing a nuisance. Most holidaymakers take a trip up the Orme on trams but the lads would jump on the sides, hold on for dear life and hitch a free ride. There'd be some old bloke saying, 'Oooh, isn't that lovely, dear?' unaware that five or six of us were clinging on either side.

There was one poor old bloke who came in for the full treatment when he was collecting the tolls at the entrance to the coast road, Marine Drive, which winds its way round the Orme with a brilliant view out to sea. He'd sit in his little cabin waiting for the cars to drive up and he'd wander over to collect the money. We'd be waiting for him to make a move and then pelt him with eggs from a little ridge high above him. As soon as he stuck his head out, we'd splatter him. All of us became great shots, so he couldn't get out to the cars and most of them would drive through.

The 'Parrots' would often camp out on the estate and run down to the beach early morning to nick the fish caught on the nightlines left by the locals. One of the most frightening experiences of my life was caving with the rest of the lads after school. We did some stupid things, but to me this rated as the worst of all. About ten of us were crawling on our hands and knees down 'the cave of seven entrances', which has now been blocked off by the Council. We went in at four o'clock in the afternoon and didn't find our way out until about half-six. Down and down we went, crawling on our knees along twisting passages that never seemed to end. I had claustrophobia – you couldn't turn round at all – and was on the verge of panic.

At one stage I couldn't get my breath. I don't know if it was shortage of air or hysteria. I honestly thought I'd never see light again. To this day I don't know how we managed to get out but I've never been so relieved. I didn't do it again.

The reputation of the 'Parrots' spread quickly. Llandudno's not New York and no one was prepared to give us any part-time work in the summer. Instead, we'd wait outside Llandudno Station with a cart and carry the holidaymakers' bags across town for a few bob. Occasionally, we got caddying jobs at the Maesdu Golf Club on the edge of town. I didn't like golf, but picked up some decent cash, bunking off school and carrying a bag for a couple of rounds.

I didn't pass the eleven-plus; I didn't even sit it. The nuns said it wasn't worth my while, so I went to the Mostyn Secondary School, better known as the Central School. I hated it, although they made me captain of the football team, a position which gave me some brilliant opportunities to skive off! On match day, I'd go round the classes and tell the other lads it was time to go.

We never had a mini-bus or anything like that, so it used to be double-deckers or trains everywhere. If we were playing in Colwyn Bay or Llandudno Junction a few miles away, I'd get the lads out of the class early and we'd go downtown for an hour or so. Sometimes we'd get to the schools early to see if we could find the girls' changing rooms for a peep.

It was football or nothing at Central; we didn't do any other sports, especially after one lad got hit in the foot with a stray javelin ... Our side was nothing special and I was nothing special in it, but like now my greatest asset was my enthusiasm and commitment. I've never had silky skills, but I've always been able to make life difficult for the opposition.

Football kept me going. I had little interest in anything else, though I quite fancied myself with the old woodwork. The teacher let us get on with it after he'd taught us the basics of hammering, chiselling and sawing. I decided to make some nameplates for the doors at home. The first one I did was 'Spion Kop'. I thought it was magnificent having spent hours chiselling out the letters and then varnishing them. After that, I made more celebratory wonders in honour of Liverpool Football Club. 'Ian St John' was stuck on our back door for years until someone pinched him. The 'Spion Kop' is still there. In my mind, I could have been carving a cathedral, I thought they were that good.

At weekends, when Liverpool were playing at home, some of the 'Parrots' would make the trip to Anfield. We stood in the Boys Pen in the early days and then graduated into fully fledged 'Kopites'. I would have liked to have gone more in the late 1960s when Roger Hunt, Ian St John, Peter Thompson and Tommy Smith were the heroes. They were like gods to me.

We'd get the train from Llandudno at about nine in the morning along with the Everton and United fans who were travelling to see their sides play. As we went up the coast picking up other supporters, there'd usually be fighting on the train by the time we got to Chester.

After Chester, we'd get into Lime Street and then walk the rest of the way in plenty of time to get fish and chips and soak up the atmosphere. I remember the Kop being packed; there was so much heaving and swaying that, once you were in, you'd always get split up from the rest. One game we got in early, but by twenty past three I couldn't see half the lads we were with. Next minute the tannoy announcer came on, 'Would Robert Lloyd please go to the players' entrance, because his friend Robert Dwyer has been hurt.'

Robert Dwyer had been pushed down to the front in the crush and Robert Lloyd was standing next to us celebrating. We were sick because he'd got to go down into the players' tunnel and we hadn't! It turned out that Robert Dwyer had broken his arm after being pushed on to a barrier. Talk about jealousy. We were calling him all sorts and reckoned it was a deliberate trick to get near to the players.

Eventually, most of the lads began playing on a Saturday afternoon with the Llandudno Estates side in the Tremorfa League. The first year we won the league and two cups. The year after, the side became Llandudno Swifts, keeping alive the name of a team that had played in the town years before. Neville Southall played in goal for them and went on to become one of the best goalkeepers in the world. Sadly, the Swifts are no longer, although there is still a team in the town called Llandudno.

The real benefit for me was to play in open football against men who knew the game and never held back in a tackle. We moved into the Vale of Conwy League, which as anyone who played in it will tell you was tough. I was 14, playing in midfield at the time and I was just quick enough to get out of the way of the madmen and with just enough stamina to get up and down the pitch.

Mickey Thomas played in the same league for Quinton Hazell, a factory side, and it helped us both when we joined the Wrexham groundstaff and were pitched in with the pros in training. They'd dish it out on occasions, but we'd seen it all before with the hard cases back home.

I've still got a number of cuttings taken from the local papers with reports on games I played for the Swifts. 'Joey Jones sent in a pile-driver from 30 yards.' I couldn't reach the goal from 30 inches now! It must have been a small pitch.

I was the only kid from our school to make the trials for the Clwyd and Conwy District at Under-15s level. I don't remember too much about them to be honest, but I know my dad was thrilled when I got through them, even though I was a year younger than most of the other lads. The first game was away at Ellesmere Port in the first round of the Welsh Schools FA Shield. It was also my first game alongside Mickey Thomas who later played for Wrexham, Everton, Manchester United and just about everyone else in the history of football! Mickey became my best mate and later my best man. The mini-bus picked him up on the way to Ellesmere Port at Colwyn Bay High School. He had a red-and-grey school tie and he'd scrawled 'Everton' all over it in blue ink. I thought, Aye, aye, this is a lad I can knock around with – he'll do for me! Even though I was a Liverpool fan, we became inseparable.

Mickey played on the left-hand side of midfield and I was on the left wing in a far-flung Peter Thompson kind of role. Barry Siddall, who later played for Bolton Wanderers, Sunderland, Port Vale and Blackpool to name but a few of his many clubs, was in goal for them – at least I think it was him. I never got close enough to be sure. I think they put me on the left wing because I was younger and smaller than most of the others; I was certainly skinnier. They probably thought I'd snap if someone tackled me.

In the second half, I lofted the ball over their full-back and ran round to burn him off with my blistering speed! I was away when I felt my leg tear at the back. They said later I'd torn a hamstring – at the time, I thought that was something you ate!

I tried to carry on, but couldn't run properly and the coaches kept shouting to me from the bench, 'Joey, are you all right?'

'Yeah, I'm fine, no problem.'

I thought there's no way I was coming off in my first game, but in the end I had to pack it in with five minutes left.

The return was due two weeks later and every night, when my dad got home from work, he'd dig out the 'Fiery Jack' embrocation and massage it into the back of my thigh. It burned like hell, but was the best suntan I ever had. It also did the trick because I was on the left wing down at our place, but only lasted five minutes before it went again. That was that and the District season was over for me for another 12 months.

In the meantime, the 'Parrots' got a team together to enter the *Daily Express* five-a-sides, which were held every summer on Llandudno beach, and we battered all-comers in front of the watching players from Wrexham. There'd always be loads of holidaymakers gathered round the pitch watching, and we always hoped that some of the Wrexham first-teamers might ask us to go training at the Racecourse. After the Llandudno tournament, we went off to Rhyl for the District finals. The 'Parrots' were on tour and the 'Parrots' won again. Mike Smith, who later managed the Welsh national side, awarded the medals.

It was the following season that things really began to fall into place with the District, the Swifts and eventually with Wrexham. It was their scout Evan Williams, who asked me to take part in club trials under the watchful eye of the Wrexham manager, John Neal, and his assistant George Showell.

Evan worked at Hotpoint with my dad and had told him I'd been doing well, but he never said anything to me. He was always careful not to let Frank or me get carried away, though he'd always tell us to compete in any game we played. 'Wherever you're playing, even if it's on the local pitch in a kick-around, there might be someone watching you. The old fellow standing watching with his dog might be a Liverpool scout, you never know.' It was a fair point and it's something I tell the young players at Wrexham.

The trials were always held at weekends and all the lads were falling over each other to impress, me included. If I put a good ball through, or more likely tackled someone, I'd shoot a quick glance over to John Neal to see if he'd seen it. They certainly couldn't miss me. I'm sure my appearance alone gave me a head start. I always had a vicious crew cut to go with my skinhead image. My socks were down to my ankles and my shirt was outside my shorts. I never wore shin-pads, but I felt comfortable without them. My legs have always been like two bits of string and with my aggression I was always likely to catch something even if it wasn't the eye.

You could never tell if you'd impressed or not; it was a case of See You Next Week if you were lucky. More and more I knew that this was likely to be my best chance, possibly my only chance, to hit the big time with a pro club. Wrexham were definitely the club for me. I was totally convinced when they bought all the lads fish and chips after one trial. This was the star treatment and I thought then that Wrexham must have been a class outfit. Fish and chips – now that was style!

Liverpool were and still are – along with Wrexham – my first love, but Liverpool seemed a million miles away from what I thought I could achieve. So, for a bag of fish and chips, I set my heart on Wrexham.

I'd hardly ever been out of Llandudno, apart from the odd day trip to Rhyl with the family, so travelling to Wrexham for training in the holidays seemed a bit like jetting off to Acapulco! It was dead handy for Glyn Davies and me because his brother Gareth gave us a lift. He still lived on the estate, despite being a first-team regular with Wrexham.

When we got there, we were put into lodgings with Mona and Bill Hughes who lived just round the corner from John Neal and just up the road from the Wrexham captain and centre-half, Eddie May. Mona and Bill had just lost their son, Martin, in a bike accident, so I guess John Neal thought us two might help take their minds off it. As it turned out, they were also the uncle and aunt of a certain Janice Griffiths, who later became my wife.

Glyn and I were like two frightened mice. We never went out at all during the week we were there; we were too scared of the big city! I remember writing home every night to my mam and dad as they didn't have a phone. They thought I'd gone soft.

Glyn and I shared a double bed and spent most of the night laughing and mucking about. He smoked and dumped the butts out of the window. Bill came home one morning after nights and told us we'd got prowlers because he'd found these cigarette stumps in a pile round the back. We nipped out quickly that morning.

It was a tremendous opportunity for both of us because we were training with the first team every day. Talk about star-struck: I was terrified of the pros. Here I was alongside the likes of Eddie May, Albert Kinsey and Dave Gaskell – he'd played in an FA Cup Final for Manchester United. As for me, I'd played against Kincade's mob on the pitch by our house.

Older players never gave you sympathy back then and it's the same nowadays. The youngsters got some right bollockings if they made mistakes. I was shy and scared stiff all at the same time, which didn't do much for my passing which has admittedly never been anything like Glenn Hoddle's at the best of times.

But these people were pros and this was their livelihood. I once clipped Eddie May's ankles in training and he got up and gave me a right mouthful. No one messed with big Eddie. Even Gareth screamed one day when I let a ball fly past me into the net. I knew I'd cocked up, but at home I probably would have laughed. Here I almost cried.

All in all, I did all right. John Neal would give me the odd word of encouragement which made me feel great. I loved playing with the grown-ups. I'd done it before and I'd get well stuck in at training, diving in for too many tackles maybe but that's what I enjoyed.

I actually learned a lot in that week about positional play and working as part of a team, and Gareth still goes on to me about the running we did. He'd told Glyn and me to take it easy and not to worry if we couldn't keep up with the levels of stamina John Neal demanded. George Showell would set up poles in a big area and we'd have to run one length and jog the other three, then run two lengths and jog the other two, and so on. I always had stamina – I needed it for all the running around I did on the estate! – and so did Glyn and we powered home in the leading group with Gareth miles back. I knew after that week I wanted to play for Wrexham. Back at school, there was nothing for me. I wasn't going to stay on past my 15th birthday; I couldn't get away quick enough.

I was selected for the District side again that season, this time on the right-hand side of midfield. We had some cracking matches against Stoke Boys, Leek Boys and Flintshire and the papers began to take notice. One report said, 'Ian Edwards played well for Flintshire, while Joe Jones performed strongly for Caernarvonshire.'

We'd played at Llandudno's ground, the ground the Llandudno Committee had chased me off three years before.

My final act as a schoolboy was taking part in a Welsh trial down in mid-Wales at a place called Knighton. Mickey Thomas and I had been selected for the North Wales side to face a South side captained by Brian Flynn. He was about the same size as he is now, but the best player on the park.

He really looked the part, but Mickey and I did ourselves no favours and, in the end, the selectors told us not to bother coming again. I still don't know if it was because we were mucking about, or that we simply weren't good enough. That was their decision, which meant I never won a schoolboy cap, the only honour I missed out on for Wales. Mind you, I never lifted the World Cup, which, come to think of it, was another one.

I wondered if my disciplinary record at school had played any part in it. Probably not, but without doubt I had been far from a model pupil. Now I was about to become an ex-pupil with no qualifications and no real future. I begged my dad to try and get me a job in the Hotpoint factory. I wanted to remain in Llandudno and stay with the 'Parrots'. It seemed the only option. The only level I had was a spirit level, but I'd hardly considered the prospect of working for a living.

Then providence intervened. Someone must have seen something they liked because out of all the kids, just two, Glyn Davies and I, were asked to go down to the Racecourse for further trials during the school holidays. Two 'Parrots' together had to be good news and, on 18 June 1970, I signed schoolboy forms with Wrexham, which meant no other club could come in for me without asking them first.

In fairness, a couple of teams had been sniffing around, but they weren't exactly battering the door down. It was rumoured a mate, Mike Jones, and I were going to Burnley, but I never heard any more about that. Then Johnnie Roberts, who managed Llandudno Swifts, took me down to Chester of all places for a trial. When I got there, I was pitched into an Under-18s game, even though I was 14. I was taken off at half-time and they said they'd let me know. I'm 50 now and I'm still waiting to hear!

The region's Arsenal scout, Maldwyn Roberts, kept in touch with me for a while. I think he had some role in discovering Liam Brady. He basically told me I'd never make the grade because I had no pace. He wasn't wrong. But I didn't really care; in fact, I never really let the old head go down because I just loved playing football, everywhere and anywhere. I'm the same now.

CHAPTER THREE

THE GROUNDSTAFF YEARS

Evan Williams has a special place in the hearts of members of the Jones household, because it's been Evan who's delivered the good news throughout my career. I was at the shops the morning he nipped round to tell my dad that Wrexham wanted me to join the groundstaff for the start of the 1971/72 season, since I'd impressed John Neal during the trials in the school holidays. Sadly, they hadn't taken Glyn Davies on, but Mickey Thomas was due to be starting the same day.

We were given a date and time to report and I dutifully set off from Llandudno with suitcases under one arm and bags of sandwiches my mam had made under the other. I met Mickey when he got on at Colwyn Bay and from that day on we've been inseparable. We were both put into digs with Mona and Bill where I'd stayed during my trials. The club paid us eight pounds a week and we were still skint! Digs cost us a fiver, the fares to and from the ground cost a few bob and, by the time you bought your dinners, you couldn't exactly paint the town red. You couldn't even give the place a thin layer of undercoat. We were constantly broke.

Wrexham picked out a tremendous crop of youngsters that year. Along with Mickey and me, there was Billy Ashcroft who made the first team and later went to Middlesbrough. Graham Whittle, brother of Everton's Alan, who was a first-teamer at Wrexham for years, was another. Then there was Dave Smallman who played for Wrexham, Everton and Wales, while the likes of Bobby Scott, Roger Mostyn, Alan Hill and Mike McBurney all came through at different times.

There were also a few others from the Liverpool area who I played alongside in the reserves, players like Billy Miller, who was as hard as nails, and Dave Fogg, who had a good league career with both Wrexham and Oxford and has since coached at numerous league clubs. He was a very funny man. Dave 'Yosser' Hughes was a good little midfield player, while Colin Edwards was a stylish midfield player who could also play at the back. Geoff Forshaw played either up front or at the back, but could certainly look after himself. There was also Brian Morgan from Wrexham who John Neal brought in to look after the young lads on the field in the Welsh National League. He would deliver bread during the week and turn out for us on the Saturday.

All of us were under the control of Johnny Edwards, who is now groundsman at the Racecourse and whose job it was to look after the reserves. Ronnie Bellis would look after the Welsh National League side, but it was Ally McGowan's job to look after us during the week. He was a tough Scot, whose playing career with Wrexham had been cut short by injury.

As groundstaff we had to do everything: scrub floors, clean baths, lay out the kit and much more besides. I hated every last bit of it. Ally was very strict with us and we were very strict with ourselves. We'd try everything to get out of it. In fairness to Ally, he never let the pros take advantage of us, which was just as well. If a pro said jump, I jumped! Mickey and I would only ever do half a job as a point of principle, and we'd skive off at every opportunity. If we were sweeping up, the dust would always get tucked under the carpet; if it was our turn to tend to the pitch, we'd run off and hide.

Our favourite hiding place was at the top of the floodlight pylons. Ally never found us up there once, yet he'd be on the prowl for ages searching for us, never thinking to look up. It shows how much I hated the jobs because I've always been terrified of heights – sometimes when you shinned up them, the floodlights would begin to sway in the wind.

Once you were up it was fine because you could lie down flat, so that Ally couldn't see you even if he had looked up, while we could see for miles. We'd be there for hours killing ourselves laughing and then whistling over to the Technical College next to the ground at the girls we fancied. I saw Ally not so long ago; he's still not forgiven us and he's still not found out where we used to hide either!

Ally did his best to keep us in check, but Mickey and I weren't in check for very long. If you were caught skiving or mucking about, you'd be hauled up in front of John Neal and given a warning. We were in his office more times than we laid the kit out! Trouble followed us everywhere. One time we had to paint the medical room and we had the ladders up and the radio on slapping the emulsion across the ceiling, the walls and ourselves. Club chairman Eric McMahon came in and chatted away, telling us what a good job we were doing and how nice the place looked. He got so carried away that he leaned back against the wall! 'Yes, lads, you're doing a fine job here. Good to see.' Both of us just stood there like dummies not daring to say a word until he went, when we both fell off our ladders laughing. He had paint all over the back of his suit and it must have been ages before he realised. He never said a word to us about it.

When he'd run out of tasks to give us, Ally sometimes got the lads to clear stones off the training pitch. We just messed about all afternoon instead, trying to form ourselves into a human pyramid on each other's shoulders. Ally told me later he'd been watching us for hours and laughing his head off, but I remember he came over and gave us a right bollocking – another warning. He stood in the doorway to John Neal's office and yelled in his broad Scots accent, 'You two-o-o-o-o. In here now.'

It's difficult to explain just how much Mickey and I hated it. We'd not really been away from home for any length of time and we were both homesick. The training and the football kept us sane, but I kept thinking the 'Parrots' would be out every night having a good laugh, while I was stuck in Wrexham with no money. I dreaded coming back after weekends at home. My mam had to virtually drag me down to the station and, when Mickey got on further down the line at Colwyn Bay, the two of us would start planning how best to skive the rest of the week. 'Right the first team play tonight, that's Monday gone. The reserves play Tuesday, that's another. Only three more days and we're home again.'

I'd ring home from Mona and Bill's to Hazel's across the road from my mam. We didn't have a phone, but she'd come across to hear my moans, night after night.

'I'm coming home, I've had enough.'

'You're not; you've got a career there. You're staying.'

She'd never soft-soap me and made me stay in Wrexham when I was all for jumping ship and heading home on the next train. I can't say how grateful I am to my mam and dad for making me stick at it.

Mickey felt the same way as I did. He once went out for a pint of milk and didn't come back for two weeks. He'd only nipped round to the corner shop, but later we found he'd nipped on a bus and legged it. John Neal had to drive to Colwyn Bay himself to get him back. Apparently he found him in a chippy, took him home, gave him a good talking to and Mickey came back. John Neal obviously saw something in us because he gave us more warnings than anyone else.

I'd sometimes come back from weekends away with the 'Parrots' with big black eyes, cuts and stitches. I looked a right state and John Neal's assistant George Showell couldn't believe the state of me. I had half-mast trousers with Doc Martens, red socks, Ben Sherman shirts and Wrangler jeans. I'd always wanted a pair; originally I had some Winfield ones, which my mam had bought from Woolies. She thought because they had a 'W' on the back pocket, they were the real thing. Later she got me a real pair and the denim was so hard you could hear me coming a mile away. When my legs rubbed together, there was a right racket. I didn't take them off for a month!

We were always bunking off back home when we should have been working at the ground, tending the pitch or clearing the dressing rooms. I was determined to get my weekends in Llandudno whatever happened, even if we were told to report. One time, our youth-team match had been cancelled because of snow and I decided there and then that I was off. Mickey and Dave Smallman both agreed and the three of us sneaked away to the bus station. In those days the first team played a lot of matches on Monday nights and we got back to the ground after the weekend to find John Neal had been digging the pitch himself in his suit because there was no one else to do it – another severe warning.

Even the football wasn't going smoothly for Mickey and me. When we first started with the youth team, we couldn't get a game because the standard was so good. We ended up being linesmen, with him on one side with a yellow flag and me on the other with a red one. Mickey would say, 'What the hell are we doing this for? We could be at home with the lads.' I now tell our young lads that at the age of 15 I was a linesman and at the age of 17 I was a regular in the first team.

When we finally did break into the side we were there to stay. We had a great youth team in 1972 and won the Welsh Youth Cup beating Cardiff City down at Knighton in mid-Wales. They'd made the final of the English FA Youth Cup, losing to Arsenal in extra-time, which showed how good they were, but we still beat them all the same – 4-3 after extra-time.

It was a tremendous season for me personally, not least because I had begun to realise what playing for a professional club was all about: travelling to places, having the best coaching and facilities and gradually settling into the routine, even if I still was a little way short when it came to standards of behaviour. Just three weeks after I'd signed for Wrexham, we were invited to Germany to take part in a special tournament in the town of Iserlohn, just a few miles from Dortmund. Iserlohn had been twinned with Wrexham and officially we were representing the North East Wales FA, which took players from Wrexham and amateur clubs in the surrounding area. In all, 14 of us travelled. We were going as part of a celebration for the Germans and we were only too happy to celebrate all the way. It turned out to be one of the best football trips I've ever been on and that includes all the times with Liverpool and Wales.

When we arrived at Iserlohn, we were split into groups to stay in lodgings all around the town. I was sent with Mickey Thomas and a few others to a hostel, which wasn't bad and we were picked up in the mornings for training and matches. We didn't really get into the sightseeing lark at all – when we had free time, we went down to the amusements. We may as well have been in Llandudno. We drew our first two games and then stuffed Iserlohn 6-1 in the final match. We got a little write-up in the newspapers back home because it was quite a novel event for the town, but headlines off the pitch were much more exciting!

Towards the end of the week, we were getting more and more noisy in the hostel: shouting and generally mucking about all night until in the end the bloke threw some of us out in the freezing cold. We didn't have enough money to get anywhere else, and we couldn't let the coaches know or we would have been for it. In the end we were forced to sleep rough in a bus shelter. It rained non-stop one night and we didn't get any sleep. In the morning we'd nip back to the hostel when the mini-bus came round to collect us to take us to training. Luckily, there was a pub across the road from the bus shelter and the landlord welcomed us with open arms. We were like the local cabaret and they thought we were completely mad sleeping rough. As soon as they opened, we'd be in buying hot dogs and hamburgers for breakfast.

The trip had a little postscript. Years later I went to Dortmund to play against West Germany for Wales. When I got to the ground I was told there was a message for me at Reception. I thought it was a bit odd that anyone should want to speak to me in Germany and, when I got to the front entrance, it turned out to be the bloke who'd thrown us out of the hostel in Iserlohn. He asked for a ticket and, fair dos, I had to admire the way he'd followed my career, but I made bloody sure he didn't get a ticket!

When we got home from Iserlohn, we were invited to take part in a festival of football down at Aberystwyth being organised by the Welsh FA who were gathering the pick of the country's young footballers to select for the national youth teams.

At that time the pros and amateurs were completely separate, so while Mickey, Dave Smallman and myself were still on amateur terms at Wrexham, the likes of Brian Flynn had already turned pro at Burnley. I was delighted when I was asked to captain a festival side in the traditional fixture against Aberystwyth Town at the end of the week. It was a tremendous honour and put me right in line for an international youth cap. Mickey, Dave and Mike McBurney also made the festival side, which was a tribute to the talent on Wrexham's groundstaff.

As captain, I was supposed to attend a meeting with the coaches on the Friday before the game, but instead I nipped off down town with a girl I'd met for a night out. It's always been the same with me: I had a habit of choosing to do my own thing when toeing the line might have been the better option.

Mike Smith was the man in charge of the festival and he was doing great things for youth football in Wales. He might have done great things for me too if I'd been at his meeting, but I wasn't so he didn't. At night I tried to sneak back into the university campus where we were staying, but I bumped straight into Mike, who was out for a stroll. He was fuming. 'You're making a rod for your own back you are. You'll never play for Wales.'

He was going mad, but I thought I'd have a go back even though it was more bluff than anything. 'I never played for the schoolboys, so what does it matter now?'

I walked off and knew I'd cocked up. I played in the festival game the next day, but, when it came round to picking national sides and handing out caps, no one came to ask me to play. Mickey Thomas and Dave Smallman earned caps that season, but I was serving my sentence for stepping out of line. No one ever said that was the reason I wasn't picked, but I'm pretty sure it didn't help my cause. I had to wait another year.

At the age of 16, it looked as if Wrexham FC thought something of me, but being away from Llandudno and my mates was becoming too much to bear. Nowadays it seems ridiculous that I could possibly have thought of throwing away the chance of becoming a professional footballer for the sake of going out with the lads on a Saturday night, but you do some stupid things when you're young.

I'd do anything to get back home for a night out following the same Saturday ritual beginning in our regular haunts like the Winter Gardens or Payne's Café Royal which was a dance hall, often with live music. We were all into soul music at that time and groups like Vocal Perfection were regulars. (They later became The Real Thing.) It was a smashing little place with a tight dance floor and balcony, a bit like the kind of thing you see in those 1960s films, *Billy Liar* and the like. We'd have a few drinks, do a spot of eyeballing with other lads and then get into a fight, which sometimes spilled out on to the streets. It was like those western brawls with chairs flying and glasses being smashed. My mam later told me that my dad often wandered into town on a Saturday to try and keep an eye on me and make sure I wasn't getting into too much bother. These days, I can appreciate his concern; indeed, my own experiences made me more protective towards my own son Darren.

I'm certainly not proud of the way I acted, but it just seemed part of my normal way of life in Llandudno and it certainly had its moments. The 'Parrots' once got into a fight in a club with a group of lads from Rhyl and it carried on outside. Suddenly, one of their lads started shouting at the top of his voice, 'Hold it. Stop, stop ... hold it for a minute.' Everyone stopped and looked at him.

'Whatever you do,' he said, 'don't smash the windows on our bus, or we won't be able to come back next week!' I had to smile.

The reputation of the 'Parrots' was certainly spreading and often gangs from Rhyl or Bangor would come down looking for a fight. But the police had singled us out. They'd come swooping down in the Black Maria to arrest us. One night a few of the lads had been caught and, while the police went looking for others, I jumped on the back of the van and opened the door. The lads legged it, but I was grabbed, handcuffed to some church railings and later slung into the cells. The rest of them were running away shouting their thanks, while Soft Joe was left chained to the railings!

In the end, the police sometimes just let us get on with it. The 'Parrots' were once in Payne's Café Royal when word spread that loads of lads had come down from Rhyl looking for trouble and there was a mass battle on the beach. Bottles and stones were flying and the police were really helpless to do anything but let it burn itself out.

How do I explain this behaviour? The only thing I can say is that I was very impressionable at the time. My tattoos have become something of a trademark down the years but I only got them done because all the other lads did the same … and now I'd give anything to be rid of them.

We used to do them ourselves with a needle and Indian ink. I had the letters J.O.E. on my fingers and a Doc Marten's boot, which I later had removed by laser. The big soul music fist with the words 'Right On' I had done professionally. When you're young, you never think they're there for life. Now they really do embarrass me when I'm in company and, though people sometimes say that they don't notice them, I know they're there and wish I'd never had them done.

Here's one final story to really sum up the type of life I was leading at the time. Ironically, it happened at the Racecourse itself during a match and it was the worst hiding I've ever taken in my life. Wrexham were playing Aston Villa, who always brought thousands of fans with them. As groundstaff, you had to act as ball boys during the game and I told everyone I was going behind the goal instead to watch like a true Wrexham fan. I wandered down the 'Tech End', which was situated at what is now the NEWI end of the ground just in time to see the two sides running out.

I hadn't even bothered to check whether the Villa fans would also be there and, just a couple of minutes into the game, I got a tap on the shoulder. 'You're from Wrexham, aren't you ...' which was more of a statement than a question.

'No,' I replied. 'I've just come to watch the match.'

Five of them began to give me a hard time and, as I turned round, this one lad smacked me in the mouth with blood flying everywhere. I knew I had no choice but to try and fight my way out, so I began ploughing into them with my arms going like windmills before making a break for it round the back of the terracing.

They tried to grab me, but I broke free. Unfortunately all the turnstiles were locked and there was no way out. And there wasn't a policeman to be seen anywhere – there never is when you need one! About 25 of them had me cornered and began to lay into me on the floor. I was in agony and – after what seemed like a lifetime – they eventually let me up. I was cut to pieces and then, to make things worse, they began feeling sorry for me and told me to come and stand with them on the terraces again.

I spent the next 70 minutes trying to be a Villa fan, hurling abuse at our lads and screaming and shouting when Wrexham were on the attack. Every time the ball came down our end, I was booing Wrexham 'keeper Brian Lloyd who's a great mate of mine. When he looked round, I ducked so he wouldn't see me. Later, one of them asked me to come back on the coach to Birmingham and I had terrible visions of being stuck in a traffic jam on the M6 with these mad Villa fans. Luckily, we started moving out of the ground and, once I saw it was clear, I legged it down into the nearby Crosville bus station, taking cover until I was sure they'd gone.

I must have been in hiding for a quarter of an hour before getting up and walking back into the ground. The first person I met was Janice, who'd been working there, and she started telling me about the terrible fighting in the Villa end. 'I know. It was me being battered!' She looked at me as if I'd gone mad, but when she saw my face she knew I wasn't messing about. I couldn't sleep for a week.

CHAPTER FOUR

LEARNING THE TRADE

John Neal made all the groundstaff take up a day-release course of their choice, the reasoning being that not every kid would make the grade and Wrexham were concerned for their futures outside the game. I had no qualifications and for me the course spelled misery. I'd spent the last ten years trying to get out of school and now I was being forced to go back again! Grudgingly, Mickey, Dave Smallman, Graham Whittle and I took up painting and decorating which seemed like one of the lesser evils at the William Aston Technical College, which is situated right next to the ground.

We began to play truant following an incident with the lecturer, Mr Swire. I'd been mucking about in class when he began poking me with his finger and telling me off. I asked him not to poke me but he carried on. I grabbed his finger and pushed him into a storeroom. The key was in the door, so I locked him in and we pissed off to town!

Mickey and I started to bunk off down town listening to records all day in Crane's record shop, which has now gone. Then we'd turn up at night to our digs and say we'd been to college. What we didn't know was that the college was sending letters to John Neal complaining about our absence.

He began to investigate what we were up to and sure enough his secretary, Madge Pike, saw us in Crane's and got word to him. We were up in his office the next day and he made us go back, but little did he know that we couldn't go back to class.

We were back the season after, this time at the Art College down the road. Again we had to enrol and pick a subject. We wanted Quarry Blasting, but settled instead for Photography. The first day we were there, the lecturer handed this camera round and told us the lens alone was worth £300, which in those days seemed like a small fortune. He was telling us to be careful when Mickey got hold of it and dropped it on the floor! I fell about laughing, which got us off on the wrong foot straight away. We lasted about three weeks, which wasn't bad until we decided to go to John Neal and ask him if we could just train on a Monday instead. He said, 'Yes, OK.'

It was around this time that I met my future wife. Janice Griffiths was the niece of Mona and Bill Hughes, who I was lodging with and, when she came to visit, I started with a bit of chatting, as you do. She told me she was doing a secretarial course (she passed, needless to say). It was then that I stumped up the courage to ask her if she'd like to go to the pictures at the Hippodrome. However, I suddenly realised this was a big mistake as I had no money to take her! We'd arranged to meet at the bus station in King Street, so I turned up and told her that the football club had put me on a curfew. Janice then caught the next bus home to Gwersyllt. Despite that disastrous first date, we soon began seeing each other on a regular basis, meeting during dinner times at the college and visiting her at her mum's house when Mickey used to chaperone me!

We never went out much in Wrexham, because we never had any money and I rarely had a drink in the week. The only time I got really drunk was after I'd left Mona and Bill's and had gone to live with another groundstaff lad, Howyn Jones. We all went out to celebrate Henry McKee's birthday and got well drunk in a pub in town after three pints. Howyn and me shared the same room and, during the night, I got out of bed and threw up in what I thought was the toilet, but which turned out to be his wardrobe. I had some sense at least, because I hit all his clothes and none of mine!

Leaving Mona and Bill's meant splitting up with Mickey. He moved to Poyser Street in Wrexham and I went to Molly and Bob Edwards who lived in Bersham Road. To maintain our friendship, the only solution, as we saw it, was for us both to go round to Janice's at night. After all, mates are mates. Janice's dad had died when she was two and I think she and her mother quite enjoyed the company. They certainly kept us stacked up with bacon butties.

We were never away – playing records, watching telly – and then Mickey and I would catch the bus home. As we were leaving, I'd tell Mickey to go and wait down the road, whilst I stayed for a while with Janice at the door – always the romantic!

Sometimes Janice and I would go to the pictures in the week. Bruce Lee, the karate king, was the big star at the time and I thought he was brilliant. His were the only films I'd watch; otherwise I'd try and get in the back row with Janice, never mind what was on the screen!

When the new league season started I was still in the reserves, then one Sunday morning in October, Evan Williams, the Wrexham scout, called round with news. 'Have you got a passport?'

'Why?' I asked.

'Because Graham Whittle's injured and John Neal's called you up for Wednesday.'

That Wednesday, Wrexham were due to be in Switzerland to face FC Zurich in the European Cup-Winners' Cup. It was the biggest tie in the club's history and it looked as if I could be making my debut.

Our place turned into a madhouse as I gathered my clothes and kit. I picked up a one-year passport the next day and on Tuesday I boarded a plane bound for Zurich. I'd never flown before and I was terrified. Even now I'm not the world's greatest flyer, but back then I really felt I'd never make it on to the plane. We arrived at Manchester Airport and, when we were called aboard, Mickey and I held hands as we were walking across the tarmac. We were both way out of our depth.

I knew this could be the big break for me, but I was nervous about letting anyone down. I was still in awe of the older pros which didn't help, but after we got off the plane and reached the hotel I began to settle.

Mickey and I went holiday-mad. It was just one big adventure. There we were, involved in the biggest match in Wrexham's history, staying in a magnificent hotel when all the other groundstaff lads were back at the Racecourse getting on with the regular jobs. We felt like royalty and spent hours mucking about in the hotel foyer. They had these massive beanbags, which certainly I'd never seen before, and they must have struck a chord with Mickey because he bought Janice and me a couple when we got married.

In the end I sat it out on the bench, while Mickey played and played well. FC Zurich was a big name in European terms. Wrexham were a small, but improving side on the verge of carving out a giant-killing European reputation. My knees were knocking together I was so nervous about going on, but I was still hoping I'd get my chance. Albert Kinsey scored the goal to take us home with a 1-1 draw.

In those days, European sides gave their opponents gifts and Zurich presented us with cufflinks, which I passed on to my dad. He said he'd have to get his wrists pierced!

I wasn't even on the bench when they came over for the second leg. Graham Whittle was fit again and I was back to being a ball boy. The groundstaff lads had to get any balls that were kicked out of the ground during the match. Wrexham won 2-1, but I was left out again when we were drawn to play Hajduk Split in the next round.

We'd beaten them 3-1 at home when I was sub, and I sat listening to the second leg on a crackling radio in Eddie Bingo's car outside the Racecourse. Eddie ran the club lottery, hence the name, and we both felt helpless as the lads went down 2-0 and lost out on the away-goals rule.

Back in the real world, I had to move digs again when Molly and Bob ran out of room. John Neal asked me if I could move in with Janice for a few days, just until he could sort something out. I went round to ask Janice's mum if it would be all right if I moved my stuff in for a short while and she said yes. That was that! I was sitting on the settee in front of the telly before she could change her mind. I saw Janice down the Wimpy that afternoon.

'I've got new digs,' I told her. 'At yours!'

She didn't believe me until she came home that night to find me lounging about in the front room with my feet up.

John Neal never mentioned digs again. He was a shrewd man. I was beginning to get into serious trouble with the 'Parrots' when I went home for weekends and he reasoned that, if I was with Janice, I wouldn't be doing too much damage to others or myself. He was right because I began to stay in Wrexham more and more in order to go out with Janice at weekends. I'd go back home now and again for a night out with the lads, but I'd take Janice with me and I'd make sure I didn't get into any fights.

Twelve lads and Janice would move from pub to pub; she must have been mad to put up with me.

At her mum's, it was strict stuff – separate bedrooms and all that. You couldn't creep down the corridor because there wasn't one; there was only about two foot square of carpet between three bedrooms. We had to stay up late if you know what I mean until Janice's mum had gone to bed. Margaret, or 'Ag' as I called her, lived with us for over 15 years. I say to the lads if I'd murdered her I'd have been out by now. But no, she's been great to both of us over the years and would always try and bung me a fiver for a pint if she thought I was short on a Sunday.

In January 1973, John Neal called me up to the first team for the Welsh Cup tie with Chester at Sealand Road – my debut at last. During the game, there were loads booked, including me, and one sent off. It started how it was to carry on really. Gareth Davies missed a penalty in the last minute and we lost 1-0. I'd been marking a winger named Dave Kennedy, and John Neal said I'd done OK, which meant I was in again for a full league debut at Rotherham on the Saturday.

CHAPTER FIVE

WELCOME TO PROFESSIONAL FOOTBALL

It was snowing heavily when I arrived at the Racecourse, but we travelled anyway because the forecast in Yorkshire wasn't too bad. The 20th January 1973 marked my first-team debut away at Rotherham. John Neal had a quiet word with me and said he'd been pleased with the way I'd played against Chester in the Welsh Cup and I nearly snapped his hand off when he asked me if I wanted to play in the league.

I had mixed feelings as we crossed the Pennines, looking out on to the white fields through the misted-up coach windows. On the one hand I was scared stiff of making a fool of myself; on the other, the chances were that the match could be off so I couldn't worry too much. When we arrived at Millmoor, the weather had eased. I'd not been there before and was well impressed with the Rotherham people as soon as I got off the coach. I sauntered into the dressing-room area and this bloke began chatting away to me as if he'd known me all his life.

He made me feel right at home, but as he walked away the rest of our team was heading into the dressing room. The game was definitely on. Gareth Davies and Eddie May asked me what he'd said and I told them.

They then told me that I would be seeing a lot of him as he was Jimmy Mullen the winger I'd be marking. He had done the rounds with a few clubs, including Reading, Charlton, Blackburn, Bury and Rochdale.

I began nervously warming up between hasty visits to the toilet. We ran out as the snow began to fall again; through the gloom I could make out Jimmy Mullen lining up opposite me about to kick off. Midway through the first half, I still hadn't had a kick. Mullen was standing next to me with the ball somewhere over on the opposite wing. Then he punched me smack in the mouth. I was more shocked than hurt, but I was fuming and completely lost my head. It was some introduction to league football! I started chasing Mullen up the wing. The crowd began screaming at us as I tried to land punches or kicks. They thought I'd gone mad. It turned out he had some pace, because I couldn't get near him and the referee had to come in and separate us before I landed the KO. Mullen didn't come near me after that, though the ref did go over to the dugout to have a word with John Neal, asking him to calm me down or he would send me off, league debut or not.

After that, I started concentrating on the game and went on to do quite well, but I never forgot Jimmy Mullen. The only time I came across him again was at Blackburn Rovers when I was in Liverpool's reserves. We ran out on to the pitch at Ewood Park and he waved to me. I gave him two fingers. He knew I'd get him if he came anywhere near me and wisely kept out of my way, although I had told the First Aid people to get a stretcher ready. I've since spoken to a number of people who are amazed when I tell them that story as they say he's a really nice feller and was never that type of player.

That was it, I'd made my impression in the first team – not perhaps as big as the dent Jimmy Mullen made in my mouth – but it was good enough to keep me in the side for the rest of the season. I had the added bonus of continued selection for the national amateur youth side, as I'd played against Ireland, England and Scotland the year before and was picked again to face Ireland in March. The Welsh FA always have the right to take an amateur away from his club to play in an international, so, to keep me at Wrexham for the league game at Bristol Rovers, John Neal offered me professional terms.

Signing pro was exactly what I had been looking for, even though it meant missing out on another youth cap. Financially, I thought I'd arrived. I'd been playing for the first team on groundstaff wages of eight quid a week, but now I'd hit the big time with an immediate increase to £25 a week with a £500 signing-on fee. After tax, that was worth about £300 and I walked out of John Neal's office feeling like a lord. He told me he'd been planning to sign me pro in the summer anyway, but he needed me in the first team now and that suited me too. His secretary Madge had a chat with Mickey Thomas and me and told us it was time to start saving, so she took us down town to help us open a building society account.

I couldn't play again for the Welsh amateur youth side, but the professional youth team called me up for the European Championship games against Scotland and France. Mickey and I were invited for a squad session at Sophia Gardens in Cardiff and we must have impressed the selectors because we both got in. It pleased us more because most of the lads there had been pros for some time: Brian Flynn, Ian Lewis and Kevin Malloy were in the First Division with Burnley; Nigel Williams was with Sheffield United and Paul Fury had been playing in Swansea's first team at the age of 16; Wayne Cegielski told us he was Mike England's understudy at Tottenham – Mickey and I were well impressed with that and a little overawed. We thought he was bound to get in, but he had to wait until the following year for a cap.

The European Championships were played on a home-and-away basis and we started badly, losing to Scotland at Newport. We then went to Partick Thistle's ground, Firhill, for the return, but the match was switched to Ayr because the pitch was frozen. We got the bus to Ayr and, on a freezing cold night in front of two supporters and a couple of dogs, we lost again.

I was marking Frankie Gray, who was with Leeds and played on the left wing. I didn't do too badly either, because they were a tidy side with Jim Blyth in goal, who went on to play for Coventry and Manchester United, and Steve Finnieston up front who was making a name for himself at Chelsea.

The real thrill was the away trip to France for the first match at a small ugly-looking ground on the outskirts of Paris. I'd flown before when Wrexham drew Zurich in the Cup-Winners' Cup, but to be representing your country on foreign soil was magnificent.

We trained in the morning, then went back to our hotel for lunch and a sleep in the afternoon. I didn't know you were meant to sleep before a game, at least no one at Wrexham had ever told me to do it. Instead I wandered down into the hotel lobby to change some money for a trip into town to buy some presents for Janice and my mam.

I was just about to set off when the manager, Mike Smith, collared me. 'Where d'you think you're off to?'

'I'm off around the town to get a few things to take back,' I replied.

'No, you're not. Get up those stairs to bed now; you're playing for your country tonight.'

'But I'm not tired and it's the only chance I'll get to look round.'

I don't think Mike Smith could believe what he was hearing. I'd had that run-in with him in Aberystwyth a couple of years earlier and I'm sure he thought I was trying to be Jack the Lad again.

'If you're not up those stairs by the time I count to five, you'll be on the first flight home.'

You couldn't see me for dust.

It makes me smile now, because on one of Wrexham's recent pre-season tours to the Isle of Man some of the young lads were messing about in the hotel the afternoon before a night match. I gave them a right bollocking about responsibility and attitude. When they'd gone, I thought back to Mike Smith and Paris ... and laughed to myself.

Sleep or no sleep, the French game was dull and I was more worried about swapping my shirt for one of the French ones than anything else. I'd clocked them in the warm-up: shiny blue nylon with a round neck and a badge. They were brilliant and, as soon as the final whistle went, I grabbed hold of one of their players and virtually ripped the thing off his back!

We'd lost 1-0, but Mike Smith said we could go into town that night, so money was clubbed together and off we went to a strip club. We all had a few beers and the stripper was doing her stuff – when she flung her bra into the crowd, it landed around my neck. That was it. I was waving it above my head like a scarf, with the lads singing, 'Walk On...' as if we were on the Kop. It was a brilliant night.

In the return match at the Racecourse, we won 2-1 and it was such an outstanding game that I can't remember a thing about it! However, I did notice in the programme a few years later that tricky winger Didier Six, who went on to play for Lens, Marseille, Vfb Stuttgart, Aston Villa, Strasbourg, Metz and Galatasaray as well as winning 52 full caps for France, actually played in that game.

On the pitch, things had never been better. Off it, things were getting steadily worse with the 'Parrots' sinking into deeper and deeper trouble. We'd got ourselves a reputation along the North Wales coast and, though I still enjoyed the nights out as much as ever, they seemed certain to end in tears. I was 17 and in Wrexham's first team and new demands were being placed on me by the club and Janice. I think the 'Parrots' had gone as far as they could go.

We were growing up and going our separate ways. Because we'd been in trouble for so long, we'd all been on the verge of a prison sentence or Borstal for some time. I'm sure the police were looking for an opportunity to put us away and I can't blame them. Janice had acted as a calming influence on me and, when I went back to Llandudno, I'd take her which meant I kept out of trouble. My big mistake was going home alone.

It was just another 'lively' Sunday afternoon in Llandudno: mods, rockers, skinheads – you name it, they had it. I was with the 'Parrots' outside a chip shop when four Hell's Angels came past barging into my chips and almost knocking them out of my hands. I gave one a mouthful of abuse, but thought nothing more of it. They were older than us and were clearly looking for a bit of trouble.

We moved round the corner, then came back. The lads were still there, so we ended up following them for a while and I knew deep down we were on the verge of a fight. Suddenly all hell broke loose. I was standing quite a bit away still eating my chips, but I did see one of the Hell's Angels take a real thumping on the ground. People were shouting and running out of their houses and we all legged it before the police arrived.

It was half-past seven the following morning when the police knocked at our door; both my mam and dad were at work. They took me away for questioning at the station, and I knew that I was going to be charged and sent for trial even though, for once, I hadn't been involved at all. They made no apologies. 'You did it. We know you did it. We've got people who saw you do it. You've had it this time.'

Although I was beginning to make a name for myself at Wrexham, they left me in no doubt they wanted me convicted. They kept saying over and over, 'You did it. You beat the bloke up.' I denied it all. What else could I do? And for the first time in my life I asked to see a solicitor. When I'd been in trouble before, I never bothered because I had always been guilty and took the punishment I deserved. This was different. It was far more serious and was threatening my career before it had really started.

They eventually let me go and I went straight back to Wrexham. On the train, it seemed like my whole life was in the balance. It was like something from one of those black-and-white films they show on the History Channel! I couldn't tell the club: I'd be in for it. I didn't want to tell Janice because she'd go mad with worry, but I knew I had to do something quickly, so I went to see a solicitor I knew called John Hughes. I told him the full tale and he said he'd help, but he also warned me I didn't have a very good case, bearing in mind my previous record.

For the rest of the week, I trained and said nothing. The following weekend my dad arrived at Janice's house after hitch-hiking down from Llandudno. 'Joe, the police are pressing charges. They're taking you to court for assault.' I went white as a sheet. I knew I was innocent, but the police were convinced I'd been involved. Janice's sister, Denise, drove my dad and me round to see John Neal. It was really embarrassing because he was having a bit of a party with some friends, but I had no choice.

'I'm sorry, but we've got to see you.' We all went into the garden and my dad explained what had happened. John Neal was calm about the whole thing and said he'd get the club solicitor to help. This was Geoff Morris, who worked alongside John Hughes. He was blunt about my chances. 'This is it. This is the be-all and end-all for Joe. If he doesn't get off, he's finished with Wrexham. The club won't have anything to do with him.'

I was still playing in the first team when the case finally came to court. It had been a horrible wait, but I don't think it affected my form in any way. I was summoned to appear before Llandudno Magistrates with the rest of the lads. They'd all pleaded guilty and one or two received custodial sentences. One of them, my best mate, shouted to the bench as he was being led away, 'I want to make it clear that Joey Jones wasn't involved in any of this.'

I pleaded not guilty and was ordered to reappear a few weeks later. When I did, John Hughes ripped the prosecution to shreds. They'd produced a witness to say she'd seen me fighting, but on oath she couldn't swear it had been me. John was brilliant and the magistrate eventually ruled 'no case to answer'.

Talk about relieved ... I couldn't watch *LA Law* on TV without thinking of

John Hughes. In later years, Janice's sister, Denise, became his secretary and he's now a coroner for North Wales. I always said he'd go far after the performance he put on for me.

How fine is the dividing line between success and failure? It's really only now I can look back and think of what might have been or, more importantly, what might not have been if the case had gone the other way. Certainly, I would have been looking at some sort of sentence and Wrexham had made it clear that I'd be finished with them if I'd been found guilty. I would have been finished before I'd even started!

I didn't go back to Llandudno much after the case and certainly didn't head out with the 'Parrots'. Effectively, the 'Parrots' were dead. We were ex-'Parrots'. And, since that day, the only trouble I've been in has been with referees.

CHAPTER SIX

MAKING A NAME FOR MYSELF

There used to be a little book lying around my house called *The Robins Story*, a brief history of Wrexham Football Club. Basically it told the story of the club down the years and picked out season 1973/74 as the best in its history.

I'd made my debut in January and played 17 games up to the end of the season. I then had a lazy summer, fishing, relaxing back home in Llandudno and generally taking it easy. I reported back to the Racecourse a first-team regular.

Pre-season at Wrexham under John Neal was a nightmare; the seasoned pros had been dreading the prospect from the moment the ref blew his whistle to end the previous season. John Neal was a believer in the 'sand treatment' for peak fitness, a case of kill or cure. We'd spend the week in Aberystwyth on the university campus, training down on the dunes at nearby Borth. Every morning we'd get on the team bus and, as we approached, we'd see the beach stretching for miles ahead of us. Pass the sick bucket.

The whole week was geared to competition and fitness, with no thought of breaking you in gently. Every run was timed; every sprint was clocked and measured to make sure we were getting fitter and faster every day. We were split into teams, with the winners at the end of the week picking up a £20 gift token. Twenty quid was no mean prize in those days, especially for those of us earning eight pounds a week. The team I was in won it a few times over the years.

The day's schedule was knackering with one exercise rolling into another; the programme was mapped out so you had little time for recovery. It kicked off with a three-mile run along Borth beach. Running on grass is hard enough, but running on sand is a killer. There'd be some hard patches and some rutted ones but worst of all were the wet bits where you'd sink and stumble. I always preferred running in bare feet; some of the lads who wore trainers ended up with bad blisters.

Mickey Thomas, Mel Sutton and Arfon Griffiths were brilliant at running. They'd be miles out in front, with the rest of the stragglers battling it out for the minor places. I wasn't bad and was always near the front without ever really setting the pace.

Mickey was just one of those sickening players, naturally fit with bags of stamina. He's the best runner I've seen in football. Even now he's a fit bugger, better still after a night out. When he left Leeds for Stoke in 1990, Howard Wilkinson reckoned he was the fittest man on his books – or so Mickey tells me!

As soon as everyone had clocked back in, we headed straight for the sand hills for the short, sharp, shock stuff. Some hills were as big as my house and, once a few of the lads had ploughed through the sand, it was murder trying to get up any speed.

Still, this is where I came into my own. I was like the roadrunner and would blast off with my legs going like the clappers. I think my build helped, being tall and skinny with no weight. I was brilliant at it. Pity we didn't play football on sand, I would have been a world-beater. In the afternoon, it would be more running on the university track, with weights thrown in for good measure. To finish, we'd head for the swimming pool to relax our aching muscles.

When John Neal left for Middlesbrough, he continued to take his sides down to Borth for pre-season. I thought I'd seen the last of it until I joined John again at Chelsea a few years later. If I'd have thought about the sand dunes when I was about to put pen to paper, I might have gone elsewhere.

God, it was tough, but we all felt tremendous when we'd finished. Stamina-wise it was superb, but there was always a feeling at Wrexham that we had a lot of knee injuries early in the season. I remember Bill Shankly criticising the style of training in the *Liverpool Echo*. He said that sand was for donkeys. I idolised Bill Shankly and what he said was gospel, though, in fairness to John Neal, I think he was having a go at other teams, who sometimes went up to Southport to run on the sand. Perhaps Bill Shankly was right, but I personally felt it helped me before the season got going.

We began well with just one defeat in seven league games and I was finally beginning to feel an accepted part of the team. I sometimes looked in wonder at the other players; it wasn't so much being star-struck but these were some of the finest players ever to pull on the red shirt: Brian Lloyd in goal played every game that season; Eddie May at centre-half, along with Gareth Davies, dominated the back four, while Arfon Griffiths ran the midfield; up front, we had Dave Smallman, one hell of a goalscorer, with Brian Tinnion on the wing banging in the crosses.

I played 41 out of 46 league games and Dave Fogg, the other full-back, played 46. John Neal said we were the best team in the Third Division. No disrespect to the others, but Eddie May and Arfon were the pick. They were the established stars and, at the back, Eddie in particular was one of the best I ever played with.

Nobody messed about with Big Eddie and he'd die for Wrexham. He was hard, the godfather of the Third Division, and he wouldn't hesitate to slap you in training if you overstepped the mark. He was always great to Mickey and me, though, keeping a special eye on us as we both came through into the first team.

By October, we'd won three, drawn three and lost three, and then we hammered Southend 5-1 at the Racecourse. The following week, we lost away to York 1-0 to a bit of a silly late goal, and Big Eddie was fuming as we came off the pitch. 'You cost us the game,' he said, turning round.

I was a bit upset to tell you the truth, because I thought I'd done all right, but he was having a go at 'keeper Brian Lloyd. As we walked into the dressing room, Eddie completely lost his head and nutted Brian who collapsed into a corner. Everyone just stared ahead of them, not daring to say anything. Then John Neal started, 'That's what I like to see, someone who cares for the club.'

I was stunned at the time, but now I think it was hilarious. It was nice to know you had someone with Eddie's commitment, not to mention size, on your side when it got a bit naughty.

In midfield there was no doubting that Arfon Griffiths could play and he could get a bit nasty if he wanted to too. He was a brilliant passer of the ball, but, if teams roughed him up or began winding him up, he wasn't so effective. In a way it was great credit to Arfon's ability that many sides began trying to rile him straight from the kick-off. For me, Arfon is arguably the best player ever to have played for Wrexham.

Arfon had made his debut for Wales as a youngster, but was then overlooked until he was 32, which I think was a crying shame for him and for Wales. His form for Wrexham earned him a recall against Austria, when Dave Smallman and I were also called into the squad for the first time. I remember Arfon doing well in that match and then throwing up on the hotel carpet after he'd guzzled a few ales. In the morning, the manager, Mike Smith, came down for breakfast and there was a right fuss, with the staff demanding that someone clean it up. Mike Smith went straight up to Dave Smallman and accused him of doing it. Dave protested his innocence and Mike Smith changed his tune. 'Well, it must have been Joey Jones then...' I got the blame! Mike Smith must have remembered me from the early days.

The experience of men like Eddie and Arfon certainly rubbed off on the groundstaff lads coming into the side, though players like Dave Smallman looked like they'd been regular for years. Dave was the rising star and made most of the headlines, deservedly so. He looked a bit like Rushie and played like him; he was quick and slim, but with great touch in the box. He was always confident, even in the early days, and amazed me by smoking 20 a day. The scouts flocked to see him, though he said his real ambition was to sit on the bench at Wembley during an England versus Wales game and then light up a ciggy. He eventually made it big when he signed for Everton. However, he was to sustain some terrible injuries, which were to curtail his career at an early age, or else he would have scored goals at the very top for years.

He certainly got the right service at Wrexham, particularly from Brian Tinnion on the left wing. 'Budgie' was the only player I've seen who wore two sets of shin-guards, one on the front of his legs and one on the back just in case ... He hated being tackled, but if he got past his man he was a brilliant crosser. 'Budgie' was a 1970s Arthur Daley figure, always buying and selling cars. He was living in Detroit when last I heard and even got a mention in Pele's book. After he left Wrexham, he'd spent some time at New York Cosmos when the American Soccer League was booming. The Cosmos' forward line was Chinaglia, Pele and Tinnion. Now he'll be able to tell people he got a mention in Joey Jones's book as well. No comparison!

We missed Mickey that season because of injury and he only came back into the side towards the end. We'd begun to build up a nice little understanding that continued with Chelsea and Wales. If anyone got past him, I got them and then I'd give it back to him to do the fancy stuff. He was as disorganised as I was. I remember him once helping Dave Gaskell in training with some extra crosses, but he kept stubbing his toe with the ball trundling along the ground. Eventually Dave called him over. 'What size boots d'ya take?'

'Nine-and-a-halfs.'

Dave pressed the toe of his boot and started laughing. Now Mickey takes sixes!

It was a season of firsts. My first real injury came away to Hereford in September. I ran back into the box to pick up from a corner and, when it was cleared, we all ran out for the offside. Next minute their big centre-forward, Eric Redrobe, booted me up the arse so hard I thought I was about to disappear over the stand. Honestly, I took off, then crashed back down like a sack of spuds. I was in agony and only vaguely aware that a big fight had started around me. Apparently, a mate of mine, John from Colwyn Bay, jumped down from the terraces to have a swing at Redrobe. Eventually, they pushed him back into the crowd after I'd got up. I still see John at Wrexham games.

After that, I was so sore I couldn't play in the Port Vale match at their place, which was a shame because they were Wrexham's great rivals back then with bags of ill feeling always close to the surface on and off the pitch. They were one of the hardest sides in the league at that time, with players like John King, who later managed Tranmere, Billy Summerscales and Tommy McLaren. Gordon Lee who'd played with John Neal at Aston Villa managed them and I believe they weren't the best of mates.

I sat on the bench and saw us go down 1-0 in a scrappy and bad-tempered match. Arfon Griffiths had lent me his coat for the evening because it was freezing; it was a long leather number with a belt – right in fashion at the time. It came with a friendly warning: 'Don't get it dirty, Joey, it cost me a fortune.'

There were tackles flying in all night and, when the final whistle went, one hell of a punch-up broke out as the players walked up the tunnel. Our centre-half, Bobby Scott, belted Tommy McLaren and we all piled in. I grabbed Tommy and held him, while Bobby got in a few more digs. Out of the corner of my eye, I could see Gareth Davies holding Billy Summerscales by the throat. When Gareth looked up and saw who it was, he let go and legged it down the tunnel. Wise move!

It took a while, but the police eventually broke it up and sent the two sides back to their dressing rooms. After half an hour, we were allowed back on the bus and, when Arfon finally got his coat back, the belt had gone. 'Where's my belt, Joey?' he enquired.

'I must have lost it in the fight. Give them a ring tomorrow and ask if it's been handed in.' Some bloody chance!

My first booking came in that 5-1 thrashing of Southend at home. I was marking Peter Taylor who I rated one of the best wingers in the Third Division. Taylor was solid, built like a tank, and he knew how to throw his weight around even if you whacked him. Some wingers would take a tackle and you wouldn't see them again. He dished out as good as he got and always came back for more.

We were having a right old scrap and both of us had been booked when I had another go at him in the second half. He lost his rag and was sent off. Now that's a first and probably a last – getting someone sent off who wasn't me. I have great respect for Taylor, who went on to play for Tottenham and England under Don Revie. He also went on to have a successful managerial career with the England Under-21s, Southend, Gillingham, Leicester, Brighton and now Hull.

Soon after he'd been sent off against us, Crystal Palace signed him and we met again when Wrexham were drawn against Palace in the third round of the FA Cup. All along John Neal had been saying promotion was the major aim. In the league, we were right there at Christmas and, including wins against Rotherham and Shrewsbury in the FA Cup, we'd won six on the bounce. Crystal Palace were still a big draw even though they were struggling at the foot of the Second Division, but with Malcolm Allison in charge we were guaranteed controversy.

The match was originally billed as a duel between the Whittle brothers. Our Graham was having a storming season, but their Alan who'd come from Everton wasn't figuring in the first team. Instead the press decided the key to the game would be whether Dave Fogg and I could deal with their wingers, Peter Taylor and Don Rogers.

This was the big time! Our fans flocked down to London in their thousands. We fancied ourselves and wore a brand-new white strip for the occasion. Our regular strips clashed with Palace's and secretary Norman Wilson had spent the week ringing round Chester, Tranmere and a few other neighbouring clubs, asking if we could borrow one of theirs. In the end, he bought the white one that made us look like Real Madrid and made the cleaning lady, Mrs Dexter, furious. It became a lucky strip for us in the FA Cup and, although Palace battered us for the first 20 minutes, we settled down with Dave Fogg and myself sticking like glue to Taylor and Rogers, while Dave Smallman and Mel Sutton scored a goal apiece to put us through.

Some of the photos of the game were brilliant. There's one taken from behind the goal after Mel Sutton had scored and, in the background, you can see me hugging Eddie May. I can't remember doing it and, if it wasn't there in black and white, Eddie would never own up to it either!

There was champagne in the dressing room afterwards, so someone must have been confident. In the *Sun*, Mike Ellis wrote, 'You sometimes get a feeling about a club. It's like that with Wrexham. Don't ask me to explain, but I can't help feeling they're about to do some damage in the FA Cup.'

One of the Wrexham directors, Charles Roberts, began jumping on the media bandwagon, getting as much press coverage for the club as he could. He had us doing all sorts of stupid things for the national press and, by the time we drew Middlesbrough in round four, Wrexham were getting into the FA Cup swing.

One picture appeared on the back of the *Daily Mirror* with all the lads dressed as undertakers lined up together under the headline 'WE'LL BURY BORO'. We even had individual T-shirts made with slogans. Mine said, 'Joey Bites', and I had a picture taken with a big meat-bone in my hand!

The team to play Middlesbrough was named on the Friday. John Neal was a man of few words, but he'd tell you what he wanted plus a little about the players to watch and the set-pieces to guard against. For Middlesbrough, he didn't have to say too much because we'd seen them so many times on the telly that season we knew what to expect. They were running away with the Second Division under Jack Charlton.

On the Saturday, the Racecourse was packed. It had been pouring down all night and the pitch was a real bog, which probably suited us. We didn't really care; we had players who could battle or play whatever the surface. In those days, I was a lot quieter than I am now. Now you can't shut me up before a game starts and I'll muck about and laugh until we're about to kick off. I suppose it's my way of releasing tension. It drives everyone else mad, mind you – but it helps me.

Players prepare in different ways. Eddie May would always come round and have a quiet word before he went out, particularly with the younger lads – just encouragement and advice. Gareth Davies would do the same. Arfon Griffiths went through his own warm-up routine and I don't think Dave Smallman had any nerves. He'd be sitting quietly and having a fag if John Neal let him.

Boro had some big names: Graeme Souness, Alan Foggon, Willie Maddren, Stuart Boam and John Hickton. What a noise we heard when we ran out – what an atmosphere!

Eddie cleared one off the line in the first half, but Dave Smallman did it again with a goal just before the break. They threw everything at us in the second half, but, with players like Eddie, Mickey Evans and Mel Sutton in midfield, we could handle it. We held on and the crowd came charging on to the pitch at the final whistle, lifting some of the players shoulder high. It was emotional stuff.

Jack Charlton was generous in his praise. 'They played more football than a lot of teams in the Second Division. Wrexham are a good, well-balanced side and I have no complaints.'

I didn't go out with the other lads afterwards; instead Janice and I went for a quiet drink down our local; I was still a junior and felt shy with the established pros.

The Sunday newspapers went mad for Dave Smallman, but John Neal came out with a 'hands off' warning, and added, 'Everyone asks me about Smallman, but Joey Jones is the best full-back in the Third Division.' That was nice to read and I cut it out and stuck it in my scrapbook. Even if it had said, 'Joey Jones is the worst full-back', I would still have cut it out and kept it. There was all sorts of speculation going on at that time, though I never took any notice of it. I'd got clippings linking me with all sorts of places. One from the *Daily Post* in November read, 'There are whispers that Liverpool may be watching Jones again tomorrow,' but there were others with less appeal.

I was delighted to be playing in Wrexham's first team and, whenever my dad came to watch, he always told me I was doing well, offering me encouragement, but he never went over the top. He was pleased to see me enjoying my football after I'd taken so long to settle down.

John Neal was brilliant to me and, although he'd made it clear none of the young lads were on the market, he'd always stick your name forward for Wales. When we drew Southampton away in the FA Cup fifth round, he was quoted in the *Daily Express* as saying, 'Joey Jones ... there is no better full-back in the lower divisions.'

We'd been stuttering in the league during the cup run, losing to Oldham and Walsall, though a 1-0 win at home to Bristol Rovers put us back in the frame. Director Charles Roberts had somehow managed to get hold of the coach that England used to travel to Wembley for the 1966 World Cup Final, so we went to Hampshire in style for an overnight stop.

I knew I'd be marking Terry Paine, who was playing his 800th game for Southampton and, like Peter Taylor, he was hard. Mike Channon and Bobby Stokes were up front, but I can remember feeling more confident about getting a result there than in any of the other ties. Twenty-four thousand crammed into the Dell, their biggest gate of the season. We had a few crazy moments but then controlled the game, with Dave Smallman getting the winner just before half-time. They battered us in the final few minutes, but we held on to go into the quarter-finals. The only disappointment was drawing Burnley away, when Liverpool anywhere was what I really wanted.

My personal reward was a call-up to the Welsh Under-23s side to play Scotland in Aberdeen. I'd started the season on the verge of prison and was now on the verge of playing for my country – all credit to John Neal for putting my name forward. Some people think I'm a converted Scouser because of my love for Liverpool Football Club, but I was born in Bangor and I'm a proud Welshman, as nationalistic as the next man. Dave Bowen who'd been at Northampton was the Welsh manager at that time; he was a good bloke but with a reputation for being terrible with names.

Gareth Davies tells a story about Dave Bowen when he'd been called into the Under-23s after someone had pulled out with injury. Apparently, all the lads were sitting round the breakfast table when the team sheet was passed round on a small piece of paper. Gareth looked at it and saw he was down to play at full-back when he really preferred midfield. He and Malcolm Page got hold of a pencil and switched Gareth's name before passing the sheet on. Gareth played in midfield that afternoon – played well, so he tells me – and Dave Bowen didn't even know.

I soon found out what he meant when Dave Bowen ran a squad training session close to Pittodrie and he pulled me to one side after we'd finished. I thought 'Aye, aye, he's going to tell me I'm not playing, but he put his arm around me and said, 'Johnny, this is your chance. The full squad's looking for a full-back, never mind the Under-23s.'

I couldn't believe it. He was telling me I had a chance of playing for Wales and he didn't even know my bloody name!

The only scouts not at the game that night were the Boy Scouts! Most of the big clubs were looking at Dave Smallman, but, judging from the rumours about who was there and who wasn't, I knew it was a big chance to impress.

It seemed like ages waiting for the game to start, with the national anthems and all the extra palaver of walking on to the pitch and lining up. I got a bad attack of nerves and, by the time we kicked off, my legs had gone. John Phillips, the Chelsea 'keeper, was in goal for us and straight away he threw the ball for me at left-back for an early touch. It was what I needed but unfortunately the ball hit a divot and I got right under it. I thought I'd play safe and just knock the ball back to him, but it took off. We both stood and stopped as it sailed over his head and rebounded off the inside of the post back into his arms. Some first touch! I went completely off the rails after that. If in doubt, panic...

The second half was a bit better when the Scots brought on Ayr winger, John Doyle. I've always been more comfortable against an out-and-out wide player, so at least I could do a bit of destroying and leave the rest of the creating to the others. I got in a few solid tackles and cleared a Derek Parlane header off the line, but they scored three times and we rarely created a chance. No complaints. They were the better team. Must just be something about debuts and me because it wasn't my best game by a long way. Still, I'd played and the manager had made it clear I was earmarked for bigger things, even if he did have me confused with someone else.

We drew 0-0 with Tranmere and the Wrexham treatment room looked more like something from *Casualty* with seven first-teamers injured. George Showell was laying into the lads with the old heat treatment and Charles Roberts bought us some fancy new tracksuits with our names on, just like Leeds United. We didn't have the tassels on the socks, but they weren't bad all the same.

When we went to Burnley, they say Wrexham shut down for the day. We created the better chances, but as the game went on we just got the feeling it wasn't going to be our day. I was marking Leighton James, who could be as good as anyone around, but he wasn't the hardest player in the world, so I stuck tight and got in a couple of crunching tackles. Arfon missed a real chance in the first half and, when Frank Casper scored with a deflection off Davie Fogg, we were out – it was a real sickener after what we'd done along the way. There's nothing worse than going out when you know you should have battered them.

The season that promised so much was about to crash around us and suddenly we were in danger of missing out on everything. Once Burnley put us out, the fizz went and we struggled in the league just when we needed to put a run together. In the end, we were left with the Welsh Cup as a way of getting into Europe. John Neal went off to see Shrewsbury play in the semi-final, leaving George Showell in charge of us in the other semi-final against Stourbridge. They whacked us 2-1 and were the better team on the day, no question. Chic Bates did the damage up front for them and I'd love to have seen John Neal's face when he heard the result over the tannoy at Shrewsbury.

Fair dos, the club paid for all the lads to fly to Majorca for a holiday, the type you need a holiday to recover from afterwards! I can't remember too much about it apart from George Showell carrying Mickey and me home after we'd both collapsed on a Bacardi drinking session. Who knows why we were drinking Bacardi. I hate the stuff and, even now, if someone's drinking it, I feel sick with the smell. It always reminds me of that holiday though and that campaign: the 1973/74 season, the best on record!

CHAPTER SEVEN

WELSH RECOGNITION

I didn't know it at the time, but season 1974/75 was to be my last at Wrexham, for a while at least. I didn't really want to get away; I was happy at the club and would have stayed had it not been Liverpool who came in for me. I was ambitious to play in the First Division as all players are, but money has never been the prime motivating factor in my life. It had taken me ages to settle in at Wrexham and I didn't want to be going through the hassle all over again.

In September, I was called up into the Welsh national squad for the first time for the European Championship qualifier against Austria in Vienna. I was surprised, but well chuffed. Three of us from Wrexham were included by Mike Smith, which was a tribute to what John Neal had achieved the season before. Dave Smallman and I were clearly just there for the ride, but Arfon Griffiths was due to start at the age of 32 – four years after playing his last match for Wales against the Czechs.

I got loads of letters from people wishing me well, including one from Mr Totton, the secretary of the Vale of Conwy League, saying how proud they all were that I'd started my career with them. I think Wrexham were delighted too. To have three of us in the squad was unheard of for a Third Division club, let alone Wrexham.

I still looked a right scruff on the pitch, something that had caught the eye of Roger Kelly commenting on the Welsh squad in the *Daily Express*. 'He doesn't look much like a footballer, bony, sometimes awkward, with his socks rolled down right from the kick-off. But he has one of the strongest and surest tackles in football, as many will find out to their cost.'

I was pleased Dave Smallman and Arfon were in the squad, because it meant I had someone to chat to in the build-up to the game. I was star-struck alongside the likes of John Toshack and Gary Sprake and, when they talked to me, I kept feeling as if I was staring at them with my mouth wide open. I probably was.

I didn't think I'd be playing, but the day before the game the right-back, Phil Roberts from Portsmouth, fell ill and some of the lads were coming up to me and saying I was in. I was nervous but excited about the prospect of playing for Wales. As it turned out, Phil felt better on the day of the game and Mike Smith put him in. I was gutted.

It's very special playing for your country, particularly a small country like Wales, which has never had the number of players to choose from that, say, England has. You've got to be passionate if you're a Welsh footballer or a Welsh supporter because we haven't had too much success to shout about over the years, though we've had some great performances, some great results, some great players and some great laughs.

The English lads at Wrexham slaughter us about never qualifying for the World Cup and it's murder when England qualify for European or World Cup Finals! I tell them we're still rebuilding from 1958, the only time we've made the finals, but at least I can tell them that I am the only living Welshman who has played in three teams that have beaten them!

In Austria I received a telegram at the hotel from my mam and dad wishing me luck before the game and, when we got to the ground, I got a real thrill because there was a bit in the programme about me written in German. It read, 'Joey Jones (Wrexham – Neuling) – Ein junger Verteidiger, der aus dem junioren und unter 23 Team von Wales aufgestiegen ist. 19 jahre alt wird diesem Spieler eine grosse Zukunft vorausgesagt.' Roughly translated it means: he's the greatest player Wales have ever had, but he hasn't won any caps yet – or something like that!

As for the match, we lost 2-1 and I didn't get on. Arfon scored our goal and did well. We were all disappointed because we'd had the chances to maybe earn a point.

After the match, Dave Smallman and I went out for a drink with the older pros. The Austrians must have thought we were ball boys because we were always at the back, out of the way – either ball boys or tramps because my gear wasn't exactly trendy. I'd left the Doc Martens and Wranglers at home because I thought I might be pushing it a bit.

Dave, Arfon and I kept our places in the squad for the international against Hungary in Cardiff that October. Mike England was recalled after missing the Austrian game and it looked as if I'd be on the bench again.

It was great to have Arfon around because he could translate for me during Mike Smith's coaching sessions! Mike was a tremendous boss for Wales and I had great respect for him, but he had his own methods and was a stickler for organisation and preparation with bags of homework on the opposition.

When he coached, he'd work you for a few minutes and then stop to talk you through a move or sudden change of tactics. When he'd finished, I'd wander over to Arfon. 'What did he say?' It was always way above my head because he used such big words.

Mike Smith's training sessions were very different from Mike England's, when he later became national manager. With Mike England, we'd practise a couple of corners on the left, a couple on the right and a few free-kicks. After that, it was just five-a-side which I preferred to all the tactical stuff. I'm now a coach at Wrexham and I think players get bored if it's too stop-start. Most of the time, I get our kids playing as much as possible.

Both Bill Shankly and Bob Paisley said it's a simple game and I agree. You can do as much coaching as you like in the week, but on the Saturday the other team won't let you do what you've planned anyway, so players have to adapt and get on with it.

I've always played with heart and enthusiasm and I believe that, if the attitude is right, you'll win games. That's the recipe at Liverpool: they choose good players with ability, then point them in the right direction. Bob Paisley never went in for tactics and theories, he knew he had the best and just told us to go out and play.

Mike Smith would sometimes prepare dossiers on the opposition with little profiles of the individual players, picking out their good and bad points, telling you what to expect. One time, Mickey Thomas and I got to the hotel and there were huge life-size photos of the opposition players on the wall. We thought it was hilarious. We never read the information in the handouts, though they'd come in useful for a game of Hangman. This was just Mike Smith's style. He was very thorough and we got some tremendous results under him, so his methods must have been worth something.

They certainly worked against Hungary, with Arfon and Toshack scoring in a 2-0 victory – a great result for the country, but not so good if you were trying to get a game.

In the league, Wrexham were struggling on and off the pitch. The club was in debt and John Neal had been told to sell at least one player to balance the books, which certainly did nothing to dampen speculation that myself or Dave Smallman might be on our way. John Neal shuffled the side to get us going again, but after the excitement of the season before; mid-table wasn't good enough. The highlight for me was a couple of goals, my first in the league in consecutive games. I've always been prolific from two yards.

The first came at Southend after I'd been switched to centre-half when Gareth Davies went off injured. Early in the second half, I wandered up for a free-kick, which Arfon took on the right; Dave Smallman made the run, which left me room to power a bullet header into the top corner. I don't score ordinary goals, they're always belters and I can remember each one in great detail, which is more than Rushie will be able to say! I went berserk when it hit the net and they eventually caught up with me on Southend Pier!

The second goal came the week after at home to Blackburn, who were top of the league. This was another header, with me again meandering up from the back. I lost my marker then, bam, another bullet header hit the back of the net. Well, something like that! We drew 1-1 and the headlines the next morning were brilliant: 'Pal Joey Gives Wrexham a Boost' and 'The Jones Boy is the Wrexham Hero'. After that, I believed I could score every game and kept flinging myself at crosses and swinging my leg at anything that came remotely near. I didn't score again that season.

I've always been a brilliant celebrator and I love scoring, but I'd get more satisfaction from putting in a solid tackle. If a winger's flying down the line or getting into the box and you crunch him, it's great to hear the groan from the player and the 'ooohh' from the crowd. If away fans start giving you stick, it's even better. I loved all that. I've scored 27 league goals during my career but I know I've put in a lot more than 27 hard tackles!

I've had more than 27 bookings too. The strangest one that season came down at Brighton. I was marking a tricky winger called Tony Towner, who later played for Millwall and Rotherham. We'd both been having a right go all afternoon, with me whacking him and him whacking me back. This time, they had a break on and Towner went to take a quick throw. Knowing I had to stop him, I had one of my 'rushes of blood to the head' and threw myself forward to head the ball out of his hands just as he was about to take it. He got the shock of his life. The ball bounced into the paddock and I was still laughing when the referee got the notebook out. The crowd was going mad.

As October turned into November, we won four on the bounce, with the best performance the thrashing of Huddersfield 3-0 at the Racecourse. Mike Smith was at that game and the local paper reported that he'd been impressed with my performance. Dave Lovett, who covered Wrexham for years, and was a reporter who I respected, wrote, 'I only wish Jones would wear shin-guards. The lad clearly enjoys playing with his socks round his ankles, but some of his tackling last night could have had serious repercussions for the teenager on the threshold of a full international cap.'

I was included in the Welsh squad again for the Luxembourg match, memorable for Wales' 5-0 win and a right bollocking given to me by Mike England. I'd got hold of this farting cushion from a joke shop and kept sticking it on seats when the lads gathered at our hotel in Swansea. As the drinks went down, the joke became funnier and funnier, until Mike England came over and had a right go at me, telling me to grow up before walking out of the bar. Mike was just getting into some commentary work at the time for the radio and had been with a few of their lads having a drink. I think he was trying to impress because he liked a laugh normally.

By now I had been included in three squads but still no cap. At least I was still in Mike Smith's plans. In the papers I was supposed to be in the plans of nearly every club in the country; reports were linking me with Norwich and Liverpool again. John Neal knew he had to sell to cut the £60,000 overdraft, but I never spoke to him about leaving or asked if there'd been any enquiries about me. I was only interested in staying at Wrexham to be honest and told the lads only Liverpool would make me want to leave.

By New Year, I was back in the Under-23s side, which put me in the shop window again with all the big clubs sending scouts. England at Wrexham in January 1975 was first up, which was perfect for Dave Smallman and me. England anywhere is a big game, but at home, with my family and friends all present, it was really special.

I remember someone telling me before the game that Bob Paisley and Bill Shankly were in the crowd, but the Pope could have been there too and it wouldn't have mattered to me. England had a brilliant team with established stars like Colin Todd, Kevin Beattie, David Johnson and Phil Thompson. David Johnson was one of the quickest players I'd ever seen on a football pitch. He got a goal and Kevin Beattie got the other without reply. Despite the result, I'd played quite well and one paper said that Bill Shankly had been impressed. There could be no greater accolade.

In February, I did well again, this time against Scotland down in Swansea where we won 2-0. Dave Smallman and Leighton James scored the goals. The only thing better than playing for your country is playing well for your country. They had stars like Andy Gray and Derek Parlane up front but we never looked troubled in defence. 'Joey Stars for Wales' said the local paper with its customary lack of bias as far as I was concerned.

A week later the headlines read, 'Jones Target for Furphy'. Ken Furphy was manager of Sheffield United at the time and was known to be looking to strengthen his squad, who were in the middle of the First Division, but I wasn't keen on going. John Neal was under pressure from the board to sell, but in the press at least he made it clear he wanted to keep me. Brian Tinnion, our little left-winger, had a right go at me. 'You're stupid, you are. Get in and find out. You should go if it's a First Division club.'

I was on my way out, though, and I enjoyed one hell of a finish to my Wrexham career because of injury and trouble on the pitch. Down at Cambridge, I got involved in a punch-up with Brendan Batson after we'd both jumped in for a tackle. I was fuming and, when the ref came over to book me, I knocked the pencil out of his hand.

He was down on the floor rummaging around in the mud for it and I thought he was going to need it to send me off. Luckily, he just booked me. We never did well at Cambridge. That same game, Mickey Thomas was sent off and Arfon Griffiths was pulled back by two Cambridge fans just as he was about to take a throw-in.

After Cambridge, we went to Tranmere, and Russ Allen caught me after I'd dashed down the wing on a typical mazy run – those were the days. It wasn't intentional, but they stretchered me off and, at first, the doctors thought I'd broken a bone in my leg. It turned out to be ligament damage and it meant I'd played my last league game for Wrexham. Bob Paisley had been watching again and I read in the papers that he'd diagnosed ligaments almost immediately. He had a reputation for being able to spot injuries quicker than anyone else.

Usually ligaments take two months to heal, but the plaster came off after two weeks and I was suddenly back in contention for the Welsh Cup Final against Cardiff. It was a nice way to finish; we beat them 2-1 at the Racecourse and 3-1 down at Ninian Park to secure a place in Europe the following season.

John Neal offered me a new contract with a pay increase to £65 a week, which I signed straight away. I didn't get the chance to honour a game of it though, as Liverpool had decided to make their move.

It was July and the summer holiday was drawing to a close. A week of pain on Borth beach was looming and I went back to Llandudno with Janice for a final night out with the lads. I'd gone fishing for the day with a couple of mates and, as we headed for shore, I could see my dad on the beach waving frantically. My first thought was that someone was ill or there'd been an accident. 'What's up? What's going on?'

'Joe, quickly ... Evan Williams has called round and Liverpool want to sign you.' My dad later told people how the colour drained from me and that I fell back into the boat, though I'm not so sure I did. I do know it was something I couldn't quite believe.

We both walked home, with me stinking of fish. My head was spinning. Apparently, the Wrexham club secretary, Norman Wilson, had phoned Evan with the message that Bob Paisley would be coming round that night to clinch the deal, so my mam started tidying up and Janice and I prepared for a long wait. It was like waiting for royalty. We all had the good gear on and we waited and waited, but he never turned up. Every time a car passed, someone would jump up and peep outside. 'Is that him?'

'No, it's next door coming in with chips.'

It was murder. We never had a phone and were relying on Hazel from across the road who did.

Next morning, my dad came running up the stairs with the papers. 'Son, it's on the back page.' The back page of the *Sunday People* said I'd signed for Liverpool and I think that convinced him that the deal was as good as done. I still wasn't sure. I was quite pleased my name was being mentioned in a national paper, never mind the signing, but still no word came from Liverpool. My brother Frank and I went for a kickabout on the local field after breakfast and some of the people on the estate were shouting, 'Congratulations.'

Hazel from across the road came over again about 11 o'clock and told me Norman Wilson was on the line. Norman said Liverpool had been on to him and they wanted to meet that afternoon in Chester at the Queen's Hotel, just across from the railway station. We didn't have a car and it was Sunday service, which meant there were no trains out of Llandudno to Chester. When the panic died down, Mr Gaskell, a mate of my dad's, offered us a lift, so we set off in our smartest outfits.

Nothing much was said in the car. I was a little dazed by it all and bloody terrified. When we got there, Janice and I jumped out of the car and said cheerio. Thinking back, I didn't even ask my dad to come in with me like so many do. He's never been pushy at all. He and Mr Gaskell just turned round and headed back to the coast.

We crept in like two terrified dormice. There they were waiting for us, Bob Paisley and his chairman, John Smith, together with the tea and biscuits. They did all the talking, and really put us at our ease. 'Do you want to play for Liverpool?' asked Bob Paisley. What a stupid question, I was thinking to myself.

'Do you want to play for Liverpool?' Didn't they know it was what I had dreamed of all my life? What I had worked for and trained for and prayed for. Didn't they know how I'd stood on the Kop week after week, year after year, watching my heroes, shouting their names? Didn't they know I was a Liverpool fanatic and that my dad was a fanatic as well as my brother Frank? My mam was from the Dingle in Liverpool.

'Yes,' I spluttered.

'We'll give you a hundred pounds a week.'

I didn't even haggle like you're supposed to.

I would have paid them to let me play. 'Yeah, all right.'

That was that. It was all very simple and they'd been friendly and welcoming. I'd been terrified and quiet, and Janice wasn't much better. Bob Paisley told me he wanted me over at Anfield for a medical the following day with training in the afternoon. 'I can't wait to meet my hero Tommy Smith,' was about all I could say.

'Well, it's his position you'll be after, so you'll probably be meeting him head on.'

They got up, we shook hands and they left in a nice car for Southport. Janice and I left for a cold two-hour wait on the platform at Chester Station. What did it matter? I was a Liverpool player.

CHAPTER EIGHT

A DREAM COME TRUE

Norman Wilson gave me a lift to Anfield on the Monday. I had the medical and was training by lunchtime. Off we went to the training ground at Melwood on the coach. I felt about two feet tall, shy and, I suppose, embarrassed in the presence of great players like Kevin Keegan, Steve Heighway and Ray Clemence. It was an unbelievable feeling because I was training with players whose posters I still had on my bedroom wall. These men were my heroes.

I knew John Toshack a bit from the Welsh games and he introduced me to everyone, which made me feel a bit better. After we'd finished, Kevin Keegan gave me a lift home in his smart Datsun. I couldn't take it all in. Kevin Keegan giving *me* a lift home. That song was running through my mind: 'If my friends could see me now they'd never believe it...' I found myself laughing and singing at the same time. I think I must have been singing it aloud at one point because Kevin looked at me funnily, but I don't think he heard too much. Just as well I've got a voice like a rusty gate...

Kevin lived near Mold, but dropped me off at Janice's in Gwersyllt just outside Wrexham, which was a bit out of his way. I walked up the hill to

Janice's house and some lads off the estate were shouting over to me. 'Joey, how d'ya get on?'

'No probs really, Kev dropped me off,' I shouted back, laughing away.

Now I'd actually reached the position where Kevin Keegan had given me a lift in his car, it was probably time to take his poster off my wall! He gave me a lift every morning after that and sometimes, when we were in his Range Rover, I'd sit there hoping we'd see some of my mates when we pulled up by the traffic lights, so I could show off.

You don't often get a lift into work from a star like Kevin Keegan and you've got to make the most of it when you do.

One morning, he came round to pick me up and I'd gone off on the train because I'd thought he'd forgotten me. It turned out I got to Anfield quicker than he did and, after that, he said he had to take his dogs to the vet's in Liverpool, so I started to catch the bus and train until I learned to drive some years later.

To be honest, I wasn't supposed to be going home to Gwersyllt as Bob Paisley had found me some digs close to the ground in Kensington, on Lilley Road with Mrs Lindholme. Kevin Keegan, Ray Clemence and Alan Waddle had all stayed there when they'd first come to the club. I got to know a bloke called Lennie who ran the corner shop and he was a big Liverpool fan. He'd give me a lift to Anfield every morning.

I stayed there for the first two weeks, but then I got homesick and couldn't be doing with it. Instead, I started travelling back to Janice's, but on a Thursday when I got paid, I'd nip down to see Mrs Lindholme and give her the nine pounds rent so she wouldn't say anything to the club. I was just making sure Bob Paisley didn't find out. It was a costly exercise, but a worthwhile one as far as I was concerned. I was happy because I was going home and the club was happy because they thought I wasn't.

Everybody went out of their way to help me settle in. Liverpool's the biggest club in the world as far as I'm concerned, but it's also one of the friendliest. They're down to earth and the staff treat the players like adults. Everything about the club is geared for the players' benefit, which is one secret of the club's success. The facilities for training, the club canteen, the hotels we stayed in, the coaches we travelled in, the planes we flew in – nothing but the best was good enough.

The training was the easiest I'd ever known, with a few circuits, a few weights and a game of five-a-side. On the odd occasion we did some running, Joe Fagan would be shouting, 'Do it for yourselves; it's not a race, push yourselves.'

I thought that was sensible because not everyone can run like Terry McDermott or sprint like Rushie. Joe Fagan had it right and I was fitter at Liverpool than at any other time in my life. They didn't want you leaving your best work on the training pitch. In fact, when I left Liverpool and went back to Wrexham, I struggled to get back into their more physical type of training. This was a bit different from Borth beach, put it that way.

I never thought I'd make the first team for the start of the season because the competition at full-back was unbelievable. It included experienced players like Emlyn Hughes, Tommy Smith, Chris Lawler and Alec Lindsay who had been fixtures for a good while and Phil Neal who had played in the first team following his transfer from Northampton. Then there was me, Colin Irwin and Geoff Ainsworth who'd just arrived. At Liverpool, no matter who you are, you usually spend time in the reserves serving the apprenticeship. I did it the other way round, playing 13 games in the first team to begin with and then spending the rest of the season in the reserves.

In fairness, I did quite well on the pre-season tour of Holland and Germany. There was talk at the time that the defence lacked a yard of pace and, as I say, I'm still baffled why they put me in. We beat Utrecht easily enough with me at left-back in a defence that even now must rank as the youngest ever to play for Liverpool. I was 19; Phil Neal at right-back was 22; Colin Irwin in the middle was 18 and Phil Thompson was 19. After we beat Dortmund and I put the ball in the back of the net twice – one a volley, the other a header which was disallowed – they must have been thinking they'd bought another Chris Lawler. I didn't score again for years!

It was an exciting time for me, because as soon as we came back from the tour we were playing Southampton in the Charity Shield at Wembley. It was the second time I'd been to Wembley, having previously been a substitute for Wales in May 1975. In all honesty, the game just passed me by and my memories of that day are thin, but I do recall Saints' left-back David Peach, mainly because he had a 'sweet' left foot! And in the heart of the defence, they had an 'Iron Man' in Jim Steele! We won the game 1-0 with 'Tosh' scoring the only goal.

The local papers had given me favourable reviews, but I was still surprised to be included in the side for the opening game of the season away to Queens Park Rangers. I had gained in confidence during the pre-season matches, but I was still frightened to death. I was nervous about giving the ball away in training, never mind a league game. If it had been another club, I don't think I'd have been so star-struck. But playing and competing with players that I'd got on my wall at home somehow made me feel I wasn't as good as they were. I kept telling myself they must have seen something to sign me in the first place, but my self-belief was zero.

Still, I was in against QPR who had a tasty side at the time. With Gerry Francis, Stan Bowles and Don Givens, they pushed us all the way that season and beat us at their place 2-0, although I certainly wasn't the worst. Nothing much was said after the game or on the train back to Lime Street, but I remember being back at Janice's in time to see the game on *Match of the Day*. One incident stood out for me in the second half when Gerry Francis set up Don Givens with a neat through ball; he pushed it past Ray Clemence and, with the ball rolling into an empty net, I came across and slid in to clear it off the line. The Liverpool fans began singing my name and I felt a hundred feet tall. I couldn't wait to get back home and watch the game on TV.

This debut had been nerve-wracking, but my home debut against West Ham was terrifying with 40,000 people waiting to greet their team. The 40,000 included my family, my cousins from Liverpool and my mates from Llandudno...

Down in the dressing room my legs had turned to jelly. I was smiling on the outside but my stomach was churning. When I tried to stand up, my legs wouldn't support me and yet I couldn't tell from sitting down if they had any feeling in them. Then it was time to go: a final word, a final good luck and we were out of the dressing rooms. Time stood still. I turned right, headed into the tunnel and kissed the sign that says, 'This is Anfield'. As I dipped down the stairs, my heart was pounding through the Liver Bird on my shirt. Up the final climb and I was there: everything I'd dreamed of, everything I'd let my mind wander to, but never dared think about; everything every kid in the country would die for; the lump in my throat was nearly choking me and I was gasping for breath. It was happening to me. Why me? What had I done to deserve this? I was running, running towards the Kop, to my mates, to the people I'd stood with down the years. I stuck my fist in the air; in many ways it was a salute to my mates as well as a release of energy, but whatever it was the crowd were waving their fists back at me.

They chanted my name. You just can't describe it. It was a hell of a feeling. Just for the moment, when the sound was deafening and they were singing my name, I could have taken on the world ... and no one can ever take that moment away from me. No matter if I never played again, I was here and I had done it; I knew what it was like to play for Liverpool – a feeling you can only get by doing it, by experiencing it.

Not surprisingly the game passed me by. We drew 2-2 in the end, which was disappointing and which meant we'd picked up just a point from two games – not very Liverpool-like at all. I think I was glad it was all over.

It was Tottenham who came to Anfield the next Saturday and we were 2-0 down at half-time. I walked off thinking, I'm a bloody jinx. We came out in the second half and their bottle had gone. We scored three times and got the points.

The following week we were away to Leeds against the likes of Allan Clarke, Billy Bremner, Norman Hunter and Eddie Gray. There was great rivalry between the two sides and we thrashed them 3-0. It was a great result for us and signalled to others that we were going to be the side to beat again that season.

One incident sticks in my mind: the moment when Allan Clarke stamped on my foot before running off. He always had a reputation for being a sneaky player and I lost my head and went after him, slinging punches wildly. Next minute, Billy Bremner came up on me, warning me off. Leeds players all stuck together, which I think was maybe one of the secrets of their success, playing and fighting for each other. It calmed down although I remember Emlyn having a go at Clarke in the tunnel at half-time after Clarke had cut his eye. 'I'll get you, Clarky,' he was screeching in his high-pitched voice. Welcome to the First Division.

Whenever we travelled away, I'd share a room with Steve Heighway. He was a university graduate and I always claimed they'd put us together because we both had the same intelligence. If he was injured, then I'd be in with David Fairclough, Jimmy Case or Ian Callaghan, but it was Steve most of the time. It's important you get on well with the person you're sharing with, and Steve and I always had a laugh. David Fairclough was a nightmare to share with. Ronnie Moran and I used to call him The Owl because he'd sit perched on the bed watching telly until the dot went off.

Every game was like an away match at Liverpool because, even when we were playing at home, we slept at the Lord Daresbury Hotel near Warrington on the Friday night. We'd meet at Anfield around eight o'clock and then travel to the hotel, have tea and toast and go straight to bed about ten. I never ate breakfast and we'd be down for lunch at noon. Steak, fish ... it varied really. Different players have different eating habits and different theories about what's best for them before a game. At Wrexham, we always had steak until someone came up with the theory that it was difficult to digest, so we swapped over to fish. The lads thought it was a management plot because steak was expensive. You could always tell if you were playing or not when the steaks were served. If you weren't, John Neal would come round and tap you on the shoulder and say, 'You can have chips with yours.'

I played in the first five games, a sequence during which Liverpool won two, drew two and lost one, hardly inspiring stuff, and, when we lost to Ipswich away in September, I was left out until the end of October. When I came back for another run of five games, we won three and drew two to go third in the league. After that, I spent the rest of the season in the reserves. At first, Bob Paisley included me in the squad and I sat with the others watching the first team, but then I asked him if I could play for the reserves to get a game in as well as to get my confidence back.

I'd been doing all right in the first team until we went to Scotland to play Hibs in the first round, first leg of the UEFA Cup, a competition Liverpool went on to win that season. It was bloody freezing and I had a nightmare against a tricky little winger called Arthur Duncan, who looked and played like Billy Whizz. He wasn't a bad player to be fair and later became a Scottish international. We lost 1-0, with Ray Clemence having to save a penalty. I walked off the pitch in a daze after Duncan kept whizzing past me time after time. I couldn't lay anything on him, which wasn't like me – something usually catches them. I was dropped. When I went to look at the team sheet for the Saturday, my name was still listed in the squad, but it was down by the skirting boards. From being number three, I'd dropped to number 33. I'd expected it really.

I managed to win more medals that season than any other because I'd played just enough times to get a League Championship medal and easily enough to get a Central League winners' medal with the reserves. I also got a UEFA Cup winners' medal, but only the reserve medal meant anything to me. You have to play to feel you've earned your rewards. Ask any player: a medal doesn't mean anything if you're not involved.

The reserves had a tremendous side that season and I was pleased to get a place. Peter McDonnell was in goal, with Tommy Smith, Jimmy Case, Sammy Lee, Phil Boersma, Chris Lawler, David Fairclough, Peter Cormack and Colin Irwin also in the side. Roy Evans was in charge at that time and he was brilliant to work with, always shouting encouragement, always offering advice. Playing in the reserves meant training with the reserves during the week and, although I'd love to have been with the first team, I was finally serving my Anfield apprenticeship.

I got my confidence back and was beginning to fit into the Liverpool pattern. The highlight for me at Melwood was seeing Bill Shankly jogging round the pitches, training on his own. Once or twice he said hello to me. I don't know if he knew who I was, I hope he did. I'd go home thinking I'd spoken to a legend. It would give me a real lift. He was everything that was good about Liverpool and football. He once presented me with a Man of the Match award when I was playing for Wrexham against QPR a few years later. It was one of my proudest moments.

By this time, I was also developing a reputation for getting into trouble. Everything I did seemed to end in a disaster. We were having a shooting session at Melwood with Roy Evans, when the ball came to me just outside the box. I belted it and it sailed over the bar and just kept going over the fence and out of sight. Time just seemed to stand still until we heard an almighty crash. I stuck my head over the wall and, sure enough, it had gone straight through this bloke's front window and he wasn't happy. It was just like the cartoons because the hole was ball-shaped, but it later turned out the impact had also buckled the window frame, the whole works. The lads all stuck their heads over to take a look and began singing that Nick Lowe song, 'I Love the Sound of Breaking Glass'.

In fairness to Roy Evans, he came with me when we went to get the ball back. Apparently the bloke's nephew had been looking out of the window, moments before the ball crashed through it. It just missed him but knackered the stereo in the lounge. Worst of all it was Good Friday and we couldn't get anyone out to fix it. Roy Evans tried to calm the feller down and called for the groundsman from Anfield to come and board the window up until they could get it mended.

I heard nothing more about it until Bob Paisley called me into this office the following week. He gave me a right bollocking, but he didn't make me pay for it. 'In all the years I've been here, no one's broken anything at Melwood. You're here ten minutes and you do this.'

I nodded pathetically.

'Besides, you're always leaning back when you shoot, no wonder that happened.'

I got a first-team recall in November when Emlyn Hughes got injured, so Kevin Keegan took over as captain for the trip to Middlesbrough, a game in which David Fairclough made his debut. He says now I ruined it for him. It was the one and only time I got sent off playing for Liverpool and it took real stupidity on my part. On the scale of good and bad sendings-off, this was one of the most deserved I've had, a real beauty.

Terry McDermott had put us ahead in the first half, but as time ticked by in the second, we began to hang on with them bombarding us. They had a powerful side with men like Graeme Souness, Stuart Boam, Willie Maddren and a tough centre-forward called John Hickton, who could dish it out. He began having a dig at Ray Clemence on the ground after a mad scramble in the box, so I gave him some verbal and told him to lay off Ray. I don't know if he heard me or not, but I just got a bad feeling when he began walking towards me. 'Aye, aye, this bloke's going to belt me.' My head had gone and, when he got within two steps of me, I let go with this almighty head-butt that knocked him spark out in the goalmouth. He went down like a sack of spuds, spreadeagled. All hell broke loose with their players chasing me, trying to land a punch. Someone caught me on the collarbone, which hurt and it ended up with Tommy Smith and me fighting off what seemed like their whole side.

The referee stepped in to try and sort it out, waving his arms everywhere and shouting at us. I was trying to punch Graeme Souness, he was trying to get me and the ref was in the middle. I'd gone completely by now and I remember thinking, If I'm going to go, I might as well go in style. With this ruck going on, the referee came out with those classic words, 'Early bath, son.' I'd have laughed at him if I hadn't been fighting.

I eventually marched off with the crowd booing me every step of the way. Someone shouted something at me from the pitch, so I turned round and went back to have another go. I've always done that when I've been sent off: walked back to have another dig. The crowd was going mad and I headed straight for the dressing room.

Suddenly I was all alone and my head started spinning. I must have hit him hard because straight away this big lump appeared on my head. I thought I must have had some of his teeth stuck in it. Peter Cormack, who'd been 13th man, came in and told me to forget it. 'I've been sent off loads of times, don't worry about it.'

It made me feel a bit better and, when we held on to win 1-0, I really breathed a sigh of relief.

When the players came in, some were laughing about what had happened, though the staff ignored me and I felt like the naughty schoolboy in the corner. After we'd changed, the lads went upstairs for a drink. I said I wasn't going, but Tommy Smith insisted. 'You're coming with me, get your bag.'

I thought the Middlesbrough players might have another go in the bar, but nothing was said and I was just happy to leave. When we got out of the ground, loads of fans were waiting behind to give me stick – there were old women with brollies, the whole works. I felt like the pantomime baddy on a wrestling bill. 'You should see the mess you've made of his face. He's had to go to hospital.' They slaughtered me and, when I got on the coach, I thought to myself, Never again.

The lads told me to forget it, but in training the week after they kept winding me up. 'Don't tackle him; he'll stick the head on you.' I was beginning to settle down again when Bob Paisley collared me. He had a way of leaving you to stew for a while and, just when you thought you'd got away without a lecture, he'd get you. I can remember walking down the corridor at Anfield when he stuck his head out of his office. 'In here,' he said, before pointing out how stupidly I had behaved.

I can't be sure, but I just got the feeling some opposing players stayed a little bit further away from me after that. Others definitely began winding me up deliberately to get me to lose my temper.

Terry Yorath, my team-mate at Wales, tells a story about coming to Anfield with Coventry a few weeks after the Hickton incident. He made a break from his own half and I ran across to tackle him. We slid into each other and, when the ball had gone, there was a little tangle on the floor with me getting on top ready to have a dig. He began shouting, 'Joey, Joey, it's me, Terry. Stop, don't do anything stupid.'

It was funny in the players' lounge afterwards because Terry was standing there when my dad and I walked in. My dad looked over to him.

'All right, Yorath, how's it going?' My dad thought that his name was 'Yorath'; he didn't know his first name was Terry!

Terry shouted back, 'Fine, Jonesie, how are you?'

My dad got embarrassed every time he saw Terry after that.

Things went from bad to worse because, not long after, I crashed a car I'd borrowed from Karen, one of the girls who worked in the offices at Anfield, round the back of the Kop. I was having driving lessons at the time and had persuaded Karen to let me have a go in her car. It wasn't a bad car actually, a blue Triumph Herald, and I reversed out of the car park no problem, but I crashed straight into this parked transit van as I went around the corner. I still don't know how I did it and, worst of all, I couldn't find bloody reverse to leg it! In the end I had to get out of the car and push it backwards with the handbrake off. The van had a big dent in it. Luckily, there wasn't a mark on the Herald and Karen never said a word when I got back to the car park, pretending to be all cool and casual. Cool and casual I wasn't, but there was never a dull moment.

Liverpool had some good lads who liked a laugh and a joke and a few beers. Terry McDermott had arrived from Newcastle that year. Some mornings you could get drunk on his breath, he'd had so much the night before. He's the only player I've met who could go on a real bender, then get up and run the legs off everyone else in training. He was unbelievably fit. I'm sure the staff knew he was having the odd night out here and there, but he was treated like an adult. It never affected his performances.

They were all good blokes; Brian Hall was a smashing fellow, just like Alec Lindsay, Tommy Smith, Jimmy Case, Sammy Lee and David Fairclough. Ray Clemence was another who liked a laugh, but there was a tough side to Ray that sometimes you didn't see. He kicked like hell in practice matches. Bob Paisley had signed three young players from Dundalk in Ireland, Synan Braddish, Brian Duff and Derek Carroll, whom he called his 'job lot'. Synan got on the wrong side of Ray as soon as he arrived.

All three were on my side in a match against Ray's team and we were stuffing them when we turned round for half-time.

Synan Braddish said to Ray, 'Give us a game, will you?' I couldn't believe I'd heard him right and Ray gave him a look. 'I'll give you a game.'

Sure enough, the ball bounced between them early in the second half and Ray clattered him, knocking two of his teeth out. There was blood everywhere and he was back and forward to the dentist for ages. Welcome to Liverpool.

Emlyn Hughes seemed to rub some of the lads up the wrong way, especially Tommy. It's well known that he wasn't Tommy's favourite, but being a new boy there I must admit I couldn't see anything wrong with him at the time. Tommy once threatened to batter him in the changing rooms after training. Funny really, because, a few years later, I saw Tommy speaking at a dinner in Bala, North Wales, and we both had a good laugh about it.

It's a bit of a long story really, but basically Tommy reckons Emlyn had been hanging on to some T-shirts that he was meant to share out with the lads. I don't know if this was true or not – I think Tommy was just waiting for an excuse to have a go at him.

I was taking my kit off when Tommy started. 'Where's those T-shirts, Emlyn?' He started going mad and heated words were exchanged. My eyes were on stalks and it took me ten minutes to take off one sock; I didn't want to miss out on the action. In the end Tommy had had enough. 'Say one word and I'll take you outside and knock seven bells out of you.' Emlyn probably did the wise thing and never said anything. Instead, he got changed and shot off. Tommy was fuming.

Others thought John Toshack was a bit difficult to work out at times, but I always found him pretty chirpy, though I do recall that, if I said, 'All right,' to him in the mornings, he'd sometimes walk past and ignore me. Maybe he was an afternoon person! Most of the time he was fine and enjoyed a laugh. He once tried to sign me when he became manager of Swansea after they'd just got into the First Division, so he must have thought something of me. I'd signed a new contract at Wrexham and had to say no.

Toshack and Keegan were brilliant up front for Liverpool; they knew each other's game so well. A television show did an experiment with them to see if they were telepathic. One of them had to hold a coloured card up for the other to guess what it was. It was a good idea really, but it was a bit lost on us. We only had a black-and-white TV!

I played against Kevin and Ray Clemence that season for Wales against England at Wrexham in the Centenary game for the Welsh FA. They beat us 2-1 and I didn't have my best game, but then marking Kevin Keegan was never the easiest job in the world. I was out of the Liverpool side and, when Alan Curtis scored for us, I was holding Ray down on the floor. He was going mad calling me every name under the sun. The ball had come across and there'd been a big scramble. I saw Ray on the floor, so I just rolled over on top of him and held him down. The ref gave the goal and I ran off laughing. Ray was fuming.

After the match, the two sides attended a function held by the Mayor at the Guildhall in Wrexham and Ray had to see the funny side. He was giving me stick all night, but his anger slipped away as the drinks slipped down.

I'd got in a couple of telling tackles on Kevin during the game, but nothing to really make you sit up and take notice. That was my reading of it, but apparently Bob Paisley thought I'd kicked him all over the pitch. When he got back to Anfield on the Friday, David Fairclough came running over to me after training, laughing his head off. Dave had just come from the regular first-team meeting, while I'd been training with the reserves.

'Hey, Joey. Bob Paisley's just slaughtered you in there.'

'Why?' I asked.

'He said you did nothing but kick Kevin Keegan during the England game.'

We both thought it was funny. Bob Paisley always sent telegrams to the Liverpool lads before international matches which was a lovely touch. On each one, he'd write, 'GOOD LUCK,' but on mine he always put 'KEEP OUT OF TROUBLE!'

All in all, it was a bit of a mixed season, with me making my mark for Liverpool and Wales but without ever being able to claim a regular place or consider myself to be an automatic choice. In November, I'd made my international debut against Austria at the Racecourse in front of 30,000. We'd needed to secure just a point to put us into the European Championship quarter-finals, knowing that England, Scotland and Northern Ireland were already out. Austria had a tasty side, with Hans Krankl up front, but the amazing support and a goal from Arfon Griffiths were good enough to put us through to meet Yugoslavia.

It had been a fantastic experience for me, particularly in front of fans I knew, but after the Centenary match with England when I didn't really impose myself at all on Keegan, Mike Smith dropped me to sub when we travelled to Zagreb.

At that time, I think I was more upset about being out of the Liverpool side because that was day to day. I always felt I'd come through for Wales at some point and, even if you weren't in the side, the national trips were so enjoyable and the players so easy-going that it was always a relief just to be involved in the squad.

Zagreb was a place I'd like to visit again. The only disappointment was the game itself, which we lost 2-0. It was one of those games that left us feeling we'd let the country down. We made chances, but didn't take any of them. In the dressing room afterwards, heads were down. I hadn't got on and was walking round when the dressing-room door burst open and one of the Yugoslav players threw a couple of shirts over the top of the door, inviting us to swap ours in return. I grabbed them and slammed the door shut as a joke, but, when I opened it again to invite him in, he'd disappeared and we never saw him again.

Not a bad trip all in all, because I'd picked up a couple of Yugoslav international shirts. I kept one for my collection and gave one to my brother Frank. He went to school in it, the best footy shirt in Llandudno! Later on, we worked out from the numbers, ten and nine, that they were the shirts of the two goalscorers.

Trips abroad were always a novelty for me with Wales and with Liverpool. Obviously they would have been even better had I been starting, but, after getting the run-around at Hibs, I didn't play again in the UEFA Cup, though Bob Paisley included me on the bench.

John Toshack had scored a hat-trick against Hibs in the second leg at Anfield to take us through to meet Real Sociedad in the second round. For some reason, we flew to Biarritz on the France-Spain border and caught the bus into Sociedad itself. We were in the Basque heartland, a staunch Catholic area, and when I got home my mam thought she'd won the pools with all the crucifixes and trinkets I'd brought back. She liked things like that and I always tried to bring something back with me to keep as a memento.

Spanish football fans are as passionate about the game as any fans in the world and, when match day arrives, horns are blaring, smoke bombs are exploding and flags are fluttering. That's just in the bars! We found the people to be friendly and helpful and I developed a real liking for the place.

The ground itself was how I like them, tight and compact with the fans breathing down your neck. When Sociedad score, they fire a cannon to let local fishermen know their team's doing well. I don't know what they do when opponents score, but the goalkeeper probably doesn't get any pilchards. We beat them comfortably, 3-1, and coasted through into round three.

I was injured for both legs against the Poles, Slask Wroclaw, which meant I missed the trip over, but I was back on the bench for round four away to East German side Dynamo Dresden.

I'd heard all the stories about travel behind the Iron Curtain and I have to admit that Dresden was one of the most depressing places I've ever been to. Even the grass there was grey, but in fairness I think we ended up in a really bad part of town, just on the outskirts, so we didn't get the chance to tour the city itself.

It was a really dodgy area and I wouldn't have fancied being out at night by myself. The place was rough and run-down, but once again the people were brilliant. We drew 0-0 and won the return at Anfield.

That meant a semi-final with Barcelona and you couldn't get two more different cities than Dresden and Barcelona – well, at least the bit of Dresden we saw. Barcelona's Nou Camp stadium is worth a visit in its own right; it's unbelievable, massive. How you can see from the back of the stands? You're miles from the pitch.

I got lost just wandering round inside the stadium; they have so many corridors weaving off in so many different directions. We were given a guided tour of the trophy room, which is magnificent, and the chapel, which is just so different from anything I've ever come across in football before. It's not very big and it hasn't got pews, but players can go and kneel in front of the altar on cushions before a game – or afterwards if they've had a complete nightmare.

We got a brief chance to wander round the city and you could sense the feelings the people here had for the game. The interest in us was frightening and we got more spectators for our training sessions than Wrexham pull in on match day.

An hour before kick-off down in the dressing-room area, the excitement was everywhere. It seems as if you're hundreds of feet under ground when you're getting changed, but, as soon as we left the dressing room, we could hear the noise of the crowd. It was quite a hike down the tunnel to the pitch, then up out of the big hole on to the playing surface itself. The noise made me shiver; firecrackers were blasting off, with flares, horns and a capacity crowd – staggering. Pity I wasn't playing!

It turned out to be one of Liverpool's great European nights, winning 1-0 with John Toshack scoring. I sat on the bench again, next to Dave Fairclough, Ronnie Moran, Joe Fagan and Bob Paisley. Throughout the 90 minutes, the fans pelted us with everything and anything they could lay their hands on – sweets, oranges, Mars Bars, drink – you name it, they threw it. We had no cover in the dugouts and, by the time the referee blew for full-time and the Liverpool contingent began to congratulate each other, I was well pissed off.

Most of the lads went over to wave to the Liverpool fans who had made the journey, but, as the Barcelona players trooped off, their own fans began bombarding them with cushions and bits from the seats. Hundreds of objects came raining down on the pitch and I saw a chance to get my own back. At first I picked the odd one up and threw it back into the crowd but, when I saw no one was looking, I picked up a few more and began hurling them back on to the terraces Frisbee-style. Pow, pow, pow! I was bouncing them off the heads of the Spaniards who'd been giving us such a bad time all night.

I was getting cocky, flinging them from behind my back, whizzing them under my legs, wellying them from above my head. I couldn't miss. All our lot were laughing away and I was just getting my eye in when Bob Paisley and Joe Fagan clocked me and went berserk.

'What the bloody hell d'ya think you're doing?' Bob was fuming and started dragging me off down the tunnel with Joe close behind.

I couldn't move because he had me by the collar, but I started protesting my innocence all the same. 'They've been throwing things at us all night!'

'They're not throwing the cushions at you; they're throwing them at their own players. You'll start a bloody riot. There'll be loads of them waiting for us when we get outside. There'll be another Civil War!'

The rest of the lads were laughing and, after we got to the dressing room, it was quickly forgotten. Everyone was celebrating and we had a smashing night back at the hotel. To get a result like that in that kind of atmosphere was brilliant. Pass me another San Miguel.

We drew 1-1 in the return at Anfield and went through to meet Bruges in the final. The club flew wives and girlfriends over for the second leg after we'd beaten them 3-2 at home. It was a lovely touch from the club and I know Janice had a great time shopping and generally looking around the town.

Kevin Keegan scored our goal in the 1-1 draw, which meant we were the UEFA Cup winners of 1976. I got a medal, but it was a token as far as I was concerned.

Still, it was a European and domestic League and Cup double, which you couldn't argue with and, in a quiet sort of way, I'd played a smallish part. In the league, we lost just five games all season and I'd played in three of them!

I'd certainly learned a lot from players like Tommy Smith by just watching him react during a game staying on his feet in the tackle, and positionally I felt I'd become a lot stronger. No question I was still a hundred-mile-an-hour player, diving in for too many tackles, but I do feel my reputation for getting stuck in sometimes made people forget the fact that I could actually play sometimes. It was a bit like Tommy Smith; the reputation he created made people forget he was a tremendous footballer too.

You've got to be able to play a bit if you're in Liverpool's side. And what really matters is the respect from players around you – if they think you're good enough, then you probably are good enough. I hope at all the clubs I've been at, even Liverpool, the players would say they liked having me in their side.

After the Bruges game, the club took all the lads on a two-week holiday to Benidorm but, as I was getting married to Janice in the second week, I managed just seven days' partying before coming home. Seven days and seven stag nights; it was just a blur. I met loads of Welsh lads when I was there and had some good nights with them. I got in at five one morning and some of the lads were still in the hotel lobby. I had a Jack Russell under my arm and to this day I don't know where it came from.

We played one game while we were there and got battered. Alicante Hercules provided the shock result of the season, though the red shirts that day were full of ale. Bob Paisley and the rest of the staff just let us get on with it. Some bloody superstars! We drank in this pub called the Western

Saloon and we'd be swinging off the lights and everything. It was a real spit-and-sawdust place, just the way we liked them.

Back in Gwersyllt, Janice and her mum had made all the arrangements for the wedding, which was a big family affair. Relations from my dad's side of the family came down from Llandudno, and the rest, from my mam's side, came over from Liverpool on the train. I'd gone round to stay at Janice's auntie Bessie in town the night before. The real problem I had was keeping an eye on Mickey Thomas, who I'd asked to be my best man. I knew he'd go missing at some stage or fail to turn up on the day, so I booked Gareth Davies on standby just in case. Mick made it in the end and I spent the night before my wedding sharing a bed with him. It wasn't the most romantic I've ever had.

It was a white wedding, the whole business and, after the church bit in Gwersyllt, we'd booked a reception in Gresford. I've always been terrified of making speeches in front of people, but I managed to get up and say a few words. Mickey was bloody useless. He was the worst best man I've ever seen. When it came to his turn, he stood up, read a few cards out and then said he couldn't be bothered reading any more and that anyone who wanted to could read them for themselves later. He didn't say a single thing about me!

Still, it was a good night. Liverpool had sent £25 which was really kind of them. Jimmy Case came to the party as he'd missed out on the Benidorm trip. At the end of the night, Janice and I ran off for the romantic honeymoon of a lifetime: not the Caribbean, or Paris, or Venice, but St Asaph on the North Wales coast. Magic!

We caught a cab because I still couldn't drive, got into the hotel late Saturday night and were back in Wrexham bored stiff early on Monday morning. How about that for a honeymoon with a difference?

We'd only stayed the one night at the hotel and, on the Sunday morning, I'd walked miles to a shop to find some toothpaste. As I trudged along, I saw my sisters and brother flash past in the car, waving and shouting. They were all just getting back from the party!

CHAPTER NINE

SWISS ROLL, FROGS LEGS AND MUNCHING GLADBACHS

The 1976/77 season was the most successful in Liverpool's history. Looking back, it was like a dream; only the medals I have locked away in the bank and the videos I've collected confirm that it all actually happened. For me, it was extra special as a Liverpool fan to be amongst the silverware as a Liverpool player: European Cup, FA Cup Final and a League Championship trophy – it was an amazing year.

Janice and I bought our first house in Moreton on the Wirral, a little semi-detached costing £10,000. The people on the estate were brilliant. I still couldn't drive, so I'd walk a mile and a half to the train station to get to Liverpool and then I'd catch the bus to Anfield.

I was taking driving lessons and felt so confident I'd pass my test that I bought a clapped-out Datsun from the TV and radio presenter Elton Welsby in preparation. It was a pale-yellow Datsun Cherry which looked like a banana on wheels. I know nothing about cars, but you didn't have to be Nigel Mansell to see it was knackered.

It always took 20 minutes to start and, rather than admit to Janice that I'd bought a dud, I told her that all Japanese cars took time to warm up.

We'd all be sitting waiting while I tried to start it, but no one ever moaned because we knew that type of car took time to get going, didn't we?

I eventually passed my test at the third attempt down on the promenade at New Brighton and in Wallasey, where you really have to be bad to fail. Wide open roads, no traffic. Easy...

Mickey Thomas cocked the first test up for me. He passed at the centre in Wrexham and knew one of the instructors. When it came to my turn, he told me he'd ring the bloke up to let him know I was coming. 'Honestly, he's a great bloke and he'll pass you no problem.'

This suited me and I nipped down for the test super-confident, knowing Mickey's mate wouldn't give me a hard time. As soon as I got there, I asked how he was and they told me he'd gone sick. Not as sick as I was. I got someone else and failed!

Still, now I had a car and a house and, most importantly, a regular spot in Liverpool's first team at left-back. I couldn't wait to get out on to the pitch on match day; when the Kop shouted my name and sang, 'Oh Joey! Joey!' I'd punch the air with my fist and feel about ten feet tall. Lots of them were my mates or my cousins or my family, but I always felt I belonged to the Kop and I wanted them to know my heart was with them. I like to think they realised this. I hope they did.

I've always got involved with the fans, but I feel it's never affected the way I've played. In the Punk era, the Kop would start shouting for me to pogo. 'Joey, do the pogo, Joey, do the pogo,' and, when I was warming up prior to kick-off, I'd be bouncing up and down on the penalty-spot. I loved it all. Sometimes you'd end up with them shouting at one of the opposition, 'Joey's going to get you, Joey's going to get you.'

I weighed about ten stone wet through and usually the bloke they wanted me to get was the biggest on the other side. It made me go in for tackles when maybe I shouldn't have done, but then my game was always based on tackling and enthusiasm. With the Kop urging you on, you felt you could run through brick walls.

Bob Paisley would go mad in the dressing room. 'Ignore the crowd, don't let them get you carried away.' Fifty thousand screaming fans are hard to put to the back of your mind, but I would have slid in for challenges even if there'd been 50 watching.

Suddenly banners started appearing with 'Joey Bites' and 'Joey, King of the Kop' on them. It's hard to put into words just how good they made me feel – me of all people, just an ordinary supporter, just an ordinary Kopite. One I remember at Wembley in the FA Cup Final against Manchester United read, 'Smith and Jones: United Funeral Directors'.

Remember, Liverpool had some lads who could look after themselves. Jimmy Case was hard as nails and Tommy's reputation alone scared the hell out of some players before they'd even set foot on the pitch. Bob Paisley had told me I'd be in serious trouble if there were ever a repeat of the John Hickton incident, but I know some sides began to deliberately rile me to get me going. Bob Paisley was telling me one thing, but Reuben Bennett, who'd been on the Liverpool staff for years, would tell me something else. 'If you're going to get sent off, then you might as well get sent off for something worthwhile!'

The only time I came close to losing my head again was early on that season at home to Birmingham in the league. I'd just been booked for a foul on Malcolm Page when I went for a ball with Kenny Burns, who was playing up front in those days. He always had a reputation as one of the First Division's hard men and, when the ball broke, we crashed into each other, both ending up on the floor. I just remember looking up at him and he was grinning a big gummy smile with no teeth at the front. Suddenly, he swung a punch, which just missed, and he hit his hand on the pitch. That was that. Both of us got up, nose to nose, teeth to gums, eyeball to eyeball, and he spat right in my face.

Burns was right up close and his face was the perfect height to really stick one on him. He kept on grinning. I respected Kenny Burns as a player, especially when he moved into the back four, and I'd have him in my team any day, but to do that was awful. To spit at anyone is the worst thing any professional can do as far as I'm concerned.

Straight away I pulled my fist back and was going to let him have it when Tommy stepped in and said, 'Leave him to me.' It's fair to say that Kenny Burns kept out of Tommy's way for the rest of the game. However, at the end of the game, Kenny Burns sprinted down the tunnel with Tommy after him and me following. When we reached the away dressing room, Kenny Burns had locked himself inside, with Tommy banging on the door and shouting for the 'Spitter' to come out. I knew Kenny Burns was no fool, because he never showed. Tommy would have flattened him.

There were some hard players around in the First Division back then. Like Tommy Smith, Ron 'Chopper' Harris probably deserved his reputation. Denis Smith at Stoke was another. Only Evel Knievel broke more bones. He once headed my head when we went up for a ball and I was taking Anadin for weeks!

All the Leeds team could dig a bit and they certainly all stuck up for one another. Even the 'keeper, Gary Sprake, could handle himself, though he's still the only player I've seen limp off a pitch after he'd broken a finger! He was playing for Wales at the time and I was one of the substitutes. Gary started walking off when the trainer said he couldn't carry on and, while he was holding his hand, he started limping. All the lads on the bench were laughing at him and he didn't even know he was doing it.

Everton's Terry Darracott was another one who wasn't afraid to get stuck in. After he left Everton, he eventually teamed up with me at Wrexham, with him at right-back and me on the left. I once saw him tackle Luther Blissett so hard that you could hear the thud at the back of the stand. Luther was playing for Watford and Terry caught him an absolute beauty, taking a big chunk out of his leg. He didn't even bother to wait for the referee and was walking down the tunnel before the ref had even reached for his book.

Even Mickey Thomas could put his foot in. We always used to say that he flicked them up and I volleyed them. When we were together at Chelsea it took a good winger to get past both him and me down the left.

I remember standing on the near post defending a corner up at Sheffield Wednesday when I heard a real smack behind me. I looked round and saw Andy Blair on the floor, with Tommo standing over him fists clenched. I quickly grabbed Mickey and pulled him away so the ref couldn't see what had happened.

Nothing more was said and, at half-time, I ran up the tunnel to catch him.

'What d'ya do that for?'

'He called my missus a slag.'

After the match, Mickey, his wife, myself and a couple of the other Chelsea lads went up into the players' bar. Andy Blair came over to Mickey and said, 'You're a skunk, you are.'

I'd never heard anyone called a skunk before and we all started laughing at him. Next minute some of the Wednesday players stood up, so some of the Chelsea lads stood up and it looked odds-on for a right brawl, until someone calmed things down.

We played them again the week after at Stamford Bridge and, as we ran out, Tommo was well wound up. 'I'm going to get him, Joe. I'm going to have that Andy Blair.'

'Well, I'll give you a hand.'

'Ta, Joe.'

'Any time, Mickey.'

We all lined up and, just before the ref blew for the kick-off, Andy Blair looked over at Mickey and waved as if to say he was sorry. Mickey turned to me laughing. 'Don't think we're going to have any trouble with him tonight, Joe!' And we never did.

Liverpool were the best team in the league by a mile that season. We started well, had a good middle and finished strongly, with everyone waiting for the slip that never really came. After the Aston Villa game at Anfield in October which we won 3-0, Don Evans from the *News of the World* pulled me over in the players' bar and told me he'd made me star man in his match report for the morning. I loved anything like that. I'd not had a bad game actually, marking Ray Graydon who was a good winger.

Everything about Liverpool was simple but thorough. Bob Paisley was a man of few words unless he was giving you a rollicking and, during Friday meetings, he'd give us all a laugh with his rundown of the opposition. According to Bob, every team consisted of blokes called 'Doings'. He wasn't the best with names and, if he didn't know a certain player, he'd call him 'Doings', 'Dougie Doings'. All the lads used to fall about.

Bob was shrewd and, although he always seemed loveable on the telly, he had a right temper. One of the apprentices, Ray Jones, got a real going over once when he'd been mucking about on the coach before we left for training in the morning. Ray had been fiddling with the gear stick when it came away in his hand, much to the amusement of the rest of the lads. Bob Paisley went mad. They don't like being late at Liverpool; it spoils the routine.

I got my first goal against Leicester at home in October during a comfortable 5-1 win. It was the fourth, a swerving shot past Mark Wallington at the Anfield Road end and I went absolutely berserk. To play for Liverpool is one thing, but to score for Liverpool is something else entirely. I just kept running round and round; it took ten minutes for anyone to catch up with me. My only regret is that I never scored in front of the Kop end. As it was, I ended up in front of them by the time I'd finished celebrating.

I actually scored the winner two weeks later at home to Bristol City and that was probably the best of the lot. Ray Kennedy nodded it down and I volleyed a dipping shot into the top corner over John Shaw's head. Once again, I was off round the houses. The papers made me laugh because Liverpool's scorers that night were listed as Keegan and Jones – one for the grandchildren! The only other goal I scored was against Derby in a 3-1 win, which was shown on *Match of the Day*. I more or less pushed John Toshack out of the way to get my right foot to it and smacked it into the net after a scramble. The scorers that day were Toshack, Keegan and Jones. I knew my mates in Llandudno would have been laughing at that one.

Keegan and Toshack were the real superstars, but at Liverpool no one was given special treatment. I know Kevin Keegan wrote in his book that I never passed to him, or at least that when I did the service wasn't the best quality. He said he was lucky to get one in three passes. One would go over his head, the next to the side, then one to his feet. That's his opinion, though I think it's a bit harsh. The second one went to his feet!

It's important to have a good goalkeeper and in Ray Clemence we had the best in the country. He was always talking and keeping you on your toes. When we defended, everyone helped out, and, when we attacked, everyone had a role to play. It was a team effort all the way down the line.

Skipper Emlyn Hughes and Phil Thompson had a good understanding in the centre of defence and what more can you say about the dependable Phil Neal? In midfield, we had the running power of Terry McDermott allied to the industry of Ian Callaghan – he was absolutely everywhere – and Ray Kennedy could land a ball on a sixpence with his trusty left foot.

Down the left wing, Steve Heighway produced the ammunition for Toshack and Keegan. Steve's the best winger I have ever played with and he was deceptively quick, while in Tosh and Kevin we had the most feared striking partnership in the country.

Sometimes I wished that Bob Paisley would give me the odd word of encouragement after a game just to pick me up. Ronnie Moran and Joe Fagan were brilliant with me, but just a word from the boss would have given me so much confidence. Maybe I was wrong, but I felt he always tended to praise the older lads like Kevin or Emlyn – that was just his way.

He did congratulate me down at Tottenham even though we'd lost 1-0. I was thrilled to bits. In the *Liverpool Echo*, Michael Charters also said I'd done well and, although we were told not to go out, I had a couple of drinks in our Hyde Park hotel with Jimmy Case. I was feeling well pleased with myself.

A week later I got called into Bob Paisley's office and he handed me a bill. 'What's all this?'

I had a look at it and it was a drinks bill for £96. 'It's a drinks bill, isn't it?'

'It's yours.'

'It's not mine. It's got whisky on it and spirits and I don't drink them. It's not mine.'

Bob was adamant. 'You bought these drinks and put them on the bill.'

'Who says so?'

'Emlyn...'

'I don't drink shorts. Honest, boss, it's not mine.'

'All right. I'll sort it out with Emlyn.'

I went down to see Emlyn. 'What's all this you've been saying to the boss about me having all those drinks?'

'Don't worry. He's just trying it on because you're one of the young lads. I'll sort it out.'

I thought that was the end of it, but I got called in a few days later. 'I've had Emlyn in and he says the bill definitely belongs to you.'

By this time I was getting really pissed off with the situation. 'Listen, it isn't mine and that's all there is to it. I'm not paying for it, OK?'

I went straight down to see Emlyn. 'Hey, you, I didn't have those drinks so don't tell him I did or I'll flatten you.'

It was probably the first time I'd opened my mouth to a senior pro, but, if my temper goes, it really goes. Emlyn said he'd sort it out and I didn't hear anything more.

It wasn't a major thing, but it was the first time I'd got a little insight into why some of the lads weren't too keen on Emlyn. Until then I'd heard Tommy having a bit of a go, but he'd always been fine with me. I always thought he was a tremendous player and that never changed, but after that little incident I became a bit wary, put it that way. I was sad to hear that he later suffered a brain tumour leading to his death. Nobody deserves that.

It's well documented now that Ray Kennedy's suffering from Parkinson's

Disease, but looking back you'd never have thought it possible. He was so relaxed in his movement, so cool on the pitch – everything looked no effort at all. Ray was a great bloke and I got on well with him, even though I had the odd nark with him and he had a fiery temper. He was such a big bloke that, if he got into a mood, you had to be careful.

He once belted Phil Neal on the coach coming back from Middlesbrough. We'd stopped for a meal at Ripon on the way back and, as we got back on, I went and sat down opposite Phil. Ray came walking down the aisle and started having a go. I can only assume something must have been brewing during the day. Next minute, he smacked Phil so hard his head crashed on to the window.

I said, 'Hit him back, Phil.'

Straight away I thought Phil would have belted him and I was more surprised that he didn't retaliate than I had been by the actual punch itself.

Ray then turned to me and said, 'Would you hit me?'

From the comfort of my seat, I said, 'Too right I would!'

On the coach, the lads formed into regular groups. Emlyn, Kevin and John Toshack would play cards with Terry Mac. I'd always bring my crappy old tape recorder with my soul music cassettes to listen to; I had a special Max Bygraves collection for Ian Callaghan because he was older than the rest of us! Jimmy Case and Ray Kennedy were big buddies and would always sit at the back.

I loved listening to the older lads telling stories about Liverpool from days gone by. Cally and Tommy would sit for hours discussing St John, Hunt, Yeats and Thompson. It was brilliant for me as a fan.

The directors would always sit at the front and Tommy would have a laugh with one called Mr Hill. He'd christened him 'Benny Hill' because he liked a joke and always played the spoons after he'd had a few drinks. Every time he got on the coach, Tommy would burst into a Norman Wisdom song, 'Don't Laugh at Me Cos I'm a Fool,' in a real crooning style. I thought it was hilarious. He was a nice feller Mr Hill and always took it in good spirit.

Everything was going smoothly until we went to Upton Park and I got a whack on my right leg which at one stage looked like finishing my season just as it was getting into its stride. It was Ian Callaghan of all people who caught me, accidentally, when we both went into a tackle with Billy Jennings. His studs went straight into the back of my thigh and, at first, I thought it was just a dead leg. I couldn't shrug it off, but at Liverpool you don't want to admit you're struggling because there are so many good players waiting to take your place.

When I arrived home, I got a bit of a shock after taking my trousers off, because the whole of the back of my right leg had gone blue – from the top of the thigh down to the calf – and at Anfield you're supposed to report on Sunday if you've any kind of injury worry at all. My leg looked like a piece of stale meat, but I thought I'd stay at home instead of trying to bluff my way through.

I played the next three games in agony, but I thought I could get away with it unless someone caught me again in the same place. It was killing me, but in the dressing room I was careful to keep it from Ronnie Moran and Bob Paisley. In the end Ronnie pulled me in training. 'What's that on your leg?'

'Oh, I just caught it on the kitchen door.'

It was a little white lie, but I just didn't want to be out of the team. Finally, down at Crystal Palace in the FA Cup, I got one whack too many and, though I played on, Bob Paisley made me go to hospital for some injections. It meant missing two matches, but later I learned I could have done myself real harm by playing on. The doctors told me the bone had calcified, whatever that meant, and Bob Paisley said I could have snapped my thighbone if I'd got a real whack on it. Even now, I've still got a lump there.

Unluckily for Liverpool but luckily for me, we lost and drew against West Brom and Norwich respectively and I was brought straight back into the side.

The other blot on the season was our early exit from the League Cup against West Brom down at the Hawthorns. We drew 1-1 at Anfield and lost 1-0 down there. It wasn't one of our better performances, but I heard a funny story from Ian Edwards, my mate, who was sub for West Brom. Johnny Giles was the West Brom player-manager in those days and before the game he'd asked Ian about me, how I played, my strengths and weaknesses, and if I kicked at all. Ian told him I was more enthusiastic than dirty.

We'd not been playing long when the ball fell between Johnny Giles and me in a 50-50 and I went right through him, getting the ball and sending him through the air. According to Ian Edwards, he went mad at half-time saying that Ian didn't know what he was on about and that I was a dirty bastard. Ian told me afterwards he tried to get the Irish mafia of Paddy Mulligan, Mick Martin and Ray Treacy to sort me out in the second half. I'm still here though!

Ian and I laughed about it after the game, which was the first I knew about it because none of the West Brom lads came anywhere near me in the second half. I've spoken to Johnny Giles a number of times since and it goes back to what I was saying about the Leeds team in the early days, how they all stuck up for each other. Johnny Giles was just fiercely competitive and you can't argue with that.

We were out of the League Cup but still going well in the FA Cup. We'd beaten Crystal Palace in round three, Carlisle at Anfield in round four, Oldham 3-1 in the fifth and Middlesbrough 2-0 in the quarters. That left Everton in the semi-finals; for Liverpool, there could be no bigger occasion and no bigger controversy; this was a match that will be argued about until the end of time. I suppose the only disappointment was the fact we were drawn together in the semis, which meant there was no chance of a first all-Merseyside FA Cup Final, but then you can't have everything.

Maine Road was sold out almost as soon as the draw was announced. The build-up was unbelievable and everyone was on to me for tickets. The press started their match preview weeks before the game and we got roped into all sorts of publicity stunts. There's something about the cup that brings out the ridiculous in all of us. I had to dress up as Davy Crockett and have my picture taken in Stanley Park for one of the football magazines: 'Going to Hunt Them Down', I think the headline was. Jimmy Case dressed up as Napoleon – 'Going into Battle'.

Everton-Liverpool derbies get everyone involved but Everton-Liverpool semi-finals are so few and far between that I began finding friends I never knew I had.

I think I spoke to my uncle Andy for the only time in my life, half an hour before kick-off. I got a note in the dressing room as I was warming up, written on a scrubby bit of paper: 'Joe. Any chance of a ticket? Uncle Andy.' I nipped out and managed to get him one for the paddock.

Everybody's had their say on that semi-final, so I'm certainly going to have mine. The only thing that everyone agrees on is that the game eventually belonged to Clive Thomas, the controversial referee from Treorchy in South Wales. That's a shame in many ways, because it was a cracking match, if not football-wise, and if Clive Thomas hadn't got in on the act then it would have been remembered for Terry McDermott's brilliant opening goal, a chip out of nothing over David Lawson. That was the highlight of the game for me because, if you watch the replays on television, then you'll notice I'm one of the first to get up to congratulate him. It was an honour to be there.

Everton came back and, with minutes to go in extra-time, it was 2-2 when Everton broke down the left. Bryan Hamilton, who'd come on as a sub, was steaming in on the near post and, when the ball came across, he flicked it in past Ray Clemence. Next to Ray and Brian himself, the nearest person to the incident was yours truly. Now I'm as red as they come – I'm not a fan of Everton and probably wouldn't go to watch them if I lived next door to Goodison – but my first reaction when I saw the ball nestling in the back of the net was despair. 'Shit, we're out!'

I thought that was it. I couldn't see anything wrong with it at all. Sure I was relieved when Clive Thomas blew his whistle to disallow it, but even now I'm not sure what it was for. I thought it was a perfectly good goal, but the whistle blew and we were heading for a replay as all hell broke loose.

One of the Wrexham directors of the time, Barry Williams, is a good mate of Clive Thomas and, when Clive used to come to the North-West to referee, he'd stay with him. Barry told me a story about a dinner he went to at Everton when Clive Thomas was invited to speak. Tommy Smith was the other guest and, when he stood up, he got a good reception even though he's a red. When Clive followed him, there was silence and someone threw a pie at him. The evening wore on and questions were invited from the floor. One bloke stood up from the back. 'Clive, why was it the Germans bombed Liverpool first instead of Treorchy?'

As for me, I didn't mind Clive as a ref, not because he disallowed that goal but because I felt he talked to players and listened to them.

The replay went on at Maine Road again on the Wednesday and we played a lot better and deserved to win. I felt Clive might have given us a bit of a head start when he awarded a penalty against Mike Pejic for a little nudge on David Johnson. I had a good view of it and, from where I was standing, it looked a bit harsh. No matter, we were still the better side and ran out 3-1 winners.

When the final whistle blew, the place went mad and those scenes will live with me forever. The Liverpool fans lifted us high on to their shoulders. It was unbelievable to know that I was going to Wembley. I could hardly take it in above the sea of screaming, shouting faces. I know the bloke who lifted me on to his shoulders. His name's Tommy Fairclough and I met him at Ronnie Whelan's testimonial dinner – a lovely feller.

We were top of the league, in the FA Cup Final and in the final of the European Cup, after we had overcome FC Zurich home and away to secure a place against Borussia Moenchengladbach in Rome. It was an unbelievable season, with everyone telling us that we couldn't do the so-called Treble, yet we kept winning and getting better and better.

European nights were always special at Anfield. We'd won the UEFA Cup against Bruges the year before, but everything that Bill Shankly had worked for, and then Bob Paisley after him, was geared to the big prize itself. Some of the games along that European route were as good as Liverpool will ever see. Saint-Etienne in the quarter-finals at Anfield was certainly the most exciting match I've ever been involved in.

We'd started slowly in the competition, only scoring twice at home against Crusaders of Northern Ireland, and it was quite intimidating playing over there in a stadium ringed with barbed wire because of the political situation. Eventually we took control and scored five goals in the second leg.

Then it was off to Turkey, to Trabzonspor, which is one of the worst places I've ever been. We flew Aer Lingus to Ankara and then changed on to a Turkish flight to Trabzon, which was where all the fun started.

The plane wasn't what you might call luxurious; we were just hoping it was safe because it looked like something out of *Indiana Jones*. There were curtains hanging off the windows and you could see the pilot at the front. The air hostesses practically had roll-ups dangling from their mouths and they wore fetching white pumps with black laces and parachutes on their backs. Not only that but the plane had an outside toilet!

The palms of my hands were sweating. I wasn't the best of passengers, but if you ever felt nervous you only had to look at Ray Kennedy. He hated flying and would often break out into a cold sweat. No wonder on this trip! As we approached Trabzon, the plane started banking steeply and I could see us heading straight for a cliff face, which seemed to rise out of nowhere. It looked like the airstrip was cut into the hill and, by this stage, I'd given up all hope of ever feeling ground beneath my feet again.

I was saying a little prayer as we eventually bounced our way to touchdown and got out, 20 Liverpool footballers, all gibbering bags of sweat.

The hotel was about as plush as the plane; in other words, it was filthy, with rooms like cells, not even very nice ones, and, remember, I'd done my fair share of bed and breakfast in the police stations of Llandudno down the years. I was rooming with reserve 'keeper Peter McDonnell, and after the nightmare plane journey all we wanted was a shower.

We swung the door open and couldn't believe what we saw. The room was dark, dingy and dirty; someone had obviously been to the local council skip to get the furniture. On the wall, there were two bits of wood with another bit of wood stuck across them in place of a shelf. A little rickety wooden table stood in the middle of the beds alongside something that looked like a wooden box, which turned out to be a radio from World War II but without the working parts. I stripped and stumbled into the shower room, which had cracked tiles and mud on the floor.

We all met for a meal in the evening and sat laughing and joking until all the lights went out and we were left in complete darkness. Apparently, it happened every night at a certain time and so they whizzed out the candles. It was like something from an Inspector Clouseau film, with everyone stumbling around. Candles were everywhere, upstairs, along corridors and, as soon as we got back to our rooms, the lights went on.

Trabzonspor weren't a bad side. It was an amazing stadium, because it was full to the capacity of 25,000, but another 2,000 or so were sitting on a massive hill overlooking the back of the terracing. Intimidating, you might call it. They held billowing banners and were screaming their heads off, with horns wailing and whistles blowing. Miss Turkey kicked off; it was that kind of carnival atmosphere.

I was marking their golden boy, Ali Camel, the Turkish equivalent of George Best, with long flowing black hair and considerable skill. I nailed him early on and played him quite well and, although they won the game 1-0, we weren't unhappy.

Unfortunately, we had to stay overnight in Trabzon, because there were no more flights, so a couple of us wandered down town to take in the local nightlife and have a drink with the locals. Ray Clemence was with us and we found a bar and settled in before some girls wandered over to talk to us. I thought they looked quite tasty, although Turkish has never been my strong point. It didn't seem to matter and we were having a chat until an English bloke who was on holiday there came up to tell us they were transvestites – Trabzon transvestites. You don't get many like that in Llandudno!

We were all having a good laugh until the bill came round and we discovered these girls/blokes had been bunging their drinks on the tab too. We tried to protest, but a load of the staff and their mates surrounded us and told us in no uncertain terms we weren't leaving until we had coughed up. None of us had enough money, so they kept us barricaded in while one of the lads went back to the hotel for extra cash. They weren't the type of crowd to argue with ...

I was marking Ali Camel again in the return, but we finished them off 3-0 and marched into the quarter-finals. It was only then that the press and the fans started to believe we had a real chance of going all the way. After the two legs with Saint-Etienne, I think the players felt too that it just might be their year. The games against Saint-Etienne were real crackers, full of high-quality football and unbelievable excitement. The return at Anfield stands out as arguably Liverpool's greatest-ever night of European football and many people still believe it was better than the final itself.

In the week before the first leg, the press had been building up their winger, Dominique Rocheteau, as the danger man. He was a real flyer and became a big star with France in the 1982 World Cup. As with Ali Camel in the previous round, I was told I'd be marking him and some French reports that filtered back to England made it clear that they thought Liverpool were vulnerable down the flanks. That meant Phil Neal and me – cheeky bastards!

Theirs was a really tight ground and it was packed out – I love that feeling of the fans breathing down your neck: it makes for a cracking atmosphere. Steve Heighway almost got an away goal when he hit the post, but they ended up 1-0 winners, a score-line we would have settled for before the game. It was also the night that the Anfield fans picked up the chant, 'Allez les Rouges, Allez les Rouges, Allez...' after their fans had been singing 'Allez les Verts' all night. (Greens and reds, for non-French-speaking readers!) When they came to Anfield, the whole ground was singing it. Such a bond developed between the two sets of supporters that many Saint-Etienne fans travelled to Rome to watch us in the final.

Over 50,000 packed Anfield that night and on the way to the ground you could feel the excitement. It was the greatest atmosphere I've ever known and, when we ran out, the sound that hit us made the hairs on the back of my neck stand up. I stuck my fist up at the Kop and a huge wave of pent-up emotion drained out of me, leaving me feeling relaxed but keyed up at the same time. It sounds stupid, but that's the only way I can describe it. I couldn't wait to get stuck in.

Right in the middle of the Kop, there was a massive banner, which read, 'Joey Bites Frogs' Legs' and, when we kicked off, I certainly got stuck in. Thousands had been locked out, but they must have known we'd scored when the place erupted only minutes into the game after Kevin Keegan's cross-cum-shot looped up over their 'keeper. When the crowd went wild, I could have done with ear plugs.

The noise must have been intimidating to the visitors, but when Batheney battered a shot from fully 25 yards, which whistled past Ray Clemence, the silence that spread round the ground was as frightening as anything the Kop were offering. It was as if someone had switched a tape recorder off. Just for a second. A second when everyone in the ground realised the ball was nestling in the back of the net. Silence, deafening silence! It was as moving as the Kop singing, 'You'll Never Walk Alone'. And everyone remained silent, until the French fans struck up with 'Allez les Verts'. Instantly, the thought dawned on all of us: Christ, we need three or we're out.

I really got stuck in after that and I've since watched the tape of the game at home; commentator Gerald Sinstadt was really quite kind to me. He said things like 'Jones is in hard there' when I've kicked the bloke up in the air. Ta, Gerald. We knew it wasn't a night for prettiness and the ref never even ticked me off.

Early in the second half Ray Kennedy put us back in it when he scored to make it 2-1, or 2-2 on aggregate, and I bet, if you asked anyone these days, they'll never remember that goal now because the winner from David Fairclough, with eight minutes to go, sent the place delirious. The fans, the players and the pigeons under the stand roof went berserk and I felt we'd won the cup there and then. What a brilliant night! I celebrated in style with a takeaway from the Chinese at the top of our road in Moreton.

After Saint-Etienne, the semi-final was something of an anti-climax. We were off to Zurich, where I'd gone on my very first trip with Wrexham. We breezed past them 3-1 over there and 3-0 at home in front of another sell-out crowd. I swapped shirts with the Swiss international Rene Botteron at the end to add another scalp to my collection, but then a few days later a Scouser came up to me claiming he'd got hold of my shirt.

'How d'you get it then?'

'My missus is a cleaner at the Holiday Inn and she was clearing up in one of the rooms and found it. One of the Zurich players had left it behind.' He obviously never thought much of my shirt!

Still, we had made progress on three fronts: we were on the verge of the First Division title; we had made it to the FA Cup Final against Tommy Docherty's Manchester United; and we were about to contest the European Cup Final against Borussia Moenchengladbach. It was my second season at the club – and my first full one. I was 22, a full international with Wales and I couldn't quite believe why it should be happening to me. If someone had sat me down and said, 'In eight months' time you'll be on the point of collecting three major medals with Liverpool Football Club, the club you've supported all your life', I'd have said, 'Pull the other one!' Now I kept pinching myself as a reminder it was really happening.

We finally won the League Championship at home against West Ham. There could have been no better place to win it, even if a 0-0 draw wasn't exactly the style the fans had come to expect from us. It didn't matter; we were the champs, the best again, and I was part of it. This time round, I'd earned my medal.

I love looking at the pictures taken during the celebrations and the laps of honour with all the lads running around in front of the Kop, parading the trophy – it was dream stuff. I'll be honest and say it all became a bit of an anti-climax when we got back into the dressing room, because I found out that Wrexham had lost at home to Mansfield to miss out on promotion to Division Two. It sort of took the shine off things for me. It meant I didn't go out or anything like that, instead I returned home for a quiet drink.

The FA Cup was different entirely. Fair dos to Bob Paisley, he left me out for the last game of the season away to Bristol City because I was one booking away from suspension. One part of me was grateful, but the other part of me said, 'Shit, I hope I'm back in for Wembley.'

From the moment we'd been carried off the pitch at Maine Road after beating Everton, I couldn't get Wembley out of my mind. I'd never been to a Cup Final, but then I'd never go to one as a fan because I was the type who loved sitting at home watching the whole day on telly from ten in the morning until it all finished about half-five, with *FA Cup It's a Knock-Out* and *On the Ball* on one side and *Football Focus* on the other. I'd get a few cans and sit in and watch the lot. I loved it all.

It seemed so strange because suddenly it was my turn: 'Joey Jones, come on down.' We were kitted out in Wembley suits – they were awful, but at the time I thought they were the business – featuring brown jackets with shiny buttons and beige trousers, set off by chocolate-brown ties, which had beige woollen crests. When we lined up for the team photo, we looked like big pieces of caramel fudge.

We were staying in a hotel called Sopwell House just outside Watford. As usual, I was rooming with Steve Heighway, who'd scored in two FA Cup Finals already. I was a bag of nerves but he and the rest of the lads were brilliant, helping me to relax.

I remember standing with Tommy Smith and Ian Callaghan in the hotel foyer when a reporter called David Miller walked in. I think he was with the *Daily Express* and Tommy turned to him straight away to have a right go. 'Look what's crawled under the door.' David Miller tried to make friendly conversation, but Tommy was having none of it. It turned out this bloke had written a piece in the paper saying that 'the Iron Man had gone rusty', or words to that effect. Tommy was furious.

The morning of the Cup Final I'd not slept too badly, but I was up early sitting reading the papers, while Steve Heighway was still asleep. I wish I hadn't because they'd done assessments of players, awarding stars to each one, and Jack Charlton had only given me six out of ten, the worst of all. Then I read a piece by Don Revie in which he said that the first time he'd seen me play, he thought I'd never make a player – another cheeky bastard! I flung the papers across the room and my confidence was in my boots by the time I got down to breakfast.

Sure enough, the telly people were there to interview us in the hotel and I kept thinking back to the time I'd been sitting at home watching others being interviewed. I just kept hoping my mates were watching. All my family had come down for the game – I don't think my sisters had ever seen me play before – and all the time Steve Heighway just kept talking to me to keep me relaxed. I'd been a bit edgy in the hotel, but, when we finally got on to the Wembley coach, I began to get into the thing, starting to focus on the job ahead. We were after a Treble, remember, but it was never talked about. It's difficult to think about anything else when you are on a coach bound for Wembley.

Driving down Wembley Way was like being involved in a movie, with cameras flashing and people shouting. They say it's a day you'll never forget and I can't remember a bloody thing. People were banging on the windows wishing us well and I even recognised some of them. The United fans were giving us 'the Vs' and, when Bob Paisley wasn't looking, I was giving them back – just sly ones!

Once we were off the coach, the police held the fans back as we walked into Wembley itself. We went up the tunnel and out on to the pitch in our 'Caramac' outfits. What a roar there was from the Liverpool fans. Then the United team came out and they got a roar from their fans along with a round of boos from the Liverpool contingent, including me.

In the dressing room beforehand, everyone seemed quite relaxed, but then most of them had seen it all before. I tried to be as cool as possible, but the giveaway came when Steve Heighway had to tie my boots for me! I remember sitting there shaking, thinking to myself that the dressing rooms weren't all they had been cracked up to be.

Telegrams were arriving thick and fast – some from my friends in Wrexham, some from my mates in Llandudno. Then they called the two teams out of the dressing room and we lined up trying not to look bothered, all thinking, Has the band started yet? And has the bloke in the white suit finished singing? Then we went out on to the pitch.

It makes me smile now when the commentators say, 'And the players are waving to their family and friends.' I was waving, but I couldn't see anyone. There were just too many people and I couldn't pick out a single face.

I think we were presented to the Duchess of Kent. She walked up our line and was very pleasant.

'Still living in Wrexham, Joe?'

'No, I'm in Moreton now.'

'Great. Have a good game.'

I was numb to be honest, and don't have a clue what she said! I just couldn't get the telly coverage out of my mind, thinking to myself I'll be on both sides: BBC and ITV.

Once the whistle blew, it wasn't too bad and, just before half-time, I nearly scored with one hell of a shot. It just fizzed over the bar – 'Ooooohhh.' Wonder if my mates saw that one back home? Hope so.

It was the second half and we'd had the best of the game. We'd battered them really, but then Stuart Pearson broke down the right, got in front of me and whacked it past Ray Clemence on his near post: 1-0. I could have brought him down because, if you remember, he ran right across me. As he went by, I was thinking to myself, I'm going to chop you down, but I also thought of all the bollockings I'd had from Bob Paisley for scything people down and decided to let him go. In the dressing room afterwards, Bob got on to me. 'Why didn't you bring him down?'

'Well, you've been telling me all season not to do it.'

Some people blamed Ray Clemence, but I didn't because Pearson struck it well. I won't blame Ray, unless he blames me for not pulling him down. If he does, then I'll say it was completely Ray's fault! Now I suppose, if I'd tripped him, I'd have been sent off for a professional foul, but in those days I would have probably escaped with a booking.

Then came the equaliser, which was created down the left with about the only dribble I've ever done. 'Here's Jones,' said the commentator as I pretended to play it with my left and cut inside Steve Coppell on to my right. I could see Kevin Keegan and Jimmy Case up in the box and clipped it in with my right foot. Jimmy brought it down and volleyed it past Alex Stepney on the turn – a brilliant goal. I'd meant to pass to Kevin! At 1-1, we thought we'd cracked it until they broke again and fluked a winner when Lou Macari flicked in a shot off Tommy's back.

I was knackered and shattered that we'd lost the FA Cup and the Treble, which had been in our grasp for so long. I was disappointed for the lads and myself, but more so for the fans. You've had your chance at winning, but they haven't. It's so frustrating having to stand and watch without being able to do anything but cheer.

Tommy Docherty came round to shake hands on the pitch after the losers' medals had been handed out. I reckon he knew they'd been fortunate to win it, but then anyone can win the cup; you just need the run of the ball on a given day. We did a lap of honour, a sad, slow lap of honour, and it all passed in a blur. I wondered if my mates were watching at home.

Straight away, Bob Paisley and Ronnie Moran were getting us going again in the changing room. 'There's a European Cup Final on Wednesday. Forget today, it's over, there's nothing more to be done.'

I'm sure that most people were beginning to wonder if we'd really blown it, believing that all the big games had taken their toll. 'Surely Liverpool couldn't win?' people kept saying after we'd lost the FA Cup Final. Rome was just four days away.

I made sure I tucked my shirt into my bag before leaving Wembley – another for the collection – and after we'd changed we were straight back on the coach. We were heading straight for the station, but there was some sort of hold-up just outside the ground and Jack Charlton got on at the front to ask for a lift.

'Don't give him one,' I shouted from the back. 'He only gave me six.' It sort of summed up the day.

ITV had their cameras on the bus and Brian Moore came round to ask me a couple of questions. I told him I was bitterly disappointed. 'In fact, I'm so bad, I'm going home to kick the cat and the dog.'

I thought no more about it until I got letters at Anfield saying I was a cruel man and shouldn't be allowed to have pets. I couldn't believe it. I'd only meant it as a joke and, as anyone who knows me will tell you, I love animals and get very angry when people are cruel to them. Besides I didn't even have a cat.

We had a few drinks on the train on the way back to Lime Street and then Janice and I stopped off at the chippy at the top of our road, before going straight to bed.

On the Monday morning, we flew straight to Rome. The wives came with us, but understandably they were staying in a different hotel. On the Tuesday, we did some light training and had our regular team talk from Bob Paisley, who was more concerned with the threat of 'Alberto Doings' than his English counterpart, 'Dougie Doings'. 'And don't do any sightseeing either,' he added, 'because there's nothing to see. I was here in the war in a tank and I knocked it all down.'

It had been one hell of a season and everyone in the press kept saying we were tired and couldn't possibly pick ourselves up after the United defeat. I don't know about the other lads, but I felt as fit as a fiddle, though let's face it you could get through FA Cup Finals and European Cup Finals on adrenalin alone.

Liverpool had experience and that's what really counts. Bob Paisley,

Ronnie Moran, Joe Fagan, they'd seen it all before. The routine was a familiar one and, as we sat round the hotel, we were all quite relaxed. Bob Paisley would sometimes get involved in the quizzes and I got him a beauty, which I don't think he ever forgave me for. A few of the lads were sitting round answering questions when I put my own in. 'Who was the last man to break a leg at Wembley?'

Bob Paisley began racking his brain to come up with the answer. He was trying all kinds of weird footballers from years ago who'd been injured in Cup Finals.

'Was it so and so in the 1935 Cup Final?'

'No.'

'It must have been thingymajig in the 1951 Final then.'

'No, give in?'

'No. I'll get it, just give me time.'

He was there for ages, coming up with name after name, and still he couldn't get it. In the end he said he'd had enough. 'Who was it then? I can't think of anyone else.'

'Evel Knievel. Wembley 1976!'

I got up and walked straight out without another word and Bob was fuming. The lads were howling with laughter.

All Tuesday, the fans began arriving in their thousands, coming into the hotel and wishing us all the best. That was the best part of it for me because at Wembley you're cut off from everyone for days and the nearest you get to your fans is when you walk out on to the pitch. Here, there were just loads of Scousers everywhere, having a laugh and enjoying themselves. They'd got there any way they could. Some fellers probably told their wives they were nipping out for a loaf and never came back. Some are probably still there now! I loved being involved with the supporters because I'm one of them.

We went down to the stadium itself on the Tuesday and it looked magnificent, even though it was empty. There were massive underground changing rooms and then you'd walk along a big tunnel up and out on to the pitch. There were a few Liverpool fans already down there having a look round and, on the coach back to the hotel, all you could see was red and white. It was like playing at home and I know it made me feel like I was going into a reserve game – I was that relaxed.

When we finally got on the bus to drive to the ground in the evening, I began to feel like I could walk through walls when I saw Liverpool fans lining every road, cheering and waving to us. It was like driving down Lower Breck Road on the way to Anfield, and that was just for starters...

It was warm without being too hot as we walked on to inspect the pitch before the game and the noise that greeted us was magnificent. It was a sea of red and white with just a touch of yellow all the way up the terracing – we couldn't see any Germans. It was an incredible sight to see so many Liverpool fans in the stadium and right in the middle of them was a massive banner, stretching across the Liverpool end. 'JOEY ATE THE FROGS LEGS, MADE THE SWISS ROLL AND NOW HE'S MUNCHING GLADBACHS.' As well as making us laugh, it gave me one hell of a boost. I don't think I've ever felt so proud in all my life. What an honour! The two lads who made it – namely Phil Downey and Jimmy Cummings – actually presented it to me some months later and I've since handed it over to the museum at Anfield, although I've still got framed pictures of it. In fact, the banner is now probably more famous than I am.

In the dressing room everyone was geeing each other up. Somehow I felt very good about our chances, as if we couldn't lose because of the fans. I suppose we were conscious of representing Britain in some way, but I didn't know I had the chance to become the first Welshman ever to win a European Cup winners' medal. Records like that are always trotted out at finals and I'm glad I wasn't aware of it until afterwards. I had enough to worry about.

I'd been much more nervous for the FA Cup Final but this was like playing at home. We had thousands more than the Germans and, when we walked on to the pitch, we had twice the noise. It's doubtful we had twice the team because they had some brilliant players, including Allan Simonsen, Berti Vogts, Uli Stieleke and Jupp Heynckes. Simonsen was the main danger and for quite a bit of the game I was marking him. It had been a tough little run for me in the competition going back to the likes of Ali Camel, Dominique Rocheteau and now Simonsen. They had one hell of a side and somehow I can't see Berti Vogts sitting at home these days and telling his mates about the greats in our side: 'They had one great team. Keegan, Heighway and Jones – what a player he was!'

I did all right in the game, got in a few tackles, supported well and kept things ticking over neatly without doing anything spectacular. I elbowed Stieleke in the mouth at one stage by accident. I remember that. He went down like a block of flats being demolished.

I've obviously got great memories of the goals, but, personally speaking, two things stick out from the game itself. First, Emlyn Hughes never passed to me (mind you, who could blame him!). If you watch the game back just count the number of times he comes to the left to knock the ball to me – very few. The second thing that really stands out came in the first half when a ball came down to me in acres of space. I tried to trap it on my foot, but unfortunately it just hit my shin and rolled into touch – terrible control. That's what I remember most about the game. In fact, the first time I saw the video I told everyone it was coming up and, sure enough, there it was.

The game was played at a slow pace because the Germans would concede space all the time and then defend in front of their box. Terry McDermott scored a beautifully worked opener for us and then Allan Simonsen scored an equaliser after Jimmy Case had given away the ball. I think it was to our credit that we came back again even though Ray Clemence did make a brilliant save and they also hit the post.

Then came that magic moment – Tommy's header. I went for a short corner from Steve Heighway and then left it for him to knock in. Next thing, Tommy bullets in a header and I was one of the first to grab hold of him. Magic! It was tremendous from a personal point of view to see Tommy Smith head us into the lead. If I wasn't to score that crucial second goal, then Tommy would have been my choice. I had always wanted to be another Tommy Smith, aggressive, hard-tackling and with a remarkable will to win.

Then we got the penalty that Kevin Keegan had earned after giving Berti Vogts a real nightmare; I just stood and watched Phil Neal walk back, saying to myself, 'Stick it in, stick it in.' He did and that finished it: we were champions of Europe. I remember thinking that there was no way they could come back from that.

The whistle went and the whole place went mad. I had a Union Jack draped round my shoulders with a big tall hat on my head. The fans were throwing scarves and hats to us as we went on a lap of honour. The big banner was waving and I just wanted to get in with the supporters. I was covered in scarves and decided to make a leap for it into the crowd. For a moment, the security guards thought I was a fan and went to set the dogs on me, but I just clung to the fence singing and shouting. That was one hell of a feeling!

In the dressing room the singing went on and on with all the cameras there. I never let my medal out of my hand once. I wanted to hide it in my pocket under my hanky, but I couldn't trust it to be safe. 'Don't lose it. Mustn't lose it.'

Back in the hotel we met up with the wives and went down for a banquet that had been laid on for us. Hundreds of fans, who came by the hotel, began celebrating with us. Alan Waddle and I opened a fire escape to let them in. It was their night as much as ours.

What a great one it was too. I got so drunk. Everyone kept buying drinks, and I was soon pissed out of my head! I threw up in the hotel room, over everything, but who cared? We'd won the European Cup. A lot of people thought I'd been involved in a ruck with Kevin Keegan when they came round the following morning. Kevin had a belting black eye, but it wasn't me who'd done it. I think he'd done it himself when someone was trying to throw him in the swimming pool.

A few of the lads stayed drinking until morning. Janice was ill because she'd drunk too much and on the plane home there were plenty of thick heads. I had a great picture taken with Janice holding the cup: I've got a denim shirt on and I look like a docker. We kept drinking on the plane all the way back to Speke Airport and then took an open-top bus tour of the city. There were thousands and thousands of people to greet us and I was grateful for the fresh air to clear my head. Even the Evertonians turned out in force, which was magnificent, and people had covered their houses in red and white. It was unbelievable.

When we got to St George's Hall in the city centre, it was packed with people as far as the eye could see, singing and waving. All the lads were introduced on the microphone which was a bit embarrassing, but for most of the time I stood at the back out of the way. Emlyn got some stick for singing, 'Liverpool are magic, Everton are tragic,' but, apart from that, things went well.

After that, it was back to the ground to pick up the cars. Everyone left while I waited 20 minutes for Elton Welsby's Datsun Cherry to start and then we all trooped back to Moreton. When we got to our street, there were banners and people out in the road welcoming us home. It was so kind. I was really touched by it. They gave me a cheer when I got out and I showed everyone my medal. It rounded the day off perfectly. After that, we went inside and had a cup of tea.

It took a while for it all to sink in and, later on, I got up and took the dogs for a walk. I think in the end I went for chips from the chippy at the top of the road because we didn't have anything in.

CHAPTER TEN

WEMBLEY WIZARDS!

Not only did I grab myself a Championship and European Cup winners' medal in 1977, but also Wales beat England at Wembley for the first time ever and I was playing at left-back. There was always a brilliant atmosphere with the Welsh lads. We didn't have the numbers to pick from like England, but the team spirit was always there on the pitch and in the bars.

There were never any cliques; everyone mucked in together. We always had a good session after a game, all going to the same club with no one slipping off by themselves. Don't get me wrong: playing for your country didn't automatically mean you became an international-class drunkard; I'm just trying to say there were never any stars. I think that's why we've been so difficult to beat down the years, because there's always been so much pride with everyone battling together.

To play for your country is the biggest honour in the game. For someone who'd hardly set foot outside Llandudno or Wrexham by the age of 17, playing for Wales gave me the chance to travel to numerous different places and play against the greatest players in the world: Socrates, Rummenigge, Beckenbauer, Platini, Dalglish, Blokhin...

While I was playing for Liverpool in Rome, the Welsh lads were gathering in Wrexham for the Home Internationals and had been watching the game on the box. When I got back, manager Mike Smith asked me if I wanted to play against Scotland at the Racecourse on Saturday and I said I'd love to. In a way, I was sad because it meant missing out on Tommy Smith's testimonial at Anfield on the Friday night – one hell of an occasion for Tommy and for Liverpool.

When I ran out to face Scotland, I received a great reception from the fans. I ran down the Kop end and waved my fist in salute. Looking back, I think I was probably knackered after all that had been happening in the last couple of weeks, but the adrenalin was pumping around my body and I was dashing around like a headless chicken. I nearly scored too, which would have topped everything. Down at the Kop end I belted the ball and it crashed against the bar. We drew 0-0.

The England match followed on the Wednesday night at Wembley. It's every Welshman's dream to beat the English at anything. As a nation we feel we get England shoved down our throats. Certainly during the Home Internationals, the papers would be full of England, England, England, with a little paragraph for Northern Ireland or us. It got on my nerves and I know it annoyed the rest of the lads. There's national pride whenever you play for Wales, but against England it's greater than ever.

On the coach to Wembley, Stoke's John Mahoney would dig out his tapes of the Welsh male voice choirs and play them full blast, getting everyone psyched up. John was a real nationalist, who taught himself to speak Welsh. He was my favourite player at that time because he never gave in – he was as hard as nails and would die for his club or country. He was also a great bloke, really funny.

The first time I joined up with the national squad, I bumped into John as I arrived at the hotel. He said, 'Hello,' like he'd known me all his life, which helped put me at ease straight away. Much like Tommy Smith, when you had John on your team, you had someone to lift the performance and give it everything. I got quite friendly with him and he'd sometimes come over to Llandudno with a mate for a few drinks.

One time I arranged to meet him in the afternoon at the Links pub on my old estate. I'd been struggling for a number of weeks with a pain in my side and in the morning my mam made me go and see the family doctor, Bell

Davis. He examined me and wrote a note, which he told me to take up to the hospital. I thought nothing about it and, when I got there, I handed it in and they told me to take my clothes off and get into bed. I was on the ward with a load of other blokes and we began having a chat.

A while later, the doctor and some nurses came up to examine me.

'We've read the letter from Bell Davis and we're going to have to take your appendix out.'

'You're not taking my appendix out; I've got to meet John Mahoney in the Links in a couple of hours.'

'But, Mr Jones, it looks like appendicitis.'

'I don't care what it is; I'm not having it out.'

They went away and I started chatting with the lads again. When they came back, I asked if I could sign myself out.

'Don't you realise that, if you do that, we can't be held responsible if the appendix bursts.'

'Yeah, no problem.'

So that was that and I signed myself out. I've still got my appendix and I've never had any trouble in that department. I said tara to the blokes in the ward and went to meet John for a few beers, none the worse for wear.

Terry Yorath was another who could mix it with the best. Before the England game in the dressing room at Wembley, word came round that the English FA were only going to play the English national anthem and not bother with the Welsh. Terry said he felt we should make some sort of protest and asked the lads for opinions. We said we agreed, so, when 'God Save the Queen' finished and the English lads broke for the kick-in, we just stood in our line looking straight ahead. The English lads didn't know whether to come back or not and the English FA officials were getting panicky. Ted Croker and other FA types began ushering us away, saying they were only going to play one anthem. After a while, we broke and ran down to the Welsh end. We'd made our point.

We eventually got two points when Leighton James slotted in a penalty – 1-0 and history made. What a season it'd been and what a feeling to beat England! We'd almost done it the year before when I was sub. John Toshack and Arfon Griffiths scored in a 2-2 draw and, when we got back to the dressing rooms, I started handing out cups of tea. I gave one to big John Roberts, our centre-half, who took one swig, looked at me and then flung the cup back over my head, smashing a mirror on the far wall! He was that wound up. It means that much when Welshmen play England.

I loved the Home Internationals; all the Welsh lads did. Most of the Liverpool team was involved for one country or another, which added to the banter in the Anfield dressing room, involving the likes of Ray Clemence and Phil Neal for England.

Alan Hansen was the one who gave me most stick after he'd seen me on television playing against Scotland at Hampden Park in 1976. It was Willie Pettigrew, the Motherwell striker, who caused the problem. Pettigrew picked up the ball just inside his own half and began running for goal. I had one of my rushes of blood and went tearing across from left-back, slid in and missed him by a mile. I was left on my arse, looking a right idiot, while he went on to beat a couple more defenders before lashing a shot into the roof of the net. Alan Hansen never let me forget it. When we were training at Liverpool, he'd get the ball to take me on and start commentating, 'Pettigrew, taking on Jones ... and Pettigrew's done him again.'

It was like a recurring nightmare which he'd shove down my throat time and time again. Luckily, I got my own back a few years later when we played Scotland down at Cardiff in 1979 – the day the Pettigrew bogey was finally laid to rest.

Alan was marking John Toshack and Tosh gave him the biggest run-around you're ever likely to see. He murdered him, scoring a hat-trick in a 3-0 victory. One special moment stands out in my mind: when Tosh slipped the ball through Hansen's legs, ran past and whacked it in. Poor Alan had a nightmare and I loved it. Put it this way, the Pettigrew incident was never mentioned again and, as soon as the whistle went, I couldn't wait to get changed and see him in the bar. I slaughtered him! I'd waited my chance and now the glory was mine.

After the match when we got back to our Glasgow hotel, Mike Smith told us not to go out because we had England in a few days and, more importantly, we were up against Yugoslavia in a vital European Championship qualifier the week after that. Places were at stake, not to mention reputations.

We got the beers from the hotel porter and, after we'd finished, we piled a big stack of empties in crates outside Arfon Griffiths's door. In the morning, Mike Smith got wind of what had been going on and, when the team to play England was announced, I wasn't in it and neither were the lads who'd been with me. I wasn't in the squad for the Yugoslavia game either and neither were they. I thought I'd had it because Mike Smith was a stickler for the rules. Arfon drove me home that night and I remember saying to him, 'I probably won't play again.' We'd been given a Gola sweater for the Home Internationals and the lads were laughing at me, saying it was a going-away present.

Despite the odd disagreement, I got on great with Mike Smith and have to thank him for continuing to pick me when he had every reason for chucking me out for good. Down the years, I've caused him enough trouble to last a lifetime, though I know too that he's often laughed about it because people have told me.

The incident I know that tickled him more than any other came when I was still in the 'Parrots' in Llandudno. A few of us were chasing after another gang one Sunday afternoon in the town and I was waving a big stick, shouting my head off.

We ran round a corner and I bumped straight into Mike Smith who was having a quiet stroll with his family. 'Hello, Mr Smith ... er ... er' – typical of my luck. I was lost for words, so I hid the stick behind my back and stopped for a chat. He never mentioned it to me, but he told plenty of others.

One of my funniest memories of Mike came on the way back from the West Germany match in Dortmund in 1977. We went to pick up our cars from the hotel in Maidenhead, and I was driving back to Wrexham with Ian Edwards, Dai Davies, Mickey Thomas and the reporter Bob Whiting from the *Liverpool Daily Post*. We started talking about the game and Mickey started having a bit of a go at Mike Smith, who had given him stick after the match. Mickey said, 'He's a baldy bastard,' and kept on moaning as you do now and then.

We'd been going for a while and were just coming into Tern Hill when I slammed on the brakes. 'Hey, isn't that Mike Smith's car in the hedge?'

Sure enough, there was his big Citroen smashed up and stuck in a hedge. We could see footballs bouncing in the gutter and various bits of kit lying on the road. It turned out a lorry had hit Mike and spun him around. We all ran back to see if we could help and found him in a nearby house, calming down and waiting for the ambulance to arrive.

'Mike, are you OK? What happened? Sure you're all right?'

'Yeah, I'm fine.'

He told us the full story and, when we were sure he was in good hands, we left and got back in the car.

I was ultra-careful driving after that, as it was pitch black and I felt a bit nervous. All of us were stunned. It was quiet for a good while until Mickey piped up from the back, 'He's still a baldy bastard!' The others cracked up and I nearly crashed through laughing – typical Mickey Thomas!

No offence meant, Mike.

Like John Neal before him, Mike Smith must have seen something in both Mickey and me because he kept picking us, no matter what we did.

After being left out of the European Championship match against Yugoslavia, I was recalled to play West Germany at Cardiff, the match where Mickey Thomas made his international debut. As always we were sharing a room on the afternoon of the game; we were sitting reading on our beds when Leighton James came in. Now Leighton's a nice feller and, on his day, I rated him one of the best wingers around, but at times he couldn't half go on. You had to take him with a pinch of salt.

He started chatting about the game and told Mickey to take it easy.

'Don't worry about Berti (Vogts),' he said.

We looked at each other trying not to laugh. 'He'll probably follow me wherever I go because I'm well known. Yeah, don't let Berti worry you.'

In his roundabout way, Leighton was trying to make Mickey feel better because Berti Vogts was due to be marking him on the left, but when Leighton had gone we burst out laughing.

When we kicked off, Vogts stayed with Mickey on the left and Bernard Dietz took Leighton on the right, despite what had been said. Dietz didn't give him a kick all night and hardly broke sweat, while Mickey gave Berti no end of trouble, snapping at him all night and, although we lost, he did bloody well. In fact it wasn't long after the match that Manchester United signed him.

In the second half, Leighton was subbed and, when we got into the dressing room after the game, he started mouthing off about Dietz, calling him all sorts instead of accepting the fact that he never had a kick all night, and telling Mickey how well he'd played. All the lads were looking at each other and I was giggling.

West Germany had one hell of a team that night. Franz Beckenbauer was captain, Sepp Maier was in goal, Karl-Heinz Rummenigge was up front and of course Berti was at right-back. Rummenigge was just beginning his career and I was marking him for the first time. I felt I did all right even though we lost 2-0. All in all, I marked him four times and, though I wouldn't say we ever became friends, we sort of got to know each other. He was quick then and just got quicker and quicker. I was slow then and didn't get any quicker!

There was one incident in that game that ranks as one of the greatest in my career. Early in the second half, a corner came over and I bulleted in a header that FRANZ BECKENBAUER cleared off the line. I couldn't believe it. I just wanted the game to finish there and then so I could get on the phone and tell everyone. 'The Kaiser' had kept one of my headers out. I'm just so relieved it didn't go in, otherwise I wouldn't have been able to boast that Franz blocked my header on the line. At the end of the game, I was about to dash up and swap shirts with him, but, when the final whistle blew and I looked round, there was already a big queue. Rummenigge was nearer so I swapped with him.

In 1979 we played the Germans again, this time in the European Championships in Cologne. When the two teams broke after the national anthems, we started kicking in and I looked over to their team and there was Rummenigge waving to me. I couldn't believe it. At first I turned round to see if he had a mate behind the goal, but he didn't, so I waved back. Now that's what I call recognition. I was thinking, Great, he's scared of me; I'll have him in my pocket all night. Twenty minutes into the game, I went in for a tackle and knackered my ankle ligaments. That was the end of my night. Off I hopped to the dressing room and down in the corridors I could hear roar after roar from the crowd, as the goals started going in. I was sitting with my foot in a bucket of ice when the lads trudged in at half-time. 'How many have we scored?' I asked. It was a serious match, but some of them couldn't help laughing. We lost 5-1 in the end, which effectively ended any hopes of qualifying, but I kept telling them it was 0-0 when I went off.

I watched the second half from the bench sitting next to one of the subs, Ian Edwards. We just stared in amazement watching Rummenigge destroy us up front, with Manny Kaltz, the right-back from Hamburg bending balls all over the place, flicking it here, shooting from anywhere. Ian couldn't believe it and gave us the only laugh of the game. 'See that Manny Kaltz,' he said. 'He's too good for the World XI!'

That night we all went out on the town. I had my ankle bandaged up, hobbling around the streets of Cologne, having a few drinks and looking for a nightclub. We ended up trying to pile our way into one, but the bouncers weren't so keen until Rummenigge (or should I say Karl-Heinz because he was my mate by then) and Manny Kaltz walked down the steps and helped us to get in.

That was it though because we got merry on the local lager and before long I was up on the dance floor throwing a few shapes – shake, rattle and rolling with my crutches in one hand and a pint in the other. Loads of the lads were bombing round the floor and I just remember at one stage looking across to see Rummenigge and Manny Kaltz sitting quietly, drinking orange juice while we were all going berserk. They must have been thinking what a load of idiots we were. No wonder we weren't going to qualify. We'd been slaughtered 5-1 and they were probably expecting us to sulk.

I always tried to make sure I swapped a shirt whenever I played. I'm a mad collector of souvenirs and programmes, but shirts were extra-special. After youth internationals, I'd dash over at the end of a game to rip the shirt off someone's back so I could take it back to Wrexham and show off to the lads. I've got shirts belonging to some of the world's greats and they've got mine. The collection includes Graeme Souness's Scotland shirt and Alan Hansen's. I had two of Kenny Dalglish's but Paul Price of Tottenham begged me to give him one after a Home International. He had Gordon Strachan's and, though I was dead keen to keep hold of Kenny's, I reluctantly agreed.

The Liverpool lads would swap amongst themselves, too. I've got Sammy Lee's and Terry McDermott's England shirts as well as a Steve Heighway Eire shirt. I'd already picked up Rummenigge's shirt and I later got hold of Bossis's of France, Nehoda's of Czechoslovakia and shirts from countries as far-flung as Iran and Canada. My only disappointment came against Brazil, when we played a friendly at Ninian Park in June 1983.

I was captain that day and went to toss up with Socrates no less. I wanted to ask him there and then if we could swap shirts at the end of the game, but thought it was just a bit out of order. When the final whistle went, our sub, Dudley Lewis, sprinted over to him and swapped. I didn't have a chance and eventually ended up swapping with one of their subs.

The team we missed out with was Kuwait, when they came over for a friendly at Wrexham in September 1977. They had the crappiest strip you've ever seen, cheap cotton that shrunk in the wash, with the name 'KUWAIT' stuck on in lettering like you get on the T-shirts on Llandudno pier. When the ref blew for full-time, one bloke swapped with me, but when I got home and stuck it in the machine the lettering started peeling off.

It was always a great thrill for me travelling abroad, seeing countries I never thought I'd ever get to see. Some of the most interesting Welsh trips have been to places like Iran, Kuwait and Turkey, where the lifestyles are so different from our own.

We went to Iran in April 1978, just before the Argentina World Cup. They'd qualified and eventually ended up in Scotland's group and took a point off them. It was also just a couple of months before the revolution and the overthrow of the Shah.

We stayed in the capital Tehran and I have to say that, when we were there, you'd never have known there was going to be such upheaval because everyone seemed so happy without a care in the world. Although it wasn't the most beautiful place I've been to, it was really buzzing. Our hotel was one of the half-finished variety and the drivers were the worst I've ever seen. Every car had a dent in it. The roads were massive, with loads of lanes and thousands of vehicles blasting their horns at each other. It was like the dodgems gone mad.

We beat them 1-0, a great result for us in front of 60,000 screaming fans. The noise was deafening, and so was the silence when Cardiff's Phil Dwyer scored the only goal. Phil later became a policeman and, boy, he was hard – he was a great bloke though.

At night, five of us crammed into a taxi and went looking for a place to drink. Phil was lying across us in the back and, when we stopped at some lights, he wound the window down and shouted something to some girls who were chatting to two fellers. Next minute, one of the blokes wandered over and, pow, he smacked Phil in the mouth so hard that he shot back across us – a real beauty. We were laughing at him and he was all for jumping out and ripping the guy's head off, which, knowing Phil, he probably would have done. Then our taxi driver suddenly put his foot on the accelerator and we flew across the lights and into the night.

After a few beers, Phil calmed down and eventually we headed back to the hotel in the same taxi. When we got there, none of us had any money left so it was one of those jobs: 'Look, mate, hang on there we'll just go inside and get some money to pay you.' It was only about three quid, but once inside we just sat round chatting with the others. Later on, people kept coming up to us saying the taxi driver was still waiting for his money. 'Tell him we've no money. He'll be gone in the morning.'

We got up next day, showered and shaved before breakfast and, when we went down into the lobby, he was still there waiting, looking filthy, tired and smelly. We felt terrible by then; we really didn't have any money left. He started asking for the cash and so we gave him some enamel lapel badges with 'Wales' on them; he was delighted. Much better than money, he told us ... and off he went!

Turkey was another good trip in 1979. It was just after we'd been hammered 5-1 by the Germans in Cologne. We had to beat the Turks in Izmir to have any chance of qualifying for the European Championships and Mike Smith took us over a day early to acclimatise. We had two training sessions and loads of their fans turned up to watch. They love their British football over there and knew quite a few of our lads. They'd get really excited even during the five-a-sides and started chanting a couple of names, including Mickey Thomas's. He loved it of course and acknowledged them by dropping his pants and showing his arse. We stood there wandering how they'd react and suddenly they mobbed him. After that, he couldn't do a thing wrong; they loved him.

Then there was the mysterious case of the missing Dai Davies when we travelled to Kuwait for a friendly in September 1978. We got to the hotel very late and, when we got up in the morning, we found the authorities had been to the hotel in the night to grab Dai and ship him out on the first available plane home. Apparently he had an Israeli stamp on his passport, so poor Dai was thrown out of the country while all the lads were nicely tucked up in bed. If we'd known I think we'd have all been out on the same flight too, but after some discussion we decided to stay and play.

The Home Internationals of 1978 stick in my mind as the most enjoyable games of the lot before the decision was taken to stop them. That was the year we lost 3-1 to England at Cardiff, a match memorable for Tony Currie's screaming 30-yarder into the top corner and John Mahoney's efforts to put him off. John was running with him and goading him. 'Go on, hit it. Hit it from here; go on, hit it then.' Wham, it flew straight in. I had to laugh. In those days they had aluminium posts at Ninian Park and you could hear the sound of the ball whacking against the bar, then the thump of Dai Davies wrapping himself around the post. Dai was about half an hour too late.

Then we went up to Scotland and got a 1-1 draw in the game where Willie Donachie scored the greatest own goal I've ever seen. Jim Blyth played the ball out to Willie at left-back and, after he'd controlled it, he knocked it back just a little bit too strong and a little bit too wide. We'd got our draw – hilarious! Hampden fell silent, though I'm sure the punters were sniggering as well in disbelief.

Once again Mike Smith told us to have a quiet night, but a good few of us sneaked across to the Chinese restaurant over the road from our hotel. We'd had a few drinks already and, when we got there, we ordered about 13 banquets, sweet and sour, crispy duck – you name it, we had it! After a few more beers, food was slopping everywhere and barbecue sauce covered the spanking new white tracksuit tops we'd been given to wear during the Home Internationals. Then we went back to the hotel.

When we lined up for the national anthems against the Irish on the Friday, 11 Welshmen were standing there in tracksuit tops covered in chow mein stains as well as sweet and sour. We were trying to fold our arms to cover up the mess. I had more on my top than I'd had on my plate!

Without doubt the most heartbreaking defeat around that time came in the World Cup qualifier against Scotland at Anfield in October 1977. Wales have been so close to qualifying for the World Cup so many times I've lost track. It always seems to be Scotland that edges us out at the death, but that night we were robbed, no question – no matter what the Scots say.

The Welsh FA were forced to move the fixture to Liverpool after there'd been trouble down in Cardiff following the game with Yugoslavia. They'd been told the venue had to be over 125 miles away from Cardiff and, although Wrexham was the obvious venue, they chose Liverpool because of the profit the Welsh FA would make from the 50,000-plus crowd.

It was all or nothing, Scotland or us – winner take all. We were hoping the Liverpool fans would come out and support us because we played in red and John Toshack and I were playing, while Kenny Dalglish was playing in dark blue! Some of our lads had never been to Anfield before, so Mike Smith took us to the ground to have a look around the day before the game. I took Mickey Thomas on to the Kop and, even though it was empty, he said it made the hairs stand up on the back of his neck.

We were based in Llangollen and trained lightly on the morning of the match. What a shock we had when we got to the ground; it looked like the whole of Scotland had been given the day off. I'd never seen so many people in the car park before; it was heaving. It took ages to squeeze the coach through and, when we finally managed to open the door, they all began shouting for tickets. When we said we hadn't got any, they started poking us with their flags and having a right go. I was just pleased to get into the dressing rooms.

What an atmosphere that night! You could feel the buzz downstairs, but I felt nice and relaxed in familiar surroundings. That all changed when I ran out on to the pitch. I'd followed my normal match routine, running down the tunnel, touching the 'This is Anfield' sign and turning right down to the Kop end to salute the fans. I thought the Kop would be full of Welshmen because that was their end, but when I got down there it was full of Jocks sticking two fingers up at me. There wasn't a Welsh fan in sight and I had to run along the goal-line screwing up my eyes to a see a few of them squeezed into a small pocket on the left. I got the fright of my life I can tell you.

The game was fairly even all the way through, but it turned on two incidents. The first seems to have been lost in history because of the controversy surrounding the second, but there's no doubt we would have won had John Toshack's shot into the top corner beaten Alan Rough. Rough will probably be remembered for the blunders he made rather than his great saves, but that night he flung himself to the left to turn away Tosh's drive. It's one of the best saves I've ever seen ... and one of the most important.

After that came the handball incident which ended with the Scots getting a penalty. Willie Johnston took a long throw and Dave Jones went up with Joe Jordan. I was only about ten feet away – closer than the referee – and I'm telling you there is no way Dave handled the ball. Besides, Joe Jordan has never come out and said he touched it, but I'm sure he knows the score. The referee was Robert Wurts from France, who at the time was thought to be one of the best in Europe, but he cocked up that night, simple as that. Don Masson stuck in the penalty and we were 1-0 down and chasing the game.

Then came one of the most embarrassing moments in my career; Kenny Dalglish did me a beauty to score the second goal. I was just across the halfway line and then the Scots began to break. I was a few yards behind Kenny, just matching his run, stride for stride. Kenny wasn't a brilliant sprinter, but he had such a quick brain and he was jogging and jogging and I was with him. Then, bam, he was gone. He left me three yards on the edge of the box and stuck in a beauty of a header – 2-0. Goodnight, Vienna, or in this case, Argentina. I was done up like a kipper and the Liverpool Jocks were top dogs that week. I still cringe every time they show it on telly, which I imagine is about three times a week in Scotland.

I was living just a few miles from Anfield on the Wirral in Moreton, but I decided to go back with the Welsh lads to Llangollen to drown my sorrows. Over the years, I've got used to just missing out with Wales. I've had some great moments. We've had some great results, but for every brilliant night there has been another 'if only' or 'what might have been'.

CHAPTER ELEVEN

THE END OF A DREAM

The summer after the European Cup Final saw Kevin Keegan move to SV Hamburg, but, being the shrewd manager he was, Bob Paisley moved swiftly to bring in a replacement for Kevin, who, in my eyes at any rate, was to be the best player ever to wear a Liverpool shirt – Kenny Dalglish. Kenny had been great for Celtic and Scotland and, for a mere £440,000, turned out to be an absolute bargain. Such was the quality of the man, he stepped into Kevin's role virtually overnight and made the position his own.

I was lucky enough to play alongside him in his first game for Liverpool. That was against Manchester United in the Charity Shield at Wembley. We drew the game 0-0, but I remember Jimmy Hill saying on TV what a memorable season it was going to be for Liverpool. A week later, Kenny made his league debut at Middlesbrough and scored early on in the game, though we ended up drawing 1-1.

Sadly, that season saw me play my last-ever game for Liverpool. I'd played in 20 league games, but then found myself out of the team following a 4-2 FA Cup third-round defeat at Stamford Bridge against Chelsea in January.

Bob Paisley switched me to right-back to mark Clive Walker because he preferred me to mark out-and-out wingers, with Phil Neal moving to left-back. To be fair, Walker had the better of me and scored twice. Not surprisingly, I was substituted though I was reluctant to come off, but when I did Bob Paisley threw me a tracksuit top and said put that on. I was upset at coming off and was all wound up, but, as I struggled to put the tracksuit top on, I remember my arm going through the sleeve and my fist hitting this flesh. As my head came through the neck, I saw Bob Paisley rubbing his face!

To this day, I don't know whether it was because I was crap in that game or whether it came down to the fact that I had accidentally punched Bob in the face, but I was never to play for the Liverpool first team again. I remained a member of the first-team squad, but I never played again. It wasn't a very good game to finish on really.

The rest of that season saw my left-back position being switched around, with first Alan Hansen and then Tommy Smith being chosen to play ahead of me. I ended up playing reserve-team football, though there were some very good players in the team which ended up winning the Central League title. In fact I'm one of the few players to have won both a Central League and a Football Combination League winners' medal (North and South reserve-team leagues at the time).

Despite losing my place in the first team, it was to be an eventful season for me in more ways than one. I also had a big fall-out with Ray Kennedy. Normally I got on with Ray, but he had this reputation for having a bit of a Jekyll and Hyde character and would flare up at the slightest thing.

Prior to playing at Manchester City, we were training on the Friday. I was mucking about with Kenny Dalglish, doing a bit of shadow boxing, when I stepped back and felt myself standing on someone's foot. I turned around and there was Ray Kennedy. Straight away, I said sorry, but he replied, 'Watch what you're doing; I've warned you before.' And with that he shoved me in the back.

I stood there looking at him and the words of my dad came back to me: if someone's going to belt you, hit them first. Before I knew it, I'd smacked him straight in the face and we began going at it hell for leather. If you were going to match us up in boxing weights, Ray was a heavyweight and I was a flyweight, but I gave as good as I got. And, to be quite honest, I fucking enjoyed it at the time! It was like a release.

We were finally pulled apart by the other players, but then Bob Paisley stormed over and told us we could both leave the club. You've also got to remember that, at the time, the Liverpool training ground at Melwood was open to fans, so this had all been in full view of the public.

Training continued with us doing sprints and Ray kept on shouting threats over to me saying he would have me after training, which I just laughed off. By this time, I'd seen his eye swelling up which made me even more confident.

We went on to our usual five-a-sides and we were on opposite teams. I went to close him down and, as I did, he gave me the hardest elbow in my face that I'd ever had. I immediately jumped on his back and began throwing punches into his head as he spun around trying to throw me off. Training was stopped and I believe it was the first time training never went the full distance, which, looking back, was embarrassing for me.

Anyway, they put us on the bus back to Anfield, which is where we changed before training. Ray was put in his usual place at the back of the coach and I was put at the front still wanting to get at him. Emlyn Hughes then came to sit by me and said, 'I'm glad someone's finally stood up to him.' I thought back straight away to the time Emlyn tried to con me with those drinks – it could have been him!

When we finally arrived back at Anfield, Ray again threatened he'd see me in the car park. I was going mad. They kept us apart as we got changed and then I went out into the car park to wait for him, but he never turned up. Looking back, it was childish really but these things happen in football.

I eventually went home to rest and pack my bag for an overnight stop since we were playing Manchester City the next day. Janice knew straight away something was up, but I never said a thing until she spotted a cut behind my ear and asked what was going on. I told her and added that, if he carried on, I'd have him again.

That evening, I went to Anfield to check in. We had to report to the boot room where Joe Fagan and Ronnie Moran were waiting for us. When they saw me, they began laughing and asked if I'd calmed down yet. I said I had, but then added, 'I tell you what, if he starts again, I'm not backing off.' With that I walked off and thought I'd go and have a chat with the night watchman who sat by the players' entrance. As I walked around the corner, the door opened and in walked Ray Kennedy. It was like a scene from the movie *High Noon*. We were like two cowboys facing each other. We were both standing there, each with a bag in our hands. I switched mine to my left as I was going to lead with my right. As we walked closer towards each other, we both dropped our bags. He then lifted his hand to shake mine! And with that he said, 'I'm sorry, Joe.'

I replied, 'It's OK, let's forget it.' And from that day, Ray and I became a lot closer and a lot friendlier, not that we hadn't been friends before.

Deep down, because I'd stood up to him, I think he had a little more respect for me because in all honesty there were only certain people he did have a go at – he'd never have a go at Tommy or Jimmy Case. However, it was all cleared up and I remember bumping into him a few years later when I was with Wrexham and he was with Hartlepool; we had a good chat about old times. Sadly, since then Ray has been diagnosed as having Parkinson's Disease.

It was shortly after I'd been dropped from the first team that Liverpool played Wrexham in the quarter-finals of the League Cup at the Racecourse. I was in the squad for the game and I remember going for our pre-match meal in the Wynnstay Hotel. Bob Paisley came up to me and asked if I knew anything about Wrexham. I watched Wrexham whenever I could, but I remember saying to him that I didn't know a thing about them! He asked about corners and free-kicks, but I wouldn't give him any information as I wasn't playing! Anyway, we won the game 3-1 with Kenny Dalglish scoring a hat-trick.

It had been nice to return to the Racecourse, but I'd love to have played in that game. One funny story from that game was that, when we left the hotel on the team bus to go to the Racecourse, we had a police motorcycle escort and, as we were getting on, I recognised one of the policemen as 'Porky' and began chatting to him. I knew him from my days with the 'Parrots' back in Llandudno, though he never mentioned it (and I have always wondered since if he realised that it was me). It hadn't been that long since he was chasing me around and now here he was escorting me on the Liverpool team bus!

That season I'd played in the early rounds of the European Cup and I remember beating Dynamo Dresden 5-1 at home quite comfortably, but it was a different story when we travelled to Dresden for the second leg. If ever a team that I have played against could have been on drugs, it had to be them. They were playing like demented men. They absolutely battered us. We couldn't get the ball off them or get near them. They raced into a two-goal lead, but we were fortunate that Steve Heighway scored to take a bit of pressure off us because we were under the cosh.

Another incident happened at half-time. Bob Paisley was obviously not happy when we returned to the drab dressing rooms – this was the place where even the grass was grey. Bob and Joe Fagan were talking to the team trying to put their points across when the lights went out. I was to blame! I'd leaned back on a switch and plunged the whole dressing room into darkness. Straight away, Bob shouted, 'Joey, put those lights back on.' By this time, I was the first suspect for anything that happened. My reputation went before me!

I was on the subs' bench for the remainder of the European Cup campaign, including the home leg with Benfica in the quarter-finals. The game was played on 15 March and we won 4-1, 6-2 on aggregate.

Though I never got on, I had more important things on my mind as I'd found out after the match that Janice had gone into labour. I went straight from the ground to the Highfield Maternity Hospital in Wallasey. I was pacing up and down like expectant fathers do and, being bored, at one stage I found a white doctor's coat which I put on. I had these women coming up to me saying, 'Doctor, can I have a word with you?' I never went in for the birth until it was over, at which point I found out that we'd had a baby son, Darren Joseph, who weighed in at 7lbs 10oz. I didn't arrive home until about 5.30 that morning and then I took the dogs out for a walk. I only had about an hour's sleep, before I was back in for training – a proud father.

A week later, I was back at Wembley, but only as a member of the squad, since I was still out of favour. We played out a scoreless draw with Nottingham Forest and met in the replay at Old Trafford. Again I wasn't even sub, but one thing that sticks in my mind from that game was stepping off the team bus and walking up the corridor at Old Trafford when I bumped into the Forest managerial team of Peter Taylor and Brian Clough. I'd spoken to Peter Taylor on numerous occasions, but I hadn't really spoken to Brian Clough before. Anyway, as I walked up the corridor, Peter Taylor stopped to talk to me and Brian Clough kneed me in my leg, which gave me a dead leg! He said to me in that tone of his, 'Are you playing, young man?'

'As it happens I'm not, but it's a good job as you've just given me a dead leg!' I replied. Thankfully, it was my one and only encounter with Cloughie.

We lost that final 1-0 to a John Robertson penalty, after Phil Thompson had brought down John O'Hare.

Having beaten Benfica in the European Cup, we came up against the team we had beaten in last year's final – Borussia Moenchengladbach. Again I was on the subs' bench for both games, as we lost 2-1 in Germany but won the second leg 3-0. In the final we met the Belgian side, Club Bruges, at Wembley, but I had to be content with a place on the bench from where I saw Kenny Dalglish score the only goal to win my second European Cup winners' medal.

Despite Liverpool winning the European Cup, as well as being League Cup finalists and runners-up in the First Division, it had been a disappointing season from a personal point of view. I'd played 20 league games, but had lost my first-team place for the second half of the season. I was just like any other professional footballer; I wanted to be playing first-team football for the club I loved.

That summer, Bob Paisley had me in the office and convinced me that I still had a future at Liverpool, so I agreed to sign a new two-year contract. He never gave me a guarantee that I would be playing first-team football and I wouldn't have expected that. However, at that time, there were rumours that he wanted to sign Alan Kennedy and I asked him if there was any truth in them. He denied it.

We then went on tour to Austria and Germany and, while we were there, Alan Kennedy flew out to join us from Newcastle United. We played against Austria Vienna and that game turned into a bit of a bloodbath. There were some dodgy tackles and I whacked one or two Austrians more out of frustration than anything else, but it almost caused a full-scale battle on the pitch! Even Ray Clemence got involved! Not surprisingly, I was taken off to try and calm things down, but really it all stemmed from the frustration of knowing that the writing was on the wall for me. It certainly wasn't a professional way to act.

Joe Fagan and Ronnie Moran later took me to one side to calm me down. They told me they understood my frustration and I settled down, although I didn't feature in many more games on that tour. In fact, I never played in Liverpool's first team again.

By October I was still playing reserve-team football, but by this time I'd

Top: The Stella Maris School football team that won the Llandudno and Conwy Primary School Cup in 1966. Back row, left to right: Robert Jones, Colin Shields, Andy Smith, Peter Alderson, Me, and Ronnie Jones. Front row: Chris Jones, Dave Watson, Paul Hayes, David Lyon and Paul Roberts.

Above: Signing schoolboy forms for Wrexham at the age of 14 watched by (left to right) Evan Williams (Wrexham Scout), Mr Jones (Warden at Llandudno Youth Club) and Johnnie Roberts (Manager of Llandudno Swifts).

Wrexham manager John Neal looks on as I sign professional forms for the club in January 1973.

Top: A delighted dressing room following our 1-0 win over Southampton.
From the left: George Showell (Trainer), Geoff Davies, Dave Fogg, Eddie
May, Gareth Davies, Arfon Griffiths, Charles Roberts (Director), Mickey
Evans and John Neal (Manager). Me and Brian Tinnion crouched at
the front.

Above: The Wrexham team in our trendy 1970s gear prior to boarding the
coach for the trip to Burnley for the FA Cup quarter-final match in March
1974. From left to right: Mickey Evans, Me, Mickey Thomas, Graham
Whittle, Dave Fogg, Brian Lloyd, Mel Sutton (Partly hidden), Brian
Tinnion, Gareth Davies, Arfon Griffiths and Eddie May.

THE FOOTBALL ASSOCIATION OF WALES
LIMITED

PATRON:
HER MAJESTY THE QUEEN.

SECRETARY:
TREVOR MORRIS.

TELEPHONE: 2425.
TELEGRAMS: "WELSOCCER WREXHAM".

**3 FAIRY ROAD,
WREXHAM,
LL13 7PS.**

16th July 1975.

MJS/EAD.

Mr. J. Jones,
c/o Liverpool F.C.,
Anfield Road,
LIVERPOOL I4 OTH.

Dear Joey,

I was delighted when I heard that you had achieved one of
your ambitions—to play for Liverpool. May I wish you
every success, and as I have said on many occasions, you
have the ability, you have the right temperament and
you are gaining composure which allows you to play better
with each game.

I am quite sure that Terry Yorath and the rest of the
lads in the Welsh Squad join me in wishing you all the
best.

Yours sincerely,

Team Manager

REGISTERED IN LONDON (ENGLAND), REG

A letter (dated 16th July, 1975)
from the Welsh manager, Mike
Smith, congratulating me on
joining Liverpool.

Inset: Liverpool manager Bob
Paisley welcomes me to Anfield
in July 1975.

Top: The famous banner at the European Cup final in Rome in 1977 made by Liverpool fans Phil Downey and Jimmy Cummings, which I've since handed over to the museum that is now set up at Anfield.

Above: The morning after the night before! On the plane back to Liverpool with Janice and the European Cup, despite me looking like a docker in my denim shirt!

Celebrating, with medal clenched tightly in hand, after our memorable 3-1 European Cup victory over Borussia Moenchengladbach. What a night!

Top: My wedding day on 5th June 1976, with my mam and dad on my right, and Janice's mum Margaret and brother-in-law, Graham, who gave Janice away on her left.

Above: Proud Grandparents! The first picture taken of Janice and I with our beautiful granddaughter Mia Louise in August 2004.

Wrexham manager Arfon Griffiths tries my new Wrexham shirt for size having just signed in October 1978.

been told that quite a few teams were interested in me. Bob Paisley had told me that Jimmy Armfield at Leeds wanted me; Middlesbrough were also interested, but so were Wrexham. The previous season they'd won promotion to the old Second Division. I also knew the manager, Arfon Griffiths, from playing with him in my first spell there.

When Wrexham came in for me, I remember Arfon asking me, 'Would you be interested in coming back?' I replied that I would rather stay at Liverpool, but I wanted to play first-team football.

Bob Paisley told me that I'd never go back to Wrexham as he wanted me to stay because I could play right-back, left-back or centre-half. However, I've always been stubborn and hot-headed and I told him that it was best if I moved on. I eventually signed for Wrexham on 19 October 1978. In all, I'd made 72 league appearances for Liverpool, scoring three goals.

I was 24 and, deep down, I know in my own heart that, if I'd stayed, I could have got back into the side. But, as I've said, I liked playing first-team football, whether it was for Liverpool or any other club and signing for Wrexham gave me that opportunity. I wasn't one to sulk either; I'd get my head down and give my all even for the reserves because that's the way I am and I can't change that.

One thing I did regret about leaving Liverpool was not seeing Bob Paisley to say goodbye to him. Unfortunately, he wasn't at the training ground when I collected my things – I think he was away scouting somewhere. Despite what had happened, I felt I got on well with him and wanted to thank him for everything he'd done for me. He was a great manager and a great feller. I was particularly proud of the fact that he saw fit to include me in his book, *My 50 Golden Reds*, in which he summed me up by saying, 'He always gave you the impression that if he hadn't been playing on a Saturday he would have been with his mates on the Kop every Saturday and there haven't been too many players who were more popular, either with his team-mates or with the fans. I'll always have a place in my memories for Joey because what he might have lacked in finesse he more than made up for with his personality which helped to make sure there were plenty of laughs in the dressing rooms when he was about.'

I couldn't really disagree with that. It had been a dream come true for me to sign for Liverpool. Even if I had only played for Liverpool the once, that would have been enough for me. Just to run out in front of the Kop where I had stood since progressing from the Boys Pen was an incredible experience. I will always be grateful to Bob Paisley for giving me that chance. He was a massive influence on my career. The same went for Ronnie Moran, Joe Fagan and Roy Evans. I wasn't a great player – I had my limitations, I knew that. I was just one of the lads who were fortunate to be out there on the pitch. To play for Liverpool was an incredible honour for me.

It wasn't long after I joined Liverpool that Bob Paisley affectionately nicknamed me the 'Wild Man of Borneo'! Bob would often tell me to calm down during a game and not get carried away by the noise of the crowd, but I suppose the name came from when I was at Wrexham where I always had my shirt out with my socks around my ankles and the fact that I didn't hold back in the tackle.

Since Kenny Dalglish arrived at Liverpool, we'd become good friends. It was funny when he was introduced to the players for the first time; he was about to shake my hand and he said, 'Fuck off, you skinny Welsh bastard,' and began laughing. He'd remembered the banter we'd previously had from some great tussles when I was playing against him for Wales against Scotland.

At Liverpool, we'd sit next to each other on the bus to away games and also change next to each other in the dressing room. I had a lot of time for Kenny; he was a smashing feller and we got on great because we had the same sense of humour. A lot of people think of him as miserable, but believe me he's not. He has an immensely dry sense of humour and everybody in the dressing room knew he liked a laugh. In fact, we used to laugh when people said he was miserable. I found Kenny to be a great feller and, as I've said before, he's the greatest player ever to have played for Liverpool.

He was more of a rough Jock really because of the way he spoke, while I thought Graeme Souness, who joined Liverpool later that season, was more of a 'posh' Jock because I could understand him. He would speak more like Sean Connery, while Kenny spoke more like Rab C Nesbitt! But they were both great players.

At Liverpool we used to take it in turns to pay the dinner money; I'd pay one week and he'd pay the next. However, when I came to leave, what with Kenny being Scottish and all, he sent me a message about getting the money for the dinners to him as it was my turn to pay that week! To be fair, after I left he sent me a telegram wishing me all the best. I also received a parcel from Liverpool. It was an adidas shoebox and with it came a message from Ronnie Moran: 'You've forgot your boots.'

When I opened the box, I found a pair of dirty, ankle-high hobnailed boots with leather studs – the kind they used to wear in the 1930s! I've still got them at home now, but that was the Liverpool sense of humour – well, it was either that or the way I played and they really thought these were what I should wear!

CHAPTER TWELVE

THEY'LL KEEP A WELCOME IN THE HILLSIDES

In a way I was home. Wrexham felt good to be around again – back with the old faces, back in the old routine. It seemed everyone was pleased to see me or at least that was the impression they gave. It certainly wasn't Liverpool. Wrexham probably never will be, but I just couldn't wait to get going again all the same. Once Arfon said he wanted me, I'd taken about two minutes to sign and it turned out to be a record transfer for the club, £210,000, which is still a club record to this day. Even then, I never felt I was worth that type of cash, but I hope over the years I've paid back every penny in blood and sweat, with the odd bit of skill thrown in as a dividend.

I came back for the same wages the other players were on at Wrexham at the time, so I went down from £300 a week to £150. It had been a hard decision for me to leave Liverpool, but it had never been a question of money as with all my moves. I was going back to the club where I started and I wanted to be part of helping the club climb to the next level.

I had the medical the day I signed. At other clubs, I'd been through all kinds of fitness tests, blood tests and spelling tests. Back at the

Racecourse, I had a piss on a bit of paper to see if I had diabetes and that was that: I was a Wrexham player again.

I'd chosen Wrexham because I thought we were good enough to get into the First Division. Arfon had got together a great bunch of players and, by breaking the transfer record, he'd shown me that both he and the club meant business. Fifteen thousand turned up when I made my debut against Crystal Palace. We certainly had some big names: Mickey Thomas, Bobby Shinton, Dixie McNeil and Dai Davies in goal, with John Roberts and later Terry Darracott at the back. Today, it would be hard to think of Wrexham in the Premiership, but then there was more than a realistic possibility of getting into the old First Division.

There was a real spirit at the club that made me think we had as good a chance as anybody of going up, but then, six weeks after I'd signed, they sold Mickey to Manchester United. In a way, I was probably being selfish thinking it would be just like the old days with him and me together again. I'd had my shot at the big time with Liverpool, why shouldn't he have his go? Bloody hell he deserved it. It was the same with Bobby Shinton. Wrexham sold him to Manchester City at the end of the season, but in fairness that was because of the new freedom-of-contract legislation. I think Bobby was the first player to make use of it. And suddenly the club's two big names had gone.

Even now, people in Wrexham talk about Bobby Shinton. He was brilliant. He looked a right hard case with his nose splattered across his face, but he had no need to be tough. With his back to goal, he's the nearest thing I've seen to Kenny Dalglish. He shielded it like nothing on earth and the crowd loved him. Unfortunately for Bob, he never really showed his best form after leaving the Racecourse.

It wasn't just the loss of Bob and Mickey that changed Wrexham's fortunes because Arfon replaced them with good lads, but somehow we never got it together in any way. I joined halfway through the 1978/79 season and we eventually finished 15th. The next two seasons, we finished 16th which showed we were consistent if nothing else. In 1981/82, we came 21st and were relegated to the old Third Division. Arfon had departed the previous season and now his replacement, Mel Sutton, lost his job and since then Wrexham haven't been anywhere near the Championship, as it is now called.

Some Wrexham fans put the turmoil the club went through in the 1980s down to those days, when the club spent money it maybe didn't have. I think it was a combination of things; you just can't lay the blame at one person's door and say this is where it went wrong. I thought Arfon bought well. I've got to say that because he bought me. But suddenly from thoughts of European Cups and League Championship medals at Liverpool, I was in the Third Division and on my way to Chelsea.

It wasn't all disappointment; we had some brilliant results at home and in Europe. I played as well in those four years as I ever played in my life. Even at the end of it, I was still only 27 and just about reaching my peak. It would have been fantastic to get into the big time with Wrexham, but you can't have everything. Results-wise, it was the least successful period of my career.

A few weeks after my debut, Arfon bought Steve Fox and David Giles from Birmingham and Cardiff for biggish fees. They both slipped into midfield and suddenly the side had a new look, certainly the dressing room did. Foxy in particular is one of the funniest players I've met in the game. All the lads loved him. We'd sit there in the morning waiting for him to come in and tell us what he'd been up to.

Because both players arrived at the same time, Arfon put them together in the Wynnstay Hotel in the town, but within weeks they'd been kicked out. Foxy had an air gun and, when they got bored, they pinned up pictures on the wall and fired at them until they made a big hole in the plaster! I was still living in Moreton at the time and sometimes stayed over with them. They'd go out into the corridors and lie on the floor, so they could shoot the full length of the hallway. When they got fed up with that, they'd ping pellets off the chef's motorbike when he was trying to get home from work. He couldn't get near it. In the end, the hotel rang Arfon and both were thrown out.

Foxy was even worse than Mickey Thomas. He'd come into training wearing his father-in-law's underpants or his shoes, because he couldn't find his own, or so he said. You never had to buy any hi-fi gear either. He'd pick up the latest model for £300, get bored with it and sell it to you for £150 the following week. His pride and joy were his tropical fish, until he came in one morning and told us he had bought a baby shark from the pet shop. He couldn't work out why he had no fish left when he put them in the same tank!

What a player though! Foxy had everything: pace, skill and he was a smashing passer of the ball – he could beat three or four men effortlessly and scored some great goals. He drove Dai Davies mad. Dai would get the ball in goal, look up and Foxy would drop back from the right wing screaming for it, even if he had three men on him. Dai would wave him away, as if to say, 'What can you do?' and they'd all start screaming at Dai. That used to make me laugh.

They were all good lads at Wrexham. The captain John Roberts was completely different to Foxy, but a character all the same. I called him the Duke because he lived in a lovely house in a place called Farndon on millionaires' row, as it is known. John was the player who threw the cup of tea back over my head after Wales had blown a two-goal lead against England at Wembley in 1976. He was in the Eddie May mould; he'd give 100 per cent at all times. Even in training, he'd go in like his life depended on it, yet off the pitch he was a gentleman.

When we played Oldham that season, John was marking Alan Young. I was at left-back and, having just knocked a ball down the wing, I heard a solid crack behind me. We'd only been going a few minutes and, as I looked round, Alan Young was getting up off the floor after John had smacked him in the mouth. 'That's just in case you're thinking of starting anything this afternoon,' says big John. A real gent off the pitch – but not one to mix with on it.

It turned out to be a disappointing season; we finished 15th. We lost loads of games by the odd goal and won just one of our last 12 matches, against Luton, a game in which my brother Frank made his league debut alongside me.

My dad would tell you it was his proudest moment. He always said he wanted to have two sons play professional football and here we were playing in the Second Division, in the same team, in the same position. Frank had come through the groundstaff ranks and deserved his chance. He did well and my dad was there to see it.

Apparently, my dad bumped into John Roberts in the car park outside the ground, and John came over to ask if he had enough tickets. Frank was taking John's place that night, but he still congratulated my dad and told him he should be a very proud man to have two sons playing in the same team. I know my dad was really touched by the gesture, but I wasn't really surprised. It was typical John Roberts. Next to Ian Callaghan, he's the nicest man I've met in football.

People said Frank and I were similar players, but I never thought he was that slow! He's much quicker than me, more reserved and he had much more skill. He must have been good because he played for the Welsh Under-21s side, which included the likes of Ratcliffe, Rushie and Neville Southall. He once played for them against Holland away and they won.

Somehow it didn't quite work out for Frank at Wrexham during my stay there and he eventually drifted into non-league. I think perhaps too much was expected of him too soon and it was never easy for him having to live up to an older brother who'd already established himself. Years later, Dixie McNeil asked Frank to come back to the club to help them out during an injury crisis. He went straight into the side at Bury and earned himself a two-year contract, playing the rest of that season. Like our dad before him, Frank now works as a porter in the hospital in Llandudno.

The biggest match of my first season back came in the FA Cup against Tottenham in January. I missed the first game at White Hart Lane, which we drew 2-2, and came back for the replay, which we lost 3-2 after extra-time. They had Glenn Hoddle, Ricky Villa, Peter Taylor and Steve Perryman, but it was a Chris Jones hat-trick in the replay that turned the game. It was a really heavy pitch and I'd just come back from suspension, and I can honestly say I've never been as tired playing football. I couldn't get my legs to work in extra-time and just shuffled up and down the left-hand side – I was pathetic. Gareth Davies told me he was on holiday in Spain once and he got talking to a bloke in the bar who'd seen the game on telly. Apparently this feller started asking him what was wrong with me that night. 'I thought he was going to collapse, he looked completely knackered.' He wasn't far wrong.

We had some cracking matches during the 1979/80 season and one of the highlights for me was renewing acquaintance with Charlton striker Derek Hales, who scored hundreds of goals in a career that went on and on. I honestly don't know how it all started, but, whenever we came up against each other, there was a right old scrap. The first little niggle I remember with him came at Liverpool down at the Kop end, when he was playing for Derby. There was a skirmish and players piled in. I grabbed the nearest Derby shirt and Derek Hales just happened to be wearing it.

The season I came back to Wrexham, we were at it again when Charlton came to the Racecourse in April. At one point the ball fell between us and I could see him going in high, so I went in a bit higher and he ended up being carried off on a stretcher. The Charlton players went mad saying I'd broken his leg, but it turned out he had a gashed shin. I have never ever tried to break anyone's leg, but in this case it was him or me, and he came off worse. A few years later when I was with Chelsea, I remember having a chat with our coach driver. It turned out he used to drive the Charlton team coach and was at the wheel the day Derek Hales was carried off at Wrexham. Apparently, Hales sat at the front of the bus and slaughtered me all the way home.

After that, people in Wrexham always wound me up about Derek Hales in the run-up to the Charlton game. Apparently, the same was going on down there because I took a friend of mine to see us play the season after and he said all the talk was about how long it would be before we started battling.

That match, Charlton kicked off and knocked the ball high on to the left wing. Derek Hales and I went for it, missed it and started getting stuck into each other straight away. Apparently, the fellers in the stand were all saying, 'Here we go!'

He got his own back on me in a big way when we walloped them 6-0 in the third round of the FA Cup at the Racecourse in January 1980. Just before half-time, I went for the ball with their midfielder Phil Warman; I was coming in from one side and he was running in from the other and, as I dived into the tackle, he waited a second and then slid into me. As we collided, he slid into my balls then flew up in the air. It could only have been accidental on his part, but I was in agony. Your first instinct is to check you've still got two and, as I put my hand down my shorts, I found that one had been pushed up into my stomach – at least that's how it seemed at the time. I quickly pushed it back down and, mission accomplished, I looked round for him. His head was lying just to the side of me and in my rage I gave him a right dig. That was that. A big scrap ensued and apparently Derek Hales ran fully 30 yards to kick me in the back of the head. I'll be honest and say I didn't even feel it, but the lads were furious. Terry Darracott went straight after him and belted him a couple of times.

Unbelievably, no one was sent off and, when I got up off the floor, I stuck two fingers up to the crowd to let them know I'd still got my full quota! In the dressing room at half-time, I put an ice pack on them straight away, but I was in agony and already they'd started to swell. The lads were more annoyed about Derek Hales and I told Arfon I was going out to get him in the second half.

I could hardly move, but, when the crowd saw me running out on to the pitch, they sensed I was coming out to have another go at Hales and gave me a right royal reception. A couple of minutes had gone when the ball was knocked over the top and Hales just ran away from me as we chased it. I couldn't go on and waved to the dugout to get the sub warmed up.

The consolation was the 6-0 win, but, by the time the rest of the lads had come in, my balls were black, blue and very swollen. Janice thought it was Christmas when I got home! All that week, I had treatment but I couldn't sleep and could hardly walk. Thankfully, we didn't have a midweek game and, by the time Saturday came, I told Arfon I could play when I shouldn't have done. Looking back, I can't believe I didn't miss a game, but the specialist made me take the ultimate precaution and, for the rest of the season, I played wearing a cricket box. It's one thing running up and down a cricket pitch with one strapped on, but playing football in it wasn't easy. At the end of the season, I had an operation to make sure everything was back in its proper place and, touch wood, I've had no problems since.

After the FA Cup game, Charlton returned to the Racecourse two weeks later for a league game. My Welsh team-mate, Leighton Phillips, who played for them rang me beforehand to see how I was. We were laughing about the 6-0 game and I told him to warn Derek Hales that I was after him. Both of us were messing about, but he rang me up again a few days before the game to tell me Hales had pulled a hamstring and wouldn't be coming. I scored in that match and we won 3-2.

The only other time I came up against him was at Chelsea and, in fairness, he caught me again. By this stage I think there was some kind of grudging respect between the two of us, though you probably wouldn't have noticed. His studs scraped down the inside of my thigh and left a scar that I've still got now. At the end of the game, we shook hands for the first time and spoke for the first time. 'Well played, Joe.'

That was it. I couldn't do anything else but admire him for the way he played. His goal scoring record spoke for itself and I'd rather have Derek

Hales on my side with his determination to win than any number of other more celebrated strikers. Fuck me he was tough though …

I scored my best-ever goal in the fourth round of the cup at home to Carlisle. We'd drawn 0-0 up there and beat them 3-1 at the Racecourse. Peter Beardsley was playing for them and, as a goalscorer, he could only stand and admire my magnificent effort! I won a tackle with Steve Ludlam on the halfway line and, instead of giving it to someone else as usual, I just kept running. I remember laughing to myself because no one could catch me and I was thinking, fuck me, they must be slow.

My mates on the Kop said they could see a smile on my face as I was coming towards them. I've seen a video of it since and the smirk's there for all to see. As the 'keeper came out, I just clipped it over him. What a beauty!

Already we knew it was Everton away in round five and, after the match, some reporters collared me for a quote. I told them I'd rather be playing Everton who were mid-table than Liverpool, who were top of the First Division, but the Evertonians took it the wrong way and, a few days before the game, I got a couple of letters warning me not to go to Goodison or I'd be killed.

'We're going to shoot you,' one said.

It didn't bother me and, when I ran out on to the pitch, I stuck my fist up to the Wrexham fans as normal and the Evertonians booed me as normal. We got beat 5-2, but I'm still here to tell the tale.

I was in trouble again when we met FC Magdeburg of East Germany in the first round of the European Cup-Winners' Cup. We won the first leg 3-2 at home; it was a cracking European night, even though they got two away goals. Dixie McNeil, Steve Fox and Steve Buxton scored for us and I had a fair old game at right-back.

They were a decent side, with a couple of East German internationals in Streich, the centre-forward, and Hoffman, the left-winger, who I was marking. He got a goal, but overall I played him quite well.

They certainly knew how to mix it, and I got in a couple of fair but hard tackles on Hoffman, who began moaning his head off in German. Their coach was up off the bench having a go at me and, when we walked off at full-time, he was waiting in the tunnel. He poked me with his finger and said something like, 'You'd better bring your pads to Magdeburg,' in broken English.

I was wound up anyway, grabbed him and slung him against the fence. Cheeky bastard! It all got broken up and I thought nothing more of it.

It was a killer getting to their place for the second leg. We flew to West Berlin and waited hours at Checkpoint Charlie, before being allowed into East Germany. Then we had a three-hour coach journey to Magdeburg and I could see the mood change as we went deeper and deeper behind the Iron Curtain. I'd been there with Liverpool and knew what to expect, but on a first visit it can shock you; it was so gloomy, grey and miserable compared to the West. Don't get me wrong; I'm not slagging off the place or saying the West was better than the East – it just wasn't as colourful, that's all. I had felt sorry for the people living there when I'd come with Liverpool and you could see the lads thinking the same thing now.

Before the game, we went out for a warm-up to get the feel of the place and I bumped straight into their coach who was standing on the touchline chatting to someone. 'That's him,' he said as I ran past. I'd not given it a second thought, but when we kicked off I was glad I'd brought my pads with me. First tackle, Hoffman went right over the top, cracked my shin-pad and after the match I needed stitches in a cut down my leg. That was just for starters.

Later on, we cleared a ball and ran out for the offside. I heard a shout from their bench and then Hoffman belted me in the mouth. Christ, it hurt. I can only imagine their bench was checking the ref wasn't looking and giving the order for Hoffman to get me. I didn't bother checking whether the ref was in the stadium or standing two feet away because I caught up with Hoffman and smacked him one back. The second punch put him on the deck. Everyone got involved and both of us were booked. We were both very lucky to stay on. We almost did it too. It was 2-2 with a minute to go, then Alan Dwyer got caught in possession and they scored. In extra-time, they ran all over us, scoring two more. Some game.

The trip back to Checkpoint Charlie was as bad as the trip out to Magdeburg. We had to wait even longer because the Russian leader Brezhnev was visiting and no one was being let through to the West. The lads went for a stroll and got some food, but we were kicking our heels for ages. In the end, a few Germans started giving us stick about the Magdeburg defeat and, although it was friendly to start with, it got a bit nastier later on. We just responded with the passport treatment. All the lads at the back of the bus started waving their passports, shouting, 'We're going out, we're going out ... you're not.' I can't believe that there is no wall now.

That 1979/80 season, we finished 15th in the league and 16th the year after. The Wrexham board soon made it clear that cutbacks had to be made. The backroom staff was Arfon, Mickey Evans, Ken Roberts and Mel Sutton, and Arfon was told he had to get rid of Mickey or Mel. He refused point blank and eventually left himself. I'm still not sure now if he resigned or was sacked, but I was sad to see him go.

He'd been badly treated in my view and I think the Wrexham board then made themselves look stupid by approaching several managers who turned them down. It was never really clear who was asked, but the press mentioned names like Alan Dicks, Richie Barker and Gordon Lee. Whether they were asked or not doesn't matter, the fact that the board ended up appointing Mel Sutton, whom they'd wanted Arfon to get rid of in the first place, looked ridiculous.

The lads weren't unhappy because everyone respected Mel, but we all felt bad for Arfon. Mel was in charge for just one season, 1981/82, and was then sacked too. He'd been on a hiding to nothing because no money was available and the best we could do was finish 21st and get relegated.

I was in a pub in Wrexham when I heard the official announcement. Grimsby had to lose for us to have any chance of escaping, but they didn't and that was that. Mel was sacked before our last match with Rotherham, which we won 3-2 with Mick Vinter scoring a hat-trick. This was ironic in many ways because that win meant Rotherham, who were managed by my former Liverpool team-mate Emlyn Hughes, missed out on promotion to Division One.

No one enjoys a laugh and a joke more than I do, but then I take defeat badly too. Relegation hit me harder than one of Hoffman's smacks in the mouth.

Everywhere you went in Wrexham, people seemed to be talking about it. In many ways, I knew we'd let the fans down, but then again we'd all given so much for Mel Sutton all season. Maybe we weren't good enough. We certainly couldn't put a run together, though we came up with one of the most amazing results in Wrexham's history that season, when we beat Nottingham Forest 3-1 at the City Ground. They'd won the European Cup a couple of seasons before and had the likes of Peter Shilton, Tony Woodcock and John Robertson still playing.

The next round saw us earn a draw against John Neal's Chelsea at Stamford Bridge. We then drew again at the Racecourse before they finally beat us 2-1 in a second replay, again at the Racecourse.

With relegation confirmed, it was time for me personally to sit down and look to the future. Wrexham looked to be showing cracks round the edges, with no money, Third Division football and Mel Sutton gone. I was playing for Wales and still a young man. It didn't take me long to realise I should ask for a move, though, when my transfer request landed on the chairman's desk, it was at the bottom of a pretty hefty pile.

I wasn't jumping ship. My commitment to Wrexham was always 100 per cent, but I needed to make sure my career wasn't about to be knocked so far backwards that the likes of Wales would forget me altogether.

During the summer, the press began running rumours that other clubs were looking to sign me; Rotherham and Watford were strongly mentioned. When it came to pre-season training, Bobby Roberts had been appointed the new boss, with Ray Bunkell as his assistant. I must admit I was still keen to go elsewhere, but under their guidance a new spirit existed and, by the time we went down to Cardiff for the first game of 1982/83, we were buzzing.

Bobby Roberts had made me team captain and we beat Cardiff 2-1, though it could have been more. I came away feeling we could walk the Third Division and made it clear to the board I wanted to come off the list.

I was as contented as I'd ever been at Wrexham until I got a call from John Neal at home one night. I must have done something right in those three cup games against Chelsea, since John asked me to come and meet him with a view to discussing a possible move. I've made it clear already I have total respect for John Neal, so although my head was saying, 'Stay where you are!' every other bit of me said, 'Go!'

John said, 'I want to meet you.'

'All right then, whereabouts?'

'You know the Red Brook Maelor Hotel just outside Whitchurch?'

I'm thinking, Nice place ... at least we'll have a good scoff if nothing else!

'Well, there's a cafe over the road from it; I'll see you in there.'

Bloody typical!

Chelsea wanted to sign me for a fee in the region of £80,000. They were in the Second Division and struggling, but obviously they were still a big club. I agreed to go down to Stamford Bridge with Janice and Darren to have a look round and discuss terms, but I felt I wouldn't be signing, no matter what was offered.

John Neal's chief scout, Ron Suart, met us at Scratchwood Services to direct us into London and, as we got deeper and deeper into the city, I became more and more convinced I wouldn't be going. In fairness, everybody was very helpful when we got there and I had a good look at the ground, but my feelings hadn't changed – and I also hadn't been able to agree terms. Ron Suart dropped us off again at Scratchwood Services and we shook hands. 'Hope to see you soon, Joe.'

'Thanks, but honestly, Ron, I don't think I'll be signing.'

That was it as far as I was concerned. Nice of Chelsea to want me, but I was Wrexham captain and I was determined to get things going there with the rest of the lads.

After the cracking start at Cardiff, we drew at Huddersfield and then lost at Lincoln and Portsmouth. Suddenly we didn't look so clever, but I believed we were still good enough to do well. Four weeks later, I got a surprise call to go and see the chairman and secretary at the club. After swapping niceties, they told me Chelsea had been back in for me, offering a reduced £30,000 this time round.

I didn't want to go, especially as I'd be losing out financially in the deal with a cut-price transfer fee, but it seemed I had no choice. 'If you don't go, we'll go bust.'

It was as simple as that and old muggins here reluctantly said all right and left the office. They'd given Dixie McNeil and Steve Fox free transfers the same day. Wrexham were broke and I was a Chelsea player.

I was in no position to say no to the Wrexham board; they'd made the situation plain, but it didn't do me any favours when it came to fixing terms with Chelsea. If I'd said 'Yes' the first time, I'd have been much better off. As it was, I signed for £300 a week, which wasn't a fortune by London standards nor by the standards of some of the salaries being paid to the other lads. I'd never played for a Southern side before and I think that made it more difficult to settle in. I wasn't welcomed with open arms by the fans, put it that way, but it didn't bother me too much. What did bother me was the reaction of the fans, which was something I hadn't bargained for at all. During the days between signing and making my debut, I received a flood of hate mail calling me a 'Welsh sheep-shagger' and a 'Scouse bastard'. Having been signed from a struggling Third Division side, I don't think they thought I was good enough to play for Chelsea, though some recalled the times I'd played against Chelsea for Liverpool.

I made my debut up at Carlisle on 30 October 1982 and I wish I hadn't. The tannoy announcer was reading out the line-ups as we ran out and, when it came to my name, the Carlisle fans booed, but so did the Chelsea fans!

What have I done here? I thought. I was warming up and both sets of supporters were giving me the Vs and slaughtering me. When I got booked early in the first half, both sets cheered!

We were crap and came off at half-time 2-0 down. I couldn't get into the changing room quickly enough. When we ran back out, I got the same treatment and I don't think I've ever felt as lonely in my life. Colin Lee pulled a goal back for us, then I slid into their centre-forward, Paul Bannon, and the ref dipped into his pocket and whipped out the red card. 'Bastard!'

It was the only cheer I got all afternoon. The Carlisle fans were going mad with delight and so were the Chelsea fans! I walked off slowly with a million thoughts whizzing round inside my head: Why me? ... Why did I do that? ... Why did that have to happen now? ... Why the hell didn't I stay at Wrexham? ... What have I done coming here?

CHAPTER THIRTEEN

BLUE IS THE COLOUR!

Stamford Bridge has changed a hell of a lot since I was a player, but at that time it had never been my favourite ground mainly because the crowd was so far away from the pitch. You run out at Anfield and the wall of noise that hits you from the Kop can take your breath away – that's the way I like it. Tight grounds with the fans on top of you are best – West Ham's Upton Park, the old Baseball Ground at Derby and Old Trafford are good examples. Chelsea's wasn't at that time.

It wasn't the fans' fault because Chelsea supporters are some of the most passionate and vocal I've come across; it's just the way the stadium was back then. The Chelsea Shed end was the Kop and the fans there lifted us all season, even though we were playing poorly. I kept wondering how much more they'd lift us, and intimidate other sides, if they were a few feet away instead of on the other side of the running track.

I'd played at Chelsea a few times with Wrexham and made my last first-team appearance for Liverpool there too, when Clive Walker ran me inside out and back to front in the FA Cup of 1978 – one way or another, it hadn't been the happiest hunting ground for me. A couple of seasons before I joined Chelsea, I'd gone down with Wrexham in the league on the day the IRA attacked Chelsea Barracks.

We'd always get the train to Euston and then a bus would take us to the ground; it was the same for West Ham, Fulham and most of the other London sides. Because of the bombings, we were diverted round the world and at half-past two were still on the bus, stuck in traffic, miles from the ground. We were sitting there having a laugh at the back, but it soon became clear that the bus driver didn't have a clue who we were. In fairness, he must have been concentrating on finding a new route to the ground and thought we were a bunch of tourists. I was sitting next to Billy Ronson and I remember us both staring out of the windows at the cramped houses with the thousands of people in and out of shops. 'I'd hate to live down here. Imagine if you played for Chelsea. I'd never move here; there's no grass anywhere.'

By now we'd reached the ground and the main entrance. Everyone was getting their kit together and beginning to stand up when the bus driver went straight past.

'Where are you going, you daft sod? We want to go in here.'

'You what?'

The bus driver stopped, wound down the window and shouted over to a copper. 'Hey, can you believe it? This lot want to go in here.'

He was pissing himself laughing. He thought we were sightseers!

'We're the bloody team, you idiot.'

'I'm not taking you in; I'll drop you off down the road.'

In the end, someone persuaded him we were the Wrexham team and had to be on the pitch playing Chelsea in 15 minutes. We went through the main gate, but lost 2-0.

After being sent off on my Chelsea debut up at Carlisle, I wasn't that keen to get through the main gates for my home debut against Crystal Palace. I knew I'd be in for a two-match ban, but from the way the Chelsea fans were booing me they must have been hoping it was a ten-match ban! It was like my early days as a youngster at Wrexham all over again. I hated it and just couldn't wait to get home.

Every new player was given a free month in a hotel and then, after that, it was fend for yourself. I was in the Hotel Lilley by Earls Court, which was fine if you liked hotels, but after a couple of nights on my own I'd had enough. In the week before the Palace match, my mate and former

Wrexham and Wales team-mate, Ian Edwards, who was playing for them, rang me up to go for a drink with him. Any chance of a bit of company seemed fine to me.

I felt like a little kid lost in London – I still do now – but Ian knew his way round and by the time I got back to the hotel I'd had a couple. I said goodnight, got the key to my room and went to bed. Next thing I knew, it was three o'clock in the morning and I was awake, standing in the corridor with no clothes on! What a nightmare. I'd obviously got up to go to the toilet, completely lost my bearings and walked out into the landing instead of the bog. I didn't half come round quickly when I couldn't get back into my room and had to creep down three flights of stairs to the main reception to ask the porter to let me back in. Joey 'Frank Spencer' Jones!

It certainly gave the porter a shock. I didn't even have a fig leaf! I just kept thinking of Inspector Clouseau when he was bollock-naked in that nudist camp. It didn't help that the porter was gay and he certainly was not going to help by giving me a coat or anything. He told me to go back up the stairs first with him walking behind! I just wanted to go home. Janice still doesn't believe me.

We drew 0-0 with Palace and the reception didn't get any better. It wasn't as bad as Carlisle, but you could still hear the booing. It also didn't help that we were crap and by now I was really thinking I'd made the wrong move. I'd been there six weeks before I played in a winning side and I'd begun to think I was a jinx. That first win was over Burnley at home, with David Speedie and Mickey Droy scoring the goals in a 2-1 win. We were still playing badly – drawing, losing and getting booed off – and to make matters worse, I was getting the impression that some of the lads weren't bothered. I was getting stick from the fans, even though I was giving it everything I had ... and yet some of the lads looked as if they couldn't care less.

In the end I pulled John Neal. 'I'm not having this. You can get me a move back up North. Some of these aren't trying.'

It wasn't the booing that bothered me; I could cope with that, but I just thought the effort wasn't worth it. John Neal knew what was happening.

'Just hold on for a bit. I agree with you and I'm going to change it.'

We lost at Middlesbrough on the Saturday, 11 December, but then beat Bolton 2-1 at Stamford Bridge the following week and that was the game where everything changed. It certainly helped that we won, but for me personally it was the moment the crowd stopped booing my every move and swung round to my side. It's funny how little things can make the difference, little moments that fans appreciate and respond to. I wasn't doing anything different at all, but, when a ball came into the box, I dived in to head it away through a crowd of players and split my head open. I just got up and carried on with blood dripping down my shirt. It didn't hurt at all. Head injuries often produce loads of blood from the tiniest nick.

I couldn't believe it. The crowd began chanting my name. They must have seen that I was prepared to stay on whatever came my way – every time I touched the ball, they'd cheer, even when I took a throw-in. That was that. Never slow to miss a chance to acknowledge the fans, I couldn't wait for the next game. That was at QPR away and we won 2-1. Clive Walker and David Speedie scored. The Chelsea fans chanted my name throughout the game and, at the end, some ran on and tried to lift us up on to their shoulders. I couldn't believe it. We'd only beaten QPR and they were going mad like we'd won the European Cup. What a feeling. What a good move I'd made!

The Chelsea fans that season were brilliant, especially away from home. We were crap most of the time, yet thousands would come away with us to places like Carlisle or Rotherham. They were as fanatical as the Liverpool fans and both of them will always be special to me. Through thick and mostly thin, they travelled in their thousands and never stopped singing throughout the game. I know they had a bad reputation at times, but every club, even Wrexham, has their bad element. I can't speak too highly of them.

From Bolton onwards, I didn't bother with warming up. I'd go running to each side of the ground to wave my fist to the stands and then the Shed. It was great getting them going and showing we meant business.

I was still bloody lonely. We'd put the house in Wrexham on the market, but I knew it would take a while to sell. I couldn't stand being on my own in the hotel and eventually started driving home to Wrexham after games ... and after training. John Neal was brilliant, letting me train the odd day with Wrexham, but the rest of the week became a routine of leaving at five in the morning and travelling down to London for training, then finishing at half-past twelve and driving straight back.

I tell people now and they still don't believe me, but that's what I did almost every day for three years. It was great when Eddie Niedzwiecki signed for Chelsea, followed by Mickey Thomas, because we could travel together and take turns driving, but for the first year at least I travelled by myself, come hail, rain or snow. I rarely went on the team bus, because, if we were playing in the North, I'd travel from Wrexham and meet up with the rest of the lads at the hotel or at the ground.

If we had no midweek game, John Neal would let me train at Wrexham on Monday and join up again on Tuesday. Straight after training, I'd be in my car and on my way back to Wrexham because we had Wednesdays off. I rarely took my days off and would go into the Racecourse, before getting my kit together and travelling down for training on the Thursday. It was handy for me because the training ground was at Harlington, near Heathrow, so I'd whizz down the M1 and be the first there every morning. Thursday afternoon I'd be back up to Wrexham and would go down again at five o'clock on Friday morning. If we were playing at home, I'd stay over. Sometimes I'd book into a hotel and other times I'd stay with different people. The reserve team physio, Jimmy Hendry, was a great bloke who let me kip at his flat. It was actually his girlfriend, Linda's flat which she shared with another girl. They were both nurses and, if the other one was away on nights, I'd nip into her bed, set the alarm early and then dive back into my sleeping bag on the settee before she came in!

I can honestly say the travelling never once affected my football and, if I had to do it again, I would. In fact, though I now live just a mile from the Racecourse Ground, I still get up at six and go for a 200-mile round trip before I get into work just to make me feel at home!

Chelsea was a friendly club and the people behind the scenes made me welcome and helped me settle as soon as I got there: Teresa Connolly in the office, Sheila Marsden the secretary, Joe Louis, the ticket officer – all of them were tremendous. When Mickey and I knocked around together at Chelsea, Joe would always see us all right for tickets and would make sure we could find our way round London. I once burst into his office wearing a rubber mask and demanded all his money. He was on the phone. 'All right, all right, wait there.'

I had to take the mask off as I was laughing so much. Joe was too relieved to go mad. 'You bastard,' he said, 'I was just about to give it you.'

Great bloke Joe!

The coaching staff were brilliant too; John Neal is the best as far as I'm concerned – not just for what he's done for me but also for his ability as a manager. He'd been brought in from Middlesbrough and, when he signed me, he was in the early stages of developing the side. He'd brought in Ian McNeil as his assistant and Ian too was a great bloke, who'd listen to you as well as have a drink with you. He had been manager of Wigan Athletic and knew the game inside out. I liked him a lot. Norman Medhurst was the physio and Ron Suart the chief scout. Gwyn Williams, who is still at Chelsea as the Academy Director, was in charge of the youngsters. He was from St Asaph and spoke fluent Welsh, a great feller, and oh yeah, I almost forgot, Ken Bates was chairman.

The first time I spoke to Ken Bates was on the phone at home in Wrexham, when John Neal rang me to ask if I'd like to come down to Chelsea to have a look round. 'Listen,' said John, 'I've got the chairman here with me, have a word with him.'

Ken Bates came on the phone. 'Have you ever had any bad injuries?'

I couldn't think of any but then remembered Derek Hales and Charlton. 'I got a kick in my boll-I mean testicles, a few seasons back, but I've not had any trouble since.'

'Oh yeah, well put it this way,' he said, 'if you don't perform for us, I'll personally kick you in the balls!'

I nearly dropped the phone. A different chairman this one, I thought.

Everything about the club was different from what I'd known and it took longer for me to mix in with the other lads than any other club I've been to. I'm not saying there was a North-South divide, but most of the blokes I got on well with were from up my way. David Speedie and Tony McAndrew were good lads, both from northern clubs. Tony had joined just before me from Middlesbrough. The first time I met him we shook hands and he started laughing. 'I've met you before ... at Anfield,' he said. Apparently, I'd had a go at him when Middlesbrough came to Liverpool. 'I was running out after the ball had been cleared and you booted me up the arse for no reason.' Doesn't sound like me that. Still I got quite friendly with Tony in the end.

There's no doubt we had some good players. Colin Pates, the captain, was magnificent. What a player: with his touch, speed and skill, I honestly thought he'd become a really big star. He was a good bloke too and later played for Arsenal. Colin Lee was another I got on well with. He played nearly every position for Chelsea, at the back and up front. If I'd had a nark with Janice, I'd buy some flowers from Colin because he'd just started up a little market stall business. I'd pay about 50 pence and tell Janice they'd cost the earth!

David Speedie was the main man. Great player and a great feller! He'd come from Darlington earlier in the season and soon began to show signs of the ability we now know he had. But what a moaner! Moan, moan, moan, moan, moan ... he made Victor Meldrew seem full of the joys of life. He never stopped on the field and was just as bad in training. He's the most fiercely competitive footballer I've ever met. Ludo, tiddlywinks, anything, he had to win. Second didn't matter, he had to be on the winning side. I'd have him in my team every time. I'm only sorry it didn't work out for him at Liverpool. If he'd gone there a few years before when he was just that bit younger, I'm sure the Liverpool fans would have loved him.

He got on a few of the other lads' nerves because of his attitude and that's probably why he ended up in the number of scraps he did, but he was a good lad to have around. He did a lot for Chelsea and, next to Kevin Keegan, he's the best I've ever seen in the air for his size. Very aggressive and he could play in midfield too – all round a tremendous asset. What a great little player!

In training, he got as fired up as he did in a proper game. He'd put in the odd late tackle and I've seen him fight with Kerry Dixon and Paul Canoville. However, he bit off more than he could chew with Canoville. He was a big lad, built like a brick shithouse, and it was more like Marvin Hagler against George Formby, when he was in one of his old black-and-white boxing films! Speedie was going in with arms flailing everywhere and Canoville just picked him off with jabs. Canoville boxed his head off.

Thinking about it, Paul Canoville was a character. He kept himself to himself most of the time and was a quiet lad, but to his credit he came through to do well at Chelsea even though some of the fans gave him stick because he was the only black player. I liked Paul and respected him. Having done all the hard work, it was bloody tough when he was forced to give up the game because of injury. We used to call him 'King'. Once I'd been getting autographs for fans and asked him to sign. I looked at his signature and he'd written 'P. K. Canoville'.

'What's the "K" for then?'

He looked at me and slowly drawled, 'King!'

From that day on he was known as King Canoville – in fact, I've got a book at home about Chelsea and under the picture of him is written 'King Canoville'.

He was a good lad, Paul, and we all used to laugh our heads off because he started bringing his mate into training when John Hollins took over as manager a couple of seasons later. George was his name and he was bloody huge. We thought he was George Foreman, a smashing feller he was too, and no one had the heart or the bottle to tell him he wasn't training with the first team. We'd all be playing five-a-side and George would be playing too. You couldn't imagine saying, 'Hey, George, you better go with the reserves and the other lads,' because George was just too big to argue with! That was that – the first team, and George.

The King didn't often go out with the other lads; instead he'd sit in his room with the biggest ghetto blaster I've ever seen, playing the music full pelt. I was just along the corridor from him when we were staying down in Aberystwyth and all I could hear was something which sounded like 'Scanga, Scanga, Scanga' blasting out.

In the end I went down to tell him to belt up. 'Who the hell's that singing?'

'It's me,' he said. 'Scanga, Scanga, Scanga.'

He'd recorded himself singing and that was it. I stayed and listened to it, once I knew it was him.

I got my first goal that season in the home game against Cambridge, the first in a 6-0 thrashing. It was about the best performance of the season. I was off round the running track like the roadrunner gone mad, waving to the fans and milking the applause. We still lost the next three games, four if you include the FA Cup fourth round away at Derby. What a match that turned out to be: we were beaten 2-1 and I was charged by the police for inciting a riot!

As I've said before, whenever I ran out on to the pitch I always saluted the fans by waving my fist in the air. This wasn't to start trouble, but to acknowledge them and let them know we were going to give it everything we had. It started at Liverpool when I'd wave to my mates on the Kop. The fans have always been the most important thing to me and waving to them was the least I could do.

Defeat at Derby brought with it all kinds of problems for the club, not the least of which was the fact we'd been dumped out of the FA Cup. When Kevin Wilson scored the winner near the end, some Chelsea fans began ripping seats out and hurling them on to the pitch. The national press jumped on the story and suddenly Chelsea was big news again for all the wrong reasons.

During the game, little Kevin Hales had been injured and was lying on the ground right in front of the Derby fans. I went over to see if he was all right and the physio, Norman Medhurst, who was known to be careful with his money, ran on too.

Next minute, a load of coins came flying at us from the Derby supporters and two hit me on the head, with another catching me just above my left eye. We were playing in our change yellow kit and soon my shirt was dripping in blood. I have to say I wasn't badly hurt, although I remember thinking to myself that I'd been very lucky to be hit just above the eye and not in it. That would have been dangerous.

Norman wasn't bothered about giving us treatment, he just picked up the money! He had about five quid in change by the time he went off! The game restarted despite all the blood on my head, but by now the Chelsea fans realised what had happened and were going mad at the far end, calling for blood (if you will excuse the phrase).

The referee came over to me in the end. 'Go down and I'll get you some treatment.'

'I'm not going down for those bastards.'

I was furious and tempers all round grew short. Both sets of supporters were chanting and, when Kevin Wilson scored, the Derby lot went mad. All hell broke loose when the ref blew the whistle and, as I was walking off, some Derby punters started having a go at me as I headed for the tunnel. 'You bastard, Jones, you caused all this.'

'Don't give me that. Your lot did this,' I said, pointing to the cut eye.

I was back in Wrexham the next day, when a photographer from the *Sun* turned up at our house wanting to take photos of the cuts on my head. I told him he had no chance, but he still sat outside my house in his car for hours, waiting and waiting.

In the meantime, the Derby chairman, Mike Wattison, rang me to apologise on behalf of the club. He was very decent about it and said I wasn't to blame in any way for the trouble that went on after the whistle. He said he was glad I was all right and that I was welcome at Derby any time. I really appreciated the call.

Having chatted to him, I decided to let the *Sun* take the pictures, hopefully as a warning to others about how dangerous throwing coins could be. When I got into training the following day, nothing was said about the game or the incident and, as far as the club was concerned, the matter was closed.

Later that week, I got a call to go and see John Neal in his office. Some police officers were there and said they were issuing a summons for me to appear in court on charges of inciting a riot. I didn't know what to say (though a few well-chosen words were on the tip of my tongue!). Apparently, some fans had complained about me waving my fist to the crowd before the game and at half-time. Their version of events was that my clenched fist whipped the crowd up into mass hysteria and my version was that I was just acknowledging the people who'd paid good money to come and see us play.

John Neal and Ken Bates were both good about it. They knew how stupid the accusations were and said they'd support me all the way. In the end, they didn't have to because, some time later, the club, and I, got a letter saying all charges were being dropped. I don't know what brought about the change of heart, but I must admit I was glad I didn't have to get further involved.

It wasn't an end to the fist waving and it wasn't an end to the complaints. The craziest one we got came in the first game of the following season down at Brighton. I was sub and stood up to get warmed up in the second half, so I pulled a few faces in fun and got on with it. The following week, John Neal told me they'd had a letter from one punter saying I was trying to incite a riot with my face. I said it always looked like that!

Later on that season up at Newcastle, the police told me after the game that they were going to press charges for inciting violence. As usual I'd waved to the Chelsea fans and, when we ran out for the second half, I stuck my fist up to get everyone going again.

The Newcastle fans were giving me loads and I had a few coins thrown at me, though all of them missed. We drew 1-1, with David Speedie scoring. The minute I'd got out of the bath in the changing rooms, the police came in and took me to a room. They'd had a complaint from a Newcastle fan about me waving my fist and they said they'd be pressing charges. But once again I didn't hear any more about it.

The whole thing was getting out of hand and, in the end, I was called before an FA disciplinary hearing at Lancaster Gate. Bert Millichip and all the top boys were sitting on the panel to investigate my behaviour. Ken Bates and John Neal came with me and told the hearing that I was doing nothing more than waving to the supporters, encouraging them to get involved.

When it came to my turn, I tried as best I could to explain. 'Funny how nobody jumped on the bandwagon at Liverpool.' I told them members of the press were only getting wound up about it because of Chelsea's reputation. 'All of a sudden, people are putting two and two together and making five; I wasn't waving at Chelsea fans in the 1970s and there was still trouble then.'

They listened and I know they weren't saying that it was only my fist waving causing trouble, but they were looking at anything and everything that might be linked to bad behaviour. 'All I'm trying to do is get the fans involved and make them feel that we're all trying for them. Besides, they pay the money to come and see us, the least I can do is acknowledge them.'

They told me that they appreciated my feelings, but said I wasn't to do it again. Ken Bates, John Neal and myself all agreed with the decision, so when I ran out at home to Rotherham the following Saturday, I did a lap of honour waving to everyone. People were laughing and cheering. I was inciting smiles, nothing more dangerous.

What a struggle it was that season. I'd started enjoying myself once the fans took to me, but we nearly went down in the end, winning just one of our last ten games. We were looking at relegation up until the last match, which for a club like Chelsea was almost unthinkable. We only scored six goals in those last ten matches, which showed how poorly we were playing. We finally got a win up at Bolton in the second to last game, which made us all but mathematically safe. The support we got that day was unbelievable. Even after the season we'd had, there were thousands there, singing all game, which doesn't half give you a boost. Against Middlesbrough in the last home match, you would have thought we were champions. We all did a lap of honour after the game and we'd only drawn. I was running round, thinking to myself what it would have been like if we were actually any good! We finished 18th and avoided the drop.

It was a smashing end to the season for me because I was the supporters' Player of the Year, the only trophy of its kind I'd received up to that point in my career (that's not entirely true, because I also got the

Liverpool Supporters Club Irish Branch award in 1977). I went to the Café Royal in London to pick it up, which seemed a million miles away from the miserable Saturday in Carlisle back in October, when I was booed on my debut and sent off. I love happy endings!

CHAPTER FOURTEEN

CHELSEA IS THE NAME

John Neal went to the sales in the close season and came up with more bargains than you'd find at a car boot sale: Kerry Dixon, Pat Nevin, Nigel Spackman, Eddie Niedzwiecki and Joe McLaughlin. It's safe to say he had the ability to spot talent. Every one of them did brilliantly for Chelsea, and Kerry, Pat and Nigel became big stars in their own right. When I joined, John Neal had said he was going to change things and he was certainly true to his word.

From being a side fighting off relegation, we became a strong side virtually overnight and went on to win the Second Division that season. We had everything – ability, flair, characters, good individuals and goalscorers: Speedie and Dixon up front were as good a pair as I've played with. The crowd took to the new lads straight away, and so did I.

Little Pat Nevin was just wizard on the wing. I loved playing with him because, if you were knackered, you could give him the ball and you wouldn't see it for another five minutes. No one would. It was tied to his foot as he weaved in and out. If anyone chopped him, then the whole team would move in.

'Which one was it, Pat?'

'Him there, I'll get him.'

'No, you won't. I will.'

'Oh, go on then.'

Mind you, if I was marking Pat Nevin, the first thing I'd do would be to try and kick him up in the air. From a defender's point of view, he has that style which cries out for you to whack him to slow him down a bit. But you had to catch him first.

I'd never seen anything like him before in football. He'd come in dressed like a tramp and we'd always take the mickey, saying he must have picked his clothes off a rubbish tip! Coming from Wrexham, it was all new to me and Eddie Niedzwiecki. We thought he was weird. Mind you, he probably thought the same about us with our flares and platforms!

Music-wise, he was into everything – everything you'd never heard of, but then three years later it'd be top of the charts. By then, he'd be on to something else. He was very brainy, very articulate. I think that's why I got on with him so well! A bit like Steve Heighway really. Pat had a regular column in the Chelsea paper, *Bridge News* – not on football, but music, films, anything trendy!

He was so laid-back he could limbo under a carpet. While we were all twitching and squirming, waiting for kick-off down in the changing rooms, he'd be warming up with his headphones on. I thought he was great. People who think footballers are thick should go talk to Steve Heighway or Pat Nevin.

Nigel Spackman's main asset was his ability to work up and down the pitch; he could run like Terry McDermott in his prime. Blimey, he was fit and a good lad too. Spackman had come from Bournemouth, Nevin from Clyde and big Joe McLaughlin arrived from Morton. Joe was a smashing feller and a solid centre-half – a Paul Young look-alike. That was his only problem; he was too good-looking. Like Kerry Dixon, all the girls fancied him. When the mail came in the morning, his would be in a massive box and mine would be in a matchbox!

'Hey, Kerry, sure you've not got any of mine there?'

Kerry was the big blond star, and could he score goals. I remember the first time we all saw him at Aberystwyth in pre-season training and he ran like a man possessed. John Neal whispered to me quietly, 'If he plays like he runs, I've got a bloody world-beater.'

Top left: My trademark clenched fist salute to the fans, which I have done at all the clubs I have played for. It was my acknowledgment to the people who'd paid good money to come and see us play - the fans.

Top right: Back in the swing of things with Wrexham, with one of my infamous tackles!

Above: Despite the death threats prior to the game, here I am trudging off the pitch at Goodison Park following our FA Cup fifth round match with Everton. I'm still here to tell the tale, but we lost 5-2!

Top: Me and my brother Frankie on leaving the pitch after a 2-0 home win over Luton Town on 7th May 1979. It was Frankie's league debut at 18, and the first time we had lined up together in the same side.

Above: My mam and dad on their first proper holiday when they went away for a couple of days to Blackpool to celebrate their 40th wedding anniversary.

Holding my Russian Samivar awarded to me after former Everton &
Wales centre-half Tommy Jones, chose me as the 'Man of the Match' for
Wales in a scoreless draw against Russia at Wrexham in May 1981.

In action for Wales against England at Wembley on 23rd May 1979. We drew 0-0.

Top left: In action playing for Chelsea.

Top right: My former Liverpool team mate Terry McDermott and I share a joke in our match against Newcastle United at Stamford Bridge.

Above: Mickey and I are reunited at Stamford Bridge in January 1984.

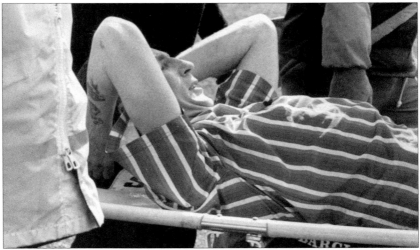

Top: Me with the silver salver that I was presented prior to a home friendly with Uruguay on the Racecourse. It was to commemorate winning my 69th cap for Wales and therefore beating Ivor Allchurch's record of being the most capped player for Wales. I have been joined on 72 caps by Mark Hughes and passed by Peter Nicholas (73), Ian Rush (73), Dean Saunders (75), Gary Speed (85) and Neville Southall (93).

Above: The end is nigh! Stretchered off at Grimsby in the last away match of the 1989/90 season. I'd broken my left ankle whilst clearing a ball upfield.

Top: My testimonial match for Wrexham in May 1993 saw Graeme Souness bring a full Liverpool side to the Racecourse. It was a fantastic occasion.

Above: It was a pleasure to line up alongside my former Welsh international team mate Mark Hughes in a Wrexham shirt for my testimonial match, and to cap it all he scored for Wrexham in front of the Liverpool fans which pleased them. Not!

Top: I partly learned my coaching methods from experience, but mostly from working alongside Cliff Sear. Hopefully, Wrexham have seen the benefits of what I picked up from working alongside such a great coach. Cliff is sadly missed.

Above: This was a 25th anniversary get together of the 1978 European Cup Final squad who beat FC Bruges at Wembley. From left to right: Ian Callaghan, Alan Hansen, Ray Clemence, Emlyn Hughes, Jimmy Case, Phil Neal, Me, David Fairclough and Ray Kennedy.

He got 34 goals in his first season and went on to spend nine years at Stamford Bridge, scoring 147 league goals in 335 games, a record that compares with the best, all credit to him. He also won eight caps for England and later played for Southampton, Luton, Millwall, Watford and Doncaster.

Kerry was a quiet lad, though. While all the dollies would be lined up for him, their grandmothers would be there for me! The only time I really saw him narked was after the Manchester City game in December, which we lost 1-0 at home. I was one of the first in the dressing room after the game with Dixon and Speedie just behind. They'd been arguing in the tunnel and, as I picked up my tea, they started getting stuck into each other. I had no idea what it was about, but they were having a right go. I got up to pull them apart and then lost interest. What the hell! Let them get on with it. I sat down to watch!

I had the feeling we were going to do well. You could just tell in training and in the early games. I still speak to Chelsea fans and many tell me that side was one of the most committed they'd seen at Stamford Bridge. Certainly we had the characters and played with real style. It was great to be involved.

Our first game was at home to Derby and we murdered them 5-0. OK, so I wasn't playing, but even when I came back into the side we were winning. We played 17 games with just one defeat, including a real thrashing of Newcastle at Stamford Bridge. They had Kevin Keegan, Peter Beardsley, Chris Waddle and Terry McDermott playing for them and to win 4-0 was as good a result as we got all season. I had a chat with Terry Mac afterwards and, during the game, someone snapped a picture of me and him sharing a joke as we waited for a corner.

In October, we whacked Fulham 5-3 at Craven Cottage and I scored with a header past Jim Stannard, which was particularly pleasing in a local derby. Then, not surprisingly, I got into a bit of trouble up at Carlisle with their boss Bob Stokoe. It's strange the way I've always had grounds at which things seem to happen. Carlisle was one of them.

Their winger, Alan Shoulder, shoved the ball past me as I came in to make a tackle and by the time I got there he was away. I deliberately obstructed him and, as he went past, his knee caught mine and he flew into the air, before crashing down on the cinder track. It was one hell of a somersault!

Bob Stokoe flew off the bench and began having a go, calling me everything. 'Ah shut up, Baldy!' I told him.

He was swearing and I was swearing back – and you'd be hard pushed to find anyone as competitive as Bob Stokoe. In the meantime, Alan Shoulder got up and started issuing threats, so I told him he'd better get me first before I got him again. It was just another quiet Saturday afternoon really.

We walked in scoreless at half-time and the crowd were booing my every step. When I looked up, I saw Bob Stokoe hanging round the tunnel area. It was the first time I'd seen him standing up and he was massive. 'Look at the bloody size of him!'

I wouldn't have started a row if I'd known he was that big.

I tried to sneak up the tunnel, but Bob collared me and started dishing out the verbals again. Luckily for me, the tunnel at Carlisle twists right then up again into the dressing room and Ian McNeil jumped in to calm things down. Bob started having a go at him and, before he turned back, I was off round the corner and in for my half-time cuppa. Poor Ian was left to take the flak. I was just glad I didn't call him anything worse than Baldy. Sadly, Bob has since passed away. There is no doubting that he was one of the game's great characters.

December was a difficult month for us as we somehow began to lose a bit of momentum, which often happened in the run-up to Christmas. After drawing 1-1 with Manchester City on 3 December, we stuffed Swansea 6-1, but then we drew with Barnsley and lost to Grimsby on consecutive Saturdays. John Neal never appeared to panic, but it was a stupid schedule we had to follow in the week after Christmas when we played four games in seven days. On Boxing Day, we won 4-2 at Shrewsbury and then drew 2-2 with Portsmouth the following day at the Bridge. On New Year's Eve, we beat Brighton at home and, straight after the match, we all travelled up to Teesside to prepare for the match with Middlesbrough on 2 January.

Eddie and I went in my car, while the rest of the lads travelled on the coach. We were first at the hotel and I went straight to the bar to grab a pint before John Neal arrived. I was just downing the last drop when he walked in and saw me. At first I thought I'd be in trouble, but to my surprise he didn't say a word, which was the cue for the rest of the lads to all pile in.

What a great night we had. Like all the best nights out, it started off slowly and, for a couple of hours, we had one eye on the staff – we expected them to tell us to go to bed at any time. During the meal, nothing was mentioned and by 11 o'clock we were all well into it. At one point, I met John Neal in the toilets and, as I left, he asked me if I was going to call it a night.

'Yeah, I've had enough.'

'Good lad, I'll see you in the morning.'

We walked out of the toilets together. He turned right towards the bedrooms as I took a left in the direction of the bar. 'I thought you'd had enough.'

'Yeah, well, I'll just finish one more pint.'

John Neal was brilliant in that way. He knew we'd all been stretched by the number of matches we'd played over Christmas and I think he was pleased we'd found a moment to relax. Besides, it was New Year's Eve.

When I got back to the bar, the other lads were chatting and having a laugh when someone said they knew of a party up the road. About seven of us decided to give it a whirl and we sneaked out across the car park. Sure enough, we found a party going on in some bloke's house down the street and we all went in, drinking cans of lager well into the early hours. I don't think they realised who we were and, at that stage, nobody really cared, but it was a smashing night.

We trained in the morning and John Neal ran us into the ground like there was no tomorrow. The next day we lost 1-0 – so much for New Year. Is there a moral in that story somewhere?

In many ways, Middlesbrough was the turning point of our season because, soon after, we went out of the FA Cup, losing 1-0 up at Blackburn, and John Neal moved in to shake us up with yet another brilliant signing just at the right time, Mickey Thomas.

I was delighted, not least because it meant I had someone to share the driving with. He made his debut on 14 January at Derby and never missed a game after that. I took him out for a warm-up beforehand and the fans gave him a brilliant welcome. As always, he was to become a folk hero.

He was still living in Colwyn Bay and had to get up at four in the morning to get to mine for about 5am. Janice would always pack my clothes and kit the night before, putting everything neatly into a bag along with my butties. I'd be stumbling around in the pitch black when I'd hear Mickey come tearing round the corner, before screeching to a halt on the drive. 'All right, Joe? What are we going to need for the next few days?'

He'd be rummaging around in the car boot for anything he could find. All his clothes were in there and anything he didn't want he'd fling back over his head on to the lawn. 'Don't need that. Might take those in case we go out. How about these?'

My clothes looked all neat and tidy and his were creased to bits. He never looks like he's been to bed anyway, but, at five in the morning in crumpled clothes, he looked a right state. Eventually, we'd get going and, when I spoke to Janice in the evening, she'd say she'd spent half the day clearing Mickey's clothes off the front garden!

I'd had my house on the market for a year and a half by this time, but we never had any realistic offers. I'd settled into the routine of travelling every day and, although a few people at Chelsea weren't happy about it, John Neal was always very helpful because he knew it never affected the way I played and besides, if I couldn't get down for training with Chelsea, I'd always be at the Racecourse with the Wrexham lads.

Just after I signed, I asked Ken Bates if he could help me with a move south and he said no. When Mickey signed, he asked Ken if he would help him with removal expenses. 'But you haven't moved.'

'Yes, I have ... from Colwyn Bay to Rhyl.'

It's 12 miles closer to London!

Travelling certainly had its moments, especially in the winter when it was foggy or snowing. One time, Mickey and I were due to play for the reserves against Swansea at Chelsea's training ground. We were both coming back from injury and John Neal was very keen for us to get 90 minutes under our belts. As always we left in plenty of time, but on the M1 we got held up behind a 27-car pile up. Seconds earlier and it would have been 28, because we escaped with just yards to spare. Both of us jumped out of the car to see if we could help, but soon there were ambulances and police cars, so there was little we could do apart from sit and wait.

By now, we were struggling to make the game and eventually we got to a phone to let them know what had happened. Luckily, they'd heard about the crash and Gwyn Williams said he'd ring Janice to tell her we were all right. When we eventually got to the ground, they'd kicked off with nine men. Mickey and I dashed into the changing rooms, got our kit on and ran over to the pitch. With half an hour gone, it was 0-0. We made all the difference and we eventually lost 1-o! We got straight into the car after the game and headed back home to Wrexham. Just another day!

The only time we cocked up on the travelling came one morning when the weather was terrible and neither of us fancied the trip down for training. We'd left at the usual time, but, with snow, wind and traffic jams on the M6, we pulled off for a cup of tea. On the radio, we heard there'd been a big pile-up on the M1, so that was that; we were straight on the phone to John Neal. I was doing the talking and got Mickey to make car noises in the background as if we'd got caught behind the pile-up like last time.

'Yeah, boss, terrible crash on the motorway. Don't think we'll be able to make it down today.'

'Whoosh, reaaaarooooooow,' went Mickey, making car and road sounds for all he was worth.

'We're stuck and don't know what to do.'

There was a silence on the end of the phone and then John Neal spoke.

'I heard about the crash on the radio, big one by all accounts. Only thing is, it's on the carriageway going north!'

Good point, we had to admit.

'All right, Mickey, cut the James Hunt stuff. We've been sussed.'

John Neal had to laugh about it and told us to go to Wrexham to train. In fairness, the weather was dreadful.

The real bonus about Mickey signing was another free month in a London hotel. Like everyone else, he was given free accommodation to help him settle and find a place, and so I took full advantage and moved in with him. It was a great hotel, much better than the one I had. He was like a starry-eyed kid in London. We both were. He couldn't spend his money fast enough. The first time we walked down the King's Road, he spent a fortune on Benetton gear: shirts, jeans, sweatshirts, anything with Benetton written on it. The next time we walked down the King's Road, he did the same thing.

'What the hell are you doing? Didn't you get enough last time?'

'Yeah, but they're dirty now!'

Spend, spend, spend: you'd swear he'd won the pools! Even when we stopped for petrol on the way home to Wrexham, I'd pay and maybe pick up a few sweets. When he was driving and it was his turn to pay, he'd come back with loads of tapes. 'There you go, Joe. Get a hold of them.'

He'd buy every tape going and stick it on his credit card.

There was never a dull night with Mickey around; it was like being kids in Wrexham all over again, except this was London and we had a few more bob. We were also a little bit more experienced. Even so, we were still like two urchins from the sticks, despite what Mickey might have you believe. It was a great laugh though.

It was a nightmare trying to find somewhere to stay when Tommo's month in the hotel was up. We couldn't be asking the lads to put us up all the time, so we'd often stay in a grotty hotel near Stamford Bridge – Heartbreak Hotel, Mickey called it. The rooms had loads of beds in them as if they were trying to squeeze more people in. The mattresses had pee stains on them and, one time, we found puke all over the floor. It was a bit like a doss house, but not so flashy! Talk about soccer stars, it was all we could afford. Mickey and I would sit at night huddled up around the TV watching the footy. One time we were with a few other lads, having a chat and a drink in the room, when one of them wandered off to see if he could borrow a corkscrew for a bottle of wine. When he came back, he told us he'd been chatting with a few of the other residents and it turned out most were homeless families who'd been put there until other accommodation could be sorted out.

At night, we'd nip along to the Stamford Bridge pub for a game of pool with the locals. I loved it because we got to know some of the lads and the night before a game Tommo and I would be in having a chat.

'Joe, Mickey, how's it going?'

'All right, lads, what about yourselves?'

'Magic.'

We were part of the scenery but we also just happened to be part of the team. We never ever had a drink the night before a game and we were always tucked up in Heartbreak Hotel at a reasonable hour.

We could only get tea and toast in the hotel, so at eight in the morning we'd be in some local café wolfing down bacon and eggs. Once again, people got to know us and they'd be shouting over wishing us luck for the game. I loved it – it was just like being part of the community. One morning I was sitting eating my bacon buttie when a dustman walked straight through the café with his bin to pick up the rubbish at the back. It was that kind of establishment.

The only place I wouldn't sleep was in the ground. Mickey did though. It was like his second home: he'd be there tucked away in the referee's room with a portable telly he'd picked up from somewhere. He'd nip in, lock the door and no one ever knew he was around. He had all the home comforts – a couple of corner flags and a whistle – and, if Stamford Bridge had gone up in smoke, then Mickey would have gone up with it. He was always first in in the mornings, put it that way. I'd nip off to Jimmy Hendry's instead.

If he got bored in the referee's room, he'd go out on to the pitch to play penalties with a couple of mates in the early hours. They'd be on there for ages in the pitch black betting on the outcome: best of five, then turn about in goal. One time, he was playing penalties at three in the morning before Everton came to Stamford Bridge in the live match. Needless to say, Mickey was Man of the Match.

Mickey had a mate called Ray, who earned his living minding massive houses in Hampstead for owners who'd gone abroad. One house he looked after was on the same street as Lulu's and Warren Mitchell lived just round the corner. It was unbelievable: outdoor swimming pool, indoor sauna, jacuzzi, snooker room and so on. The baths had gold taps and the beds had radios in the headboards. You could have marked out a five-a-side pitch on the landing. The new tenants were J Jones esq and M Thomas, along with Ray. Just to make it a bit more homely, we bought a dartboard which we stuck in the lounge on the cork tiling, so it didn't mark when we missed. Sometimes if we were in having a quiet drink, Mickey would perk up. 'Should we nip round to call for Lulu?'

Ray had the use of the house's stretch limo and, after one Wales game at Wembley, he persuaded us to stay down in London to make a night of it. 'Get to the main entrance after the match and I'll pick you up.'

Sure enough, we were outside Wembley in the pouring rain after the game and there was Ray in the limo waiting for us. It had about seven doors and a telly, with frosted glass and mini bar. George Berry, Kevin Hales (a Chelsea team-mate), Rushie, Mickey and I got in and Ray took us cruising down the West End. I couldn't take it all in. We were downing cans of ale and watching the telly, while Mickey mucked about with the sunroof. We flashed down Piccadilly. Now that was living.

The most difficult part of being in London was passing time between games, travelling and training. If we weren't going home and had nowhere to stay, we'd both do anything to while away a few hours. Most of the time, we'd go star-spotting down the Kings Road. We were like private eyes stalking people.

'I'm sure that's him out of Culture Club.'

'Which one? Where? Boy George?'

'No, the guitarist, what's his name?'

'Oh yeah, I know the one. Nah, it's not him; he's got pink hair.'

We saw all the big names down there. Remember that one in Slade with the straight hair at the front – Dave Hill was his name – well, we saw him. Marilyn Cole, we saw her, or was it Nat King Cole?

I once went into a shop to buy a coat and the woman serving started looking at me funnily. 'You were in the "Parrots", weren't you?' Talk about the past catching up with you. Apparently they'd had a RentoKill man in the previous week and this girl had told him I'd been in the shop. The bloke told her to ask about the 'Parrots' next time I was in because he was from Llandudno. I got the shock of my life.

When we were really bored, we'd take the special tourist trips around the city to see the sights: the Tower of London or Buckingham Palace. We were walking through Harrods one day, when the commissionaire collared us near one of the exits. I thought we were about to be accused for shoplifting, but it turned out he was a Chelsea fan and he asked Mickey and me to sign the visitors' book reserved for special guests!

At night, we'd wander down to Soho to see what was happening and, like naughty schoolboys, we'd be in and out of the peep shows. You had to put 50 pence into a slot and then the women would dance. I'd be on one side laughing away at Tommo who'd be on the other waving to me. Then he'd come running out and we'd be off somewhere else. Last of the Big Spenders!

The Chelsea lads thought we were barmy and they were probably right, but if there's someone laughing and keeping you relaxed it doesn't half help. Right up to the kick-off, Mickey would be messing about and sometimes it would only be me joining in because as I say he's crackers and I'm on the same wavelength. Many of the others didn't get the joke.

At the best of times, Mickey never keeps still – he's always fidgeting and moving around. With these peep shows in Soho, he was worse than ever, going straight out of one and into another. I was standing by one of the minders on the door when Mickey came running out dropping his money all over the floor. 'Come on, Joe, let's get into this one here. No, hang on, that looks a good one over there.'

He was picking up his money dead quickly and this feller was looking at me.

'I'm sure that's Mickey Thomas, did you see him?'

'I don't know, mate, what does he look like?'

'Scruffy hairstyle. I could have sworn it was him.'

Meanwhile, Mickey was up and off again. 'Come on, Joe, let's nip over here.'

Down the years, hundreds of people have asked me to describe him, to sum him up, but it's impossible. Mickey, along with Eddie Niedzwiecki, is my best mate and we've known each other for over 30 years. It's fair to say that I know Mickey as well as anybody, but then you never really get to know Mickey inside out. In many ways, that's his secret because he always does his own thing and you can never tell what that's going to be. People will remember him for being completely off his head – which he is, no question – but they should also remember him for being one hell of a player. He won 51 caps for Wales and had spells with Manchester United, Everton, Leeds United and Chelsea, of course, and you don't play those sides if you're not a good player.

He was lucky in that he was one of those players who was naturally fit; that's why he played until he was in his late-thirties. Even then he looked a class apart in the Wrexham team, but when people talked about his wayward lifestyle, then all I could say was he hadn't done too much wrong to play so well at that age.

He's always been very nervous and fidgety and, even when we were kids on the Wrexham groundstaff, he couldn't keep still. By his own admission he says silly things, a lot of which he doesn't mean, but most are against himself, not about other people. He's one of the most generous people I've ever met and he'd give you his last penny. In a sense, he's too generous.

Before Wrexham knocked Arsenal out of the FA Cup, Mickey told everyone his performance was down to drinking Guinness and a lot of people got the impression he was a boozer. Nothing could have been further from the truth. Sure he enjoyed the odd pint, but then who doesn't? But that was as far as it went.

I have to say he's completely eccentric, which he admits himself. That's why he had so many clubs because they couldn't pin him down and make him conform. If you try to do that, then you might as well forget it. John Neal was the manager who got the best out of him because he just let him get on with it away from football and reaped the benefits on the pitch.

When John Hollins took over at Chelsea, he made the mistake of trying to make Mickey toe the line. John Neal made the point to me later that Kerry Dixon was banging in 35 goals a season when Mickey was in the Chelsea side, but, when John Hollins took over and dropped Mickey, he couldn't understand why Dixon's goals suddenly dried up.

He was brilliant to have in the dressing room. Ask any player at any club he's been to and they'll tell you he was great to have around because he was so funny. In a way, he played the way he was, buzzing around, hassling players and making them hurry. He'd always make things happen and had a great ability to get forward, fizzing in crosses with his left foot. He was scared of no one and would always come up with a vital goal at the right time.

It's the same now, bags of skill, but he could mix it with the tough lads and, when Mickey and I played down the left, it took a good winger to get past both of us.

CHAPTER FIFTEEN

A BRIDGE TOO FAR

Mickey Thomas became the missing piece in John Neal's title-winning jigsaw that season, because, after we beat Derby 2-1 on his debut on 14 January, we didn't lose again in the league and Mickey played in every game. He scored twice against Sheffield Wednesday on 21 January in a 3-2 victory and the crowd who'd given him such a welcome down at Derby fell in love with him.

It wasn't just Mickey because everyone in that team could play. John Neal, Ian McNeil and John Hollins were men of few words regarding tactics or pre-match talks. We knew what our job was and we had the ability to mix it or play our way out of trouble. Dixon, Speedie, Spackman, Nevin, Pates, Mickey and Eddie 'Niedz' were some of the best players to pull on a blue shirt during that era. John Neal would just wander round the dressing room before a match. 'C'mon, my bonny lads.'

Everything was simple which suited me. John was always very shrewd; he never ranted and raved during or after a match. In fairness, he didn't need to that season.

My only low point came against Fulham, when we won 4-0 at the Bridge on 7 April. The scorers were Kerry Dixon with two, Dave Speedie and Pat

Nevin, but just before half-time I went in for a 50-50 ball with Paul Parker and he went down like a sack of spuds. It wasn't deliberate on my part, but I caught him high up in the groin. A few of their lads dashed in to have a go at me, but it died down and I apologised to him at half-time as we walked off and he told me to forget it. He had treatment but carried on for the rest of the game. End of story ... or so I thought.

The morning papers gave me a right slagging and really made a meal of it, hardly mentioning the fact that we'd won 4-0. Fulham boss Malcolm Macdonald said people who had been in the top tier of the stand and could see my foot coming – it was that high. That was his opinion and he was welcome to it, but not one reporter asked me for mine. As I read the reports, I became more and more angry. Steve Curry in the *Daily Express* gave me a particularly hard time and the message seemed to be that I could get away with it in the Second Division, but the First Division hard men would sort me out if we got promotion.

They seemed to forget that I'd played in the First Division for Liverpool and I told a couple of journalists I wasn't happy about the coverage, particularly the fact that not one had come to get my view. I told them I wanted a word with Steve Curry and I'd catch up with him some other time.

I got my chance at the Racecourse of all places after a Wales-England game, which we won 1-0. After the match, I met up with Janice and a few friends for a drink in the bar and I spotted Steve Curry with the press lads over the far side. I had to laugh because, as I was standing there, one reporter came past me and started whispering out of the corner of his mouth. 'Joe, he's over there behind that pillar.'

I told Janice to wait and walked over to have a word. As I did, a couple of others tried to block my way, but I pulled them aside and spoke to Steve Curry.

'I want to see you.'

He said it was no problem.

'Come on outside then.'

He put his drink down and started walking behind me, but when I turned round he'd stopped. 'What's the problem, Joe?'

'You know what the problem is: what you wrote about after the Fulham match and the tackle on Paul Parker.' By now, people in the bar were beginning to take note and I felt myself becoming more and more annoyed.

'I used to respect you as a reporter but you never had the decency to ask for my opinion after the match. Parker never went off, but you didn't want my view.'

He apologised and said he respected me as a player, but I thought it was too little too late. I knew it had been a bad tackle, but I've taken worse many a time. I felt I was being made out to be a hatchet man.

It was just dying down when Janice suddenly appeared and began having her two-pence worth. 'Yes, and you've upset all the family too.'

'Get out of the way, Janice.'

I pushed her clear and Steve Curry started talking again. 'Listen. Give me your phone number and I'll ring you to get your side of the story.'

Needless to say, I'm still waiting for the call. I'm no angel, I've never claimed to be, but I'm sure if you ask reporters up and down the country they'll say I'm fair as well as easy to contact. They know they can get my phone number if they want it, but sometimes players are given no right of reply. The press are entitled to their opinions, but I thought a report that made me out to be such a villain deserved a response from me.

The incident against Fulham was merely a hiccup, though, as we got promotion by beating Leeds 5-0 with four league games to go. What a result that was. Kerry Dixon scored a hat-trick and all the players walked up on to the balcony to take the applause of the fans who'd invaded the pitch. We threw our shirts, shorts and boots to them as they celebrated and, on the electronic scoreboard, someone had put up the message: 'Hard Luck, Leeds. Better Luck Next Year.' It wasn't meant as a mickey-take, but one Leeds fan must have taken it that way because soon after it had gone up someone threw a piece of wood right through it.

We still had to win the three remaining games to claim the title and, after beating Manchester City away and Barnsley at home in front of 30,000, we went to Grimsby for the last match of the season. I'd been injured since the City game and had started a suspension, which kept me out of the side. But the way the lads were playing they clearly didn't need me.

Thousands had made the trip up from London and Kerry Dixon netted the only goal. The whole place went berserk and, even though I wasn't playing, I loved every minute of it. It was a special moment for all of us – not least John Neal – and most importantly for the supporters who'd stuck by us in the grim days of the season before. They certainly made the most of it.

In the dressing room there was champagne and Ken Bates came in to congratulate everyone, doling out a bob or two for the lads to get a drink. Mickey and I weren't going back on the coach with the rest of them, so I asked him what we could have. 'What about me and 'Tommo' who have to drive home to Wrexham?' He gave us a tenner each! We didn't really mind because it was a cracking trip home with all the Chelsea fans waving at us and beeping their horns. I looked in the rear-view mirror and all you could see was a trail of blue-and-white scarves hanging out of the windows.

In the distance behind us, I suddenly saw Ken Bates catching us up in his Rolls-Royce and Mickey told me to pull over. 'It's him, I'm telling you, get in the middle lane quickly.' I moved over and, as he got nearer, the Chelsea fans started waving at him. He pulled alongside, and Tommo and I were at the windows sticking the Vs up, laughing our heads off. We were only messing about, but unfortunately his wife saw us because she was in the front. We didn't mean anything by it – and we certainly didn't mean it towards his wife because she was a lovely woman – and Ken Bates never said anything to us about it. The only time he mentioned it was in his book, when he said that two Welsh internationals who had played for the club, showed they had no respect for the chairman and his wife.

It was a time for real celebration, but already I was having difficulty agreeing terms for a new contract that would have tied me to the club for another two years. I'd been in to see Ken Bates, who dealt with all the players directly, and asked him for a £50-a-week rise. I was on a lot less than some of the other lads and I felt I'd earned a few bob for helping the club win the title, but Ken Bates didn't agree. 'I only want a £50 rise and, if we get relegated, I'll give it you back. I can't be fairer than that.'

He told me in no uncertain terms that I couldn't have it, so I told him he could stick it. 'I'll see out the remaining year of my contract and then I'm off.'

It wasn't as if it was a fortune, but with all the travelling and my mortgage I was struggling. I've said it before in the book, but money has never been that important to me. This time I needed it, but I didn't get it.

A few weeks afterwards, I was called in again to see him and he went on the attack, trying to get me to sign the new two-year deal. 'If you don't sign this contract, you won't play in the first team here.'

It was typically straight of him, but I've never been shy about speaking my mind. 'Listen, it's not some apprentice you're talking to now. You can't frighten me that way.'

Suddenly he started backtracking. 'I didn't mean it that way.'

'Yes, you did. I'll see out my contract and that's it.'

Fair dos to Ken Bates, he's a man who says what he means and he was right. I didn't play a first-team game on our return to Division One until 22 December. I was sick. All that work to get back into the First Division, all that effort, and I was nothing more than a bit-part player all season. It was doubly hard for me because I was so fit and desperately wanted to show I could still play at the top level, but, whether it was on Ken Bates's say so or whether it was down to the new boss John Hollins, I wasn't ever a regular in the side again.

It had been a difficult summer for the club because John Neal was taken ill and had to undergo heart surgery, which meant John Hollins stepping up to manager in his absence. John thankfully made a full recovery, but John Hollins continued to run the coaching side, and had already begun to shuffle things round.

I'd always got on with John Hollins as a player and I liked the way he coached, keeping us playing with the ball without too much messing round on the tactical side. He was great at encouraging and supporting the players, but I knew he was never keen on Mickey and me travelling down from North Wales.

The season was always going to start badly for me because I was suspended, which meant missing the opening games with Arsenal away and Sunderland at home. To make things worse, Doug Rougvie had been bought from Aberdeen to play at the back and he had a storming debut at Highbury and kept his place. All I could do was sit on the sidelines and watch, but, having worked so hard to earn a place back in Division One, it was frustrating to say the least.

In September, we lost 4-2 at Aston Villa and were absolutely crap. I asked John Neal, who was still very much involved, if I was ever going to get back in the side. He told me I'd definitely be back to face West Ham the following week, which was good enough for me. It really gave me a lift because I was playing for Wales on the Wednesday against Norway and, when I met up with the lads, they were chuffed for me that I was on the way back.

I can always remember walking into Stamford Bridge on the Friday to find I'd been picked for the reserves again and that was enough as far as I was concerned. I wrote out two transfer requests immediately and gave one to Ken Bates and one to John Neal.

'Writing notes to me now, are you?' said Bates.

'Just read it.'

It didn't really make any difference apart from making me realise I wasn't ever going to be first choice again. They still wanted me to sign a new contract, but after West Ham I was determined to go.

In fairness, the side was doing well and I couldn't see a way back, even though I thought I was still worth a place. I had to wait until 22 December for my first game away to Everton of all sides. We won 4-3 and everyone played well; Gordon Davies netted a hat-trick for us. The Everton fans booed me, but that was no surprise. The most important thing was keeping my place away to Queens Park Rangers on Boxing Day.

We drew 2-2 at Loftus Road and Kerry Dixon hit in two penalties. The first came following a scuffle between Gary Chivers and myself after I'd gone up for a corner. I was waiting for it to come over and felt a real belt to the side of my face. I thought it could only have been him, so I whacked him one back and everyone piled in. When the referee sorted it out, he gave us a penalty, which I couldn't understand and Gary Chivers couldn't believe.

We were waiting for the penalty to be taken when Chivers started having a go at me, so I had a few words back. Suddenly Mickey jumped in.

'C'mon then,' he said to Chivers. 'C'mon then, now.'

'Get out of my way, Mickey, I can deal with this.'

We were like Batman and Robin!

On the Saturday we lost at home to Manchester United and, although a few people had been saying I was doing well, I was left out again. We were all sitting in the dressing room before the game with Nottingham Forest when the team was announced and I wasn't even sub. Straight away I got up and asked for a word with Ian McNeil.

'How come I'm not playing?'

'Well, you said you weren't going to be here next season.'

'Yeah.'

'Well, big Doug's back in.'

I just stormed out of the ground, got in my car and drove back to Wrexham. It was one hell of a lonely night.

It was clear I was second choice and that was their opinion, but as time went by I began to feel I was just being messed about. I was playing in the reserves one week, called up for the first team the next, and then left out again.

In January, the first team played Sheffield Wednesday at home in the Milk Cup, as the League Cup was called back then, and drew 1-1. I'd been in Wrexham, watching them play instead and wandered home after the game to find Janice in a panic.

'Ian McNeil's been on the phone asking where you are.'

At half-ten the phone went and it was Ian McNeil. 'Where are you?'

'You know where I am. If no one can be bothered to tell me what's happening, how am I supposed to know you're looking for me.'

'You'd better get over to Sheffield tomorrow because you're playing in the replay on Wednesday.'

I eventually travelled over early in the morning and wandered into the hotel just as the lads were having their breakfast. They were giving me stick and calling me a 'rebel'; I was in a foul mood. One minute they wanted me and the next they didn't.

We trained and I let it be known I wasn't happy by going off by myself to do my own work. In the end Ian McNeil came over and had a word.

'You're playing at right-back.'

'Oh yeah?'

'Listen. If it's any consolation, Sheffield United want you.'

I just looked at him and ran off.

It turned out to be a tremendous game, as we came back from 3-0 down to eventually draw 4-4. I can remember sitting in the dressing room at half-time and, although we were three down, all you could hear was the Chelsea fans singing and singing. We didn't need a team talk because it inspired us so much that we came out like madmen. The fans were brilliant that night.

We scored straight away and pulled it back to 4-3 before they equalised again. I got loads of letters after the match saying it was one of the best performances the fans had seen from Chelsea and a number said it was good to see me back in the side. It really lifted me. The match had been on telly and was also the occasion that Mickey walloped Andy Blair after he'd said something about his wife. In the second replay, Blair waved to Tommo beforehand and we knew we'd won the battle. We won the game 3-2.

Victory meant we were in the semi-finals against Sunderland. I was back in the first-team picture and suddenly the season that had been on the point of turning into disaster looked like providing a tasty little extra in the form of a possible trip to Wembley. I should have known better really because, in the first leg up on Wearside on 13 February, we lost 2-0 to two penalties, the second of which Eddie saved but one of their lads knocked in on the rebound.

The replay was even more disappointing in front of almost 40,000 at Stamford Bridge. Dave Speedie put us ahead after six minutes and the place was going mad, but then as time ticked by and we pushed further and further forward, Clive Walker scored to kill the tie. That was just the start of it really because the Chelsea fans went wild and there was scuffling with the police. It was the first time I'd ever seen any trouble at the Bridge and, at one point, a fan ran on the pitch shouting that he was going to get Clive, who was a former Chelsea player. I could see what was going to happen and grabbed him. I urged him to get back into the crowd before the police got to him, but he was adamant he wanted to have a go at Clive and eventually the police nabbed him. Pat Nevin hit in a late goal for us, but the headlines the next day were all about the trouble. Clive Walker told the press lads what had happened with the fan trying to get to him and thanked me for helping out. I bet Clive wishes he'd never scored because Sunderland went on to lose 1-0 to Norwich in the final and he missed a penalty!

It was too little too late for me because I was in and out for the rest of the season, playing at left-back, right-back and centre-half at Watford, where we won 3-1. The following week we beat Sunderland 2-0 at Roker Park, but I was dropped straight away. Just before deadline day, Mick Buxton of Huddersfield rang and asked me to sign for him, but I told him I'd prefer to wait until the end of the season. I just kept hoping Chelsea might decide to pick me regularly, but I think I knew deep down I hadn't any real chance of that.

I played against West Ham at Upton Park and was then left out again until Liverpool away in a noon kick-off, which was the match I wanted to play in more than any other. I was only sub, which was disappointing, but at least I was back at Anfield. What a reception I got from everyone on the way to the ground and down in the corridors before the game. It was lovely to be back. I sat in the dugout watching the game and in fairness it was a cracker. At Liverpool, the dugouts at that time were split with a wall in between, which meant the manager, coach and physio could sit in one part and the subs could sit in the other. Throughout the game I kept putting my hand over my mouth and shouting to John Neal, 'Get Jones on. Get Joey Jones on now.' I was pretending it was the crowd in the paddock, but John Neal never budged until eight minutes from time.

Someone shouted to me to get warmed up and, with seven minutes and 59 seconds of the match to go, I was stripped and ready to go on. The entire Liverpool bench were laughing because I'd just ripped my kit off I was that desperate to play.

Sure enough I ran on and both sets of fans gave me an ovation that will stay with me all my life. The Chelsea fans were singing my name, but most importantly so were the people in the Kop. It was the only time in my life that both sets of supporters have been on my side. What a fantastic moment!

For the seven minutes and 58 seconds I was on, I only touched the ball about twice and instead ran round waving to everyone. It was brilliant, saluting the Chelsea fans and then the Kop. The Kopites were chanting my name and I was sticking my fist up to them, so then the Chelsea fans started up and I was waving back to them. What a feeling. We lost 4-3, but it was a brilliant day for me.

Later on, it turned into a brilliant night because after the match a few of us joined Sammy Lee at his bar on Smithdown Road in Liverpool for a drink. It was funny really because myself, Eddie Niedzwiecki and Ian Rush were all supposed to be going out that night with our wives, but after a couple of hours down at Sammy's everything sort of drifted. We must have got in there at half-two and the first time I looked at my watch it was half-six.

I knew I was in for a right bollocking from Janice and persuaded Rushie and Eddie to ring their wives and tell them to get over to my house. Brilliant thinking really, because, when I got back with the two of them, Janice had to bite her tongue though I could see she was fuming. It was soon forgotten when we all nipped down to the pub at the bottom of our road for more drinks. Typically, Rushie signed autographs all night and, when last orders were called, we got a few more takeaways and went back to ours.

It was five o'clock when we eventually turned in and Janice laughs now because, at one stage, Rushie and I were spinning round on our backs trying to break-dance in the hall. We still had our suits on and, in the confusion, one of my dogs ran off into the night. I went to bed as poor Rushie went wandering after it!

Eddie and I were due to be in London on the Sunday because we were playing Sheffield Wednesday on the Monday. I got a call from Rushie on the day of the game telling me he'd been straight into the nearest bookie's to put a big bet on Sheffield Wednesday stuffing us. Eddie and I had the last laugh because we won 2-1 and both of us had blinders.

Eddie rarely had anything else; he was a brilliant 'keeper and was just so unlucky that injury forced him to quit playing at the relatively young age of 28. I've always thought that Neville Southall was one of the best 'keepers I'd played with, but Eddie pushed him close. Like so many other 'keepers, Eddie suffered at international level because Neville was so good. He only got one cap against Norway and even then he was only on for 45 minutes. I say it isn't really a cap, more of a sun-visor! Eddie had been brilliant at Wrexham, but he was better at Chelsea. He later stayed on at Stamford Bridge in a coaching capacity for a number of years, before becoming reserve-team coach at Arsenal under Arsene Wenger. He also helped out at national level with Wales when Mark Hughes was manager, but when Mark took charge at Blackburn last year, he took Eddie with him as his first-team coach. I still speak to him frequently on the phone and I like to think of him as one of my very best friends.

I played in the last four matches that season and we finished sixth, which wasn't bad for a first season back in Division One. My last game was at home to Norwich, which was a nice way to finish, even if we did lose 2-1. It didn't matter to the fans who gave us a standing ovation as we did a lap of honour in the driving rain. I've said it before, but it's worth saying again: Chelsea fans are magnificent. It's as simple as that.

I think the fans knew it was the end for me and they gave me another great reception. At one point I dived headfirst into a huge puddle and began pretending to do the breaststroke. I took my shirt off and threw it into the crowd. Then I took my boots and socks off and threw them in too. In the end I had my jockstrap left and that was it. They were singing my name and I couldn't ask for more than that.

In the end, I got changed and left the dressing room for the final time.

Nobody made a fuss and I hardly said a word on the way out. David Speedie wished me all the best in the corridor, but that was about it. I packed what was left of my kit into the car and headed for Wrexham. It was a sad trip home in many ways because I'd had a wonderful time at Chelsea and have great affection for the club, particularly the fans. I'd been part of the Championship-winning team the season before and had done my bit when called on in the First Division. I still get letters from Chelsea fans now, which is brilliant, and a few years back I did an interview for the fanzine down there. Many letters say the Second Division Championship-winning team was one of the best that they'd seen at the Bridge, which is pleasing. It was certainly a privilege to play in it.

As I turned off the M6 and moved on to the quieter back roads to Wrexham, I felt unsure about the future. Although there'd been talk in the press about one or two other teams being interested, I didn't have a club. I was still playing for Wales and knew I had to get fixed up quickly to make sure I remained in the international set-up. I admit I was worried but then, as I got within a few miles of home, I began to think of the great times I'd had at Chelsea, the great players and the tremendous fans. I regretted not playing as often as I'd have liked to in the First Division, but I couldn't complain.

I'd made my debut for the club at Carlisle and the fans had booed me on to the pitch. In my last game, they chanted my name and wished me all the best. That's what matters – at least that's what really matters to me.

I gave my all for Chelsea every time I pulled on the blue shirt. It was the only way I could play and I think the fans realised that. And that's the nice thing about writing a book: it gives me the chance to say thank you to all of them.

CHAPTER SIXTEEN

YORKSHIRE TERRIER ...
OR PUDDING!

The 27th March 1985 was one of the truly great nights for Wales – one of the nights that you look back on in a career and say to yourself, 'I'm glad I was there.' It was Scotland versus Wales at Hampden Park, Glasgow in the World Cup-qualifying competition and, having taken just two points from our first three matches in Group Seven, it was win or say goodbye.

We were staying in a hotel outside the city. We knew how important the game was; I certainly knew it would be my last chance to make it through to the finals of a major competition. I was struggling to get a game for Chelsea and had turned down the chance of a new contract. It was going to be a time of change one way or another.

Some things stayed the same, like the lads' last night out on the Sunday before the game. We'd had a few drinks in the bar then nipped off to a club up the road for a quiet couple more, before sneaking back to bed. The next morning we sauntered down for breakfast and Mike England was already there chatting away to the hotel staff. At one point, he was talking to one of the waitresses asking her if she knew or recognised any of us. Straight away we clocked what was happening and started making for the door just as she answered. 'I know them all. I met them in the nightclub up the road last night.'

Mike nearly choked and was completely lost for words. We all legged it before he could go too mad.

On the afternoon of the game, I was sitting quietly in my hotel room chatting to Mickey Thomas when I got a call from Chelsea manager John Neal. 'Huddersfield have come in for you and you can speak to them.' Brilliant timing: the day of one of the biggest games of my life and he tells me that!

I had to laugh because straight away Mickey was out with the pen and pencil telling me what money to ask for. I couldn't get the phone call out of my mind, so in the end I rang the manager, Mick Buxton. He told me he wanted me, but I knew Mike England would have gone berserk if he'd known what was going on so close to kick-off.

Although I'd been in and out of the first team at Chelsea, I'd put a few good games together and wondered again if maybe I had a future with them. It was just before transfer-deadline day and I told Mick Buxton I'd like to think about it before committing myself. I told him the terms I wanted and he agreed. Mickey Thomas was sick. 'I told you to ask for more,' he said. It was stupid trying to negotiate my future when I should have been looking forward to the game that night.

'Listen,' said Mick Buxton. 'I know you're playing tonight so I won't keep you but I'll ring you at midnight.' In a strange sort of way the phone call actually lifted me; it was nice to feel that someone wanted me.

At night, I went out and played one of my best games ever for Wales at centre-half alongside Kevin Ratcliffe. Rushie scored a beauty and we won 1-0 and, sure enough, at midnight Mick Buxton called again. I was as high as a kite by this stage because some of the Scottish lads had come up after the game and said I'd done well. I'd spoken to Janice after the game and told her about the Huddersfield interest but suddenly I was in a frame of mind that said stay in Division One with Chelsea.

'Mick, I don't know what to do, but at the moment I think it would be best if I left it until the end of the season.'

'Look, sleep on it and I'll ring you in the morning.'

He put the phone down before I could say anything and, when he did ring, I said the same thing.

'I'll tell you what,' he said, 'you're flying into Birmingham; I'll meet you there and we'll talk about it.'

Rather than dive into anything, I told him I was definitely going to leave it until the end of the season, but told him that if he was interested after that to get in touch.

Unfortunately, there was no way back at Chelsea and I was in and out of the side again, which meant that in the summer I was out of contract and without a club. I was getting worried and made sure I kept myself fit until Ian McNeil phoned, telling me that Leicester wanted to speak to me. I had a chat with their boss, Gordon Milne, who'd been at Liverpool before I'd arrived there. We arranged to meet in a hotel in Birmingham, where I agreed terms.

'Have you spoken to anyone else?'

'Yes, Huddersfield.'

'How much did they offer you?'

I told him exactly and he nodded his head in approval. 'I knew what they offered you.'

He was testing me, but, unlike some players, I wasn't in the business of lying over cash. I shook on the deal, but on the way back to Wrexham I had a terrible feeling that I'd made the wrong move. I just didn't get the same feeling about Leicester that I'd had about Huddersfield after talking to Mick Buxton. It wasn't anything to do with Gordon; it was just a gut feeling that I'd made a mistake. Gordon had told me he was signing two Scottish players the same day, Ally Mauchlen and Gary McAllister, which showed he had a bit of judgement if nothing else.

He had a bit of money, too, because he was offering more than Huddersfield, but I still felt I'd done the wrong thing. I was training with Wrexham over the next few days when I got a call from Gordon Milne.

'Sorry, Joe, but we'll have to call the deal off.'

'Really, why's that?'

'Trouble with the transfer fee.'

'Oh, what a shame.'

Apparently, Chelsea wanted too much money and it had all fallen through. 'You've done nothing wrong.'

'Ah well, can't be helped. Thanks for telling me.'

I was jumping around the room, delighted it had all gone wrong. It didn't help any because I still didn't have a club and I'd even rung Huddersfield to tell them I was joining Leicester. Luckily, Mick Buxton phoned a few days later and I told him what had happened. He said he still wanted to sign me, and so I went training with them on the Wednesday before the league season started.

In the end, the tribunal fixed the fee at £35,000, which was precisely £1,000 more than the Blues had paid Wrexham some three years previously. Chelsea had got their money back on me and I was delighted to be at Huddersfield.

It happened so quickly that I'd not even played any pre-season matches, but Mick Buxton told me I was in the side at centre-half for the big kick-off at home to Millwall. Typically, it was red hot and on the way to the ground I began to get a bit edgy, wondering what type of reception I'd get. I'd been sent off on my debut for Chelsea when my own fans had booed me on to the pitch. Surely it couldn't be as bad as that?

I parked the car and walked down to the ground and a bloke came across to have a go at me immediately. 'I'm never coming to watch again now you've signed, Jones.'

I could hardly believe it. I knew some Huddersfield fans would take time to be convinced because I'd played at Leeds Road for Chelsea and given the fist salute to the fans before the game. But a lot of people wished me all the best and, when I ran out on to the pitch, they started shouting my name. I whacked up the fist in acknowledgement; a new period of my career was up and running.

Unfortunately, running was something I didn't do much of that afternoon, mainly because I was absolutely knackered! I'd not played a competitive match since the season before and, after 20 minutes, I couldn't breathe. It didn't matter really because we held on to win 4-3 in a brilliant game and, despite the odd doubter in the crowd, I'd shown I meant business and already I felt at home.

I loved it at Huddersfield. I absolutely loved it. Everything about the place was brilliant as far as I was concerned – with great lads, great management and great people behind the scenes. Chelsea or Liverpool it certainly wasn't, but I was dying to get stuck into the new season. In a way it reminded me of Wrexham. The training ground was half a mile away and we had to run there past a canal, then set the goalposts up before we could start. It was freezing even in the summer, never mind the winter. After training we had to take down the goalposts again and run all the way back, but everybody mucked in together.

For years at Huddersfield, there'd been an initiation ceremony for newcomers which meant getting thrown in the canal after training with all the kit on. Everybody went in at some point, but I told the lads that, if anyone so much as laid a finger on me, I'd belt them. Fair dos, they let it lie for months and, when I was least expecting it, they grabbed me – four of them, each taking an arm or a leg.

'I can't swim, I can't swim. Honestly, I'll batter you.'

It didn't matter. Brian Cox, the big 'keeper, Paul Jones, the equally big centre-half, Dave Cork, a little midfielder, and Dave Cowling, all of them swung me back and forward until they let go. In I went. I felt as if I'd gone down 50 feet when it must have been five, but when I came up I was covered from head to toe in green slime and I could see them all dashing off into the distance. I had to laugh. I'd been initiated and, after that, I was all for it. I couldn't wait for the next new signing to come along!

I was still travelling from Wrexham every day, but after Chelsea it seemed like a jog round the corner. I'd make my way to Junction 17 on the M62 just north of Manchester, dump the car and then meet up with four other lads who lived my side to get a lift the rest of the way. There was me, Malcolm Brown, the right-back, Dave Burke, the left-back who lived in Bolton, Steve Doyle, a cracking little midfield player, and Brian Stanton, a little Scouser who later had a loan spell with Wrexham. We'd take it in turns to drive and, mile after mile, we put the world to rights with our views on everything under the sun. Sometimes we even talked about football.

The Leeds Road ground has since been demolished and the impressive McAlpine Stadium built in its place. The old ground had real character. The pitch was superb and, when the fans got behind us, there was a cracking atmosphere on match day. The changing rooms were big and modern and, like all the other clubs I've been to, the backroom staff were brilliant. Nellie, the tea lady, was probably the biggest character; she'd come marching into the dressing room when some of the lads were starkers and wouldn't bat an eyelid. 'You've seen one, you've seen them all,' she'd shout as everyone struggled to cover up their crown jewels!

Mick Buxton was the main reason I'd come to the club because I'd been so impressed talking to him on the phone and I'm glad to say I still speak to him now. He'd done a great job at Huddersfield bringing them up into Division Two without having pots of money and he was a manager the players could look up to and learn from. Mick did have a temper when he wanted and gave us some right goings-over.

After the tremendous win over Millwall on my debut, we kept things going, beating Crystal Palace 3-2 away in another thriller, Bradford 2-0 at home in a local derby and Leeds 3-1 at home in the biggest game of the season on 5 October. By then, we'd played eleven, won four, drawn five and lost just twice. We were seventh in the league and I thought we were on for a hell of a run. As it turned out, we didn't win another game for three months and, by the middle of December, we were bottom! We weren't playing too badly, just not scoring enough goals.

I scored my first goal in the Milk Cup away at Shrewsbury in a brilliant 3-2 win. I scored my next goal up at Middlesbrough on New Year's Day, sliding in from a corner. I think the nerve ends were beginning to get a bit raw by this stage because, when we went down to Portsmouth on 1 February, we got hammered 4-1 and I had a blazing row with Mick Buxton. We were losing 1-0 at half-time and I thought we were doing all right, but, when we got in the dressing room, Mick was going mad. I'd been playing at centre-half on the left, with Ian Bray at left-back. Vince Hilaire hadn't really seen much of the ball on their right wing, but Mick started asking for more responsibility from Mally Brown and myself and told Ian Bray to get tighter to Hilaire. In the end I snapped.

'You don't know what you're on about, you.'

'You what?'

'You heard.' I was out of order, but it was too late.

'Joe, what's the matter?' But at this stage the bell went and we were back out for the second half. That really was a nightmare because we eventually lost 4-1.

Nothing was said after the game but, on the coach, Mick's assistant John Hazeldine came up to the back to have a word with me. 'I don't think the boss meant what he said.'

'John, it was my fault. I was out of order, but it's finished with as far as I'm concerned.'

It was funny really because on Monday we had a big team meeting and Mick started going on at us, saying he was sick and tired of being answered back. All the lads were silent, but I was on the verge of the giggles because I've never been the best at keeping a straight face. I thought I was in for a bollocking when Mick suddenly turned elsewhere. 'And as for you Brian, Stanton, if you ever answer me back again...' All the lads were laughing to themselves because he'd not said anything to me! 'Now get out training the lot of you.'

They all got up to leave when he called me over. 'Joe, can I have a quick word in the office?'

I thought that now he really was going to have a go, but instead he began asking me how my ankle was and talking about everything, except Portsmouth.

In the end, I felt I had to say something. 'Listen, I was wrong on Saturday. I shouldn't have said what I said: it's my fault and I apologise.'

'Say what?' asked Mick.

'Oh, that stuff at half-time. I've forgotten it already.'

That was the end of the meeting, though I think Mick wanted to make sure we understood each other, even though he was cagey. I wouldn't fall out with Mick Buxton over something as trivial as that. I had far too much respect for him and still do. If I could have played under Mick Buxton throughout my career, I would have been happy.

After Reading put us out of the FA Cup, our season suddenly depended on avoiding the drop. We'd put a bit of a run together during January and February, but then slipped back into the danger zone in March. It was then that John Hazeldine came to ask me about Duncan Shearer, who I'd played with at Chelsea. I told him he'd get goals.

'We've got a chance of getting him for five grand.'

'Five grand!'

I couldn't believe it. 'Take him.'

'We're thinking of taking him on loan.'

'For five grand, get him now because he'll get goals wherever he plays and, if he receives the right service, he'll get as many as Kerry Dixon.'

They went ahead and bought him and the rest, as they say, is history.

Duncan scored seven times in the last seven games and kept us up, as simple as that. What a player and what a lovely feller! Duncan's quiet, but he can be really dry. I'd got on well with him at Chelsea and always felt he'd been unlucky to be around at the same time as Kerry. In a way they were similar players. Mickey Thomas always gave him terrible stick because he didn't have any front teeth.

Duncan's goals made the difference between Divisions Two and Three for us, because we avoided relegation despite losing our last two matches to Fulham and Wimbledon. In the Wimbledon game, Terry Curran and Paul Raynor were sent off before half-time and I remember John Fashanu wandering over to me and having a quiet word. 'Hey, Joe, can't you get your lads to calm down a bit?' I thought that was a bit rich coming from a player who became a member of the 'Crazy Gang' a few years later. Wimbledon finished champions that season.

I suppose staying up represented success for us and was delighted when I was made Player of the Year by the supporters, the local paper and the junior supporters. It's the only treble I've ever won! We finished 16th in the end and showed we were consistent by finishing 17th a year later, though once again Duncan came up with the goods by scoring 21 goals.

At that time, the 1986/87 season, the Second Division was one hell of a league with teams like Sunderland, West Brom, Leeds, Crystal Palace, Oldham, Derby and Sheffield United in it – we had a poor start without a win in the first five games. We never had the resources to compete in the transfer market, but Mick Buxton was slowly bringing in young lads that he'd picked up cheaply.

The big centre-half, Paul Jones, had gone and then, five games into the season, captain Steve Doyle was signed by Sunderland. I was delighted that Mick made me his replacement, but still we couldn't find a winning run. By December, we'd only won four matches and, after losing 2-1 to Crystal Palace at home, Mick Buxton was sacked.

There was a team meeting and the chairman, Keith Longbottom, came in to talk to the players and, just looking at the faces in the room, you could tell everyone was sick for Mick Buxton. I was disgusted.

'Has anyone got anything to say?'

I looked around and knew that no one would open their mouth, so as usual I stuck my foot in mine and said what I knew all of us were thinking.

'Yes, I have.'

He looked up. 'Oh yes, what's that then?'

'You're a fucking twat!'

I went on to say that I thought Mick had been treated terribly after all he'd done for the club and said it didn't matter who they brought in, they wouldn't be able to do a better job than the man who had been sacked.

'You'll get somebody in and, if we do well, you'll say, "Look, he's successful," and, if we do badly, you'll say, "It's Mick Buxton's fault."'

'Yes, that's right.'

And that was that: end of meeting: And end of everything that had been good about Huddersfield as far as I was concerned. I'd said my bit – in with two feet as always – but I hate to see unfairness and I thought the sacking was unfair.

Mick was a great bloke, who'd brought me to the club, and he had the respect of all the players. A few days later, he invited us in for a farewell drink and the players drank the cabinet dry. I had a quick orange juice and drove back to Wrexham. It wasn't a celebration that I wanted to be part of.

Sure enough, we went out and won 2-1 at Blackburn in the next game, the first under new manager Steve Smith, a former player, who'd been promoted from the youth team. As new managers do, Steve obviously wanted to make his mark and, before the Blackburn game, he walked into the dressing room and told Ian Banks he was the new team captain. All the lads looked at me and I was about to say my bit, but instead bit my tongue and went out to play as normal.

It was a great win for us and then, the next day, we battered Bradford City 5-2 at home on 27 December in front of our biggest crowd of the season. What a match that was! We were 4-0 up at half-time and I knackered my ankle ligaments. The injury was really killing me, but the sight of George running on with his fingers about to dig deep into my ankle somehow did amazing things for my powers of recovery. He strapped it with plaster on the outside of my boot to get me through to the break and, when the whistle blew, I hobbled towards the tunnel.

It had been a brilliant half for us, but, as we were walking off, our centre-forward that day, Dave Cork, began having a go at the lads in defence. In a way it wasn't really surprising because Corky was the club moaner, the Huddersfield equivalent of David Speedie. I loved him because he was a cocky so and so who was always winding me up, but just at that moment when he moaned I snapped. Looking back, I think it was the straw that broke the proverbial camel's back because just recently Mick had been sacked, I'd had the captaincy taken away from me and now I'd done my ankle ligaments – I knew I'd be out for weeks.

It wasn't Corky's fault but, when he started having a go, I went for him. 'Hey, you lot,' he said. 'Get the ball up to us quicker.'

I couldn't believe that, at 4-0 up, he still wasn't happy, so I just swung a punch and cracked him one in the mouth as we got to the players' tunnel. The Bradford lads must have been wondering what we did to each other when we were 4-0 down. Next there was a scuffling of aluminium studs on concrete as I chased after him into the dressing room. It was like the Keystone Kops because I was limping around the physio's table trying to get hold of him, but, when Steve Smith came in, it all died down instantly. I sat in one corner and Corky sat in the other and, within minutes, we started laughing about the whole thing. I apologised to him and he accepted it.

It sounds a crazy thing to have done, but I think I'd just about had my fill and sometimes you do strange things – besides Corky was always winding me up and had been the main instigator in chucking me into the canal for my initiation. The police came in soon afterwards and told us to calm down; Steve Smith was still looking round the room wondering what the hell had gone on. Corky and I just sat there laughing. We eventually won 5-2 and Duncan Shearer scored four of the goals.

After beating Bradford on 27 December, we had a scoreless draw at home to Grimsby, then went up to Leeds and drew 1-1. After that, I went in to see Steve Smith to have a word about the captaincy. He was as nice as could be and I told him it didn't matter if I was captain or not, I'd still give everything I had for the club. But I had to laugh when he told me the reason he'd made the change.

'D'ya know, I completely forgot you were the captain.'

'Don't give me that; the chairman told you to do it, didn't he?'

'Yes,' he replied.

It was clear to me I was paying for opening my mouth when Mick Buxton was sacked. I knew then the writing was on the wall for me at Leeds Road and, when we started negotiating another contract, things began to turn sour. I wanted two years and even offered to move to Yorkshire, but the club would only offer me one. In the end, we were getting further and further apart, but at this stage in my career I needed some kind of security and it was obvious they weren't prepared to give me it.

The contract saga dragged on all the time I was out with my ankle ligaments and, when I finally came back to face Birmingham on 23 March

1987, I knew I'd be playing for someone else the following season. We were still three off the bottom and relegation was looking a real possibility again, but we must have toughened up our defence because we put together a six-match unbeaten run. I had a real laugh before the Birmingham game with referee John Lloyd who comes from Wrexham. I was having a pre-match look at the pitch when he came over and started chatting.

'Hey, John,' I said, 'I've been out for seven weeks and my timing's a bit off. Let me have a couple of free swipes at Wayne Clarke.'

'Don't give me that, Joe.'

'But, John, I've been out for so long I'll need a bit of leeway.'

Sure enough, we kicked off and after a few minutes I couldn't breathe. I was so knackered I caught Wayne Clarke a couple of crackers after the ball had gone, but John never booked me. In the end, I had about four digs and John just kept coming over wagging his finger, having a little word.

'Come on, Joe, that's four times. No more now.'

'Cheers, John.'

It was some weeks later when I met John again. He told me the referee's assessor had been at the game and, in his report, he'd said that the referee had let the number six get away with far too much without booking him! No prizes for guessing who had number six on their back!

It was deadline time and Steve Smith decided to let Paul Raynor and Andy Thackeray go. He also told me Swansea were keen to sign me. I spoke to their manager Terry Yorath, but said I'd prefer to stay at Huddersfield, still hoping there might be the chance of a two-year deal if we stayed in Division Two. But Huddersfield refused to offer any more than a year, so that was that. I was disappointed because I loved the club and at 31 still felt I had plenty to offer. I certainly gave everything I had to keep us up in the remaining games and thankfully we survived. We needed to beat Millwall in the last game of the season to make sure and the fans probably knew it was going to be my farewell appearance.

Oddly enough, my first game for Huddersfield had been against Millwall and it was a boiling hot day like this one, too. Early in the first half, I moved up for a free-kick on the right-hand side down at the Cow Shed end. Over it came and I flew in to stick a header into the bottom corner, my first goal at Leeds Road in my last game. I did a lap of honour that Linford Christie would have been proud of. We won 3-0 in the end, which was just as well because Shrewsbury had also won, but still went down. It was a special way to finish a special time in my career. I said goodbye to everybody after the game and told them I wouldn't be back.

I was still only 31 and had only just finished playing for Wales. A number of clubs showed interest in signing me at the time, including Tranmere and Shrewsbury, but when Dixie McNeil at Wrexham came in for me I decided it was time to head home. I'd been travelling for five years and felt enough was enough. I'd started at Wrexham and now I was going to end my career there.

I've returned to Huddersfield a few times since with Wrexham, but the first time I went back was when I was invited to do a bit of a question and answer session held by the 'Patrons Association'. It was a great evening and I stayed on for ages afterwards, chatting with everyone about the times I'd had at the club. I used to get so nervous speaking in front of people and I was sweating more than during a game, but it went well and they presented me with my number six shirt which had been framed. I still have it to this day.

The second time I went back was for Frank Worthington's testimonial. Frank was a massive favourite at Huddersfield and I was delighted when he rang me to take part. I was even more delighted when I found out the teams. I told him I'd run over broken glass to play because we had Joe Corrigan in goal. The Preston manager Les Chapman was at right-back, Frankie Gray played left-back, with Frank Stapleton and me in the middle of defence. The midfield was a tasty little line-up of Phil Thompson, Kenny Dalglish and Graeme Souness. Up front, we had John Hendry, Simon Stainrod and Roger Palmer. We were up against the current Huddersfield team and it was a great day. It finished 4-4 and I actually scored with a flick header from a corner. Soon after, I chased a ball out to the left and whizzed in a cross which Frank Stapleton bulleted into the net. Some goal and, as I ran back, Kenny Dalglish started shouting that they'd give me Man of the Match. 'It's the first time you'll have got it, mind!'

Frank Worthington came on for the second half and the referee awarded a penalty against us which Souness and Dalglish were furious about. They weren't messing about either. Graeme Souness was so livid that the crowd started having a right go at him. It was typical of those two; they hated losing, that's why they were such winners. Even in the bath afterwards they were moaning about the penalty. I just sat there laughing.

CHAPTER SEVENTEEN

ENGLAND FOR WALES

Mike England began his reign as manager of Wales with a game against England at Wrexham in May 1980. He'd come in to take over from Mike Smith and guide us through to the 1982 World Cup in Spain. Mike Smith had done wonders for Welsh football at almost every level, but if anyone was going to take over then I was glad it was Mike England because all the players had a deep respect for him.

He'd finished his own playing career in the American Soccer League and, when we gathered for his first team talk at the Bryn Howell Hotel in Llangollen, there was the usual anticipation. He went through each player individually, telling us what to do and what to expect, but then he lapsed into a slow American drawl. 'Right, when the ball's cleared, I want you dee-fence to get the hell out of there.'

It sounded just like a John Wayne movie – 'dee-fence'. We were trying not to laugh as he talked on and on, but from then on his nickname was 'Howdy'.

His approach was completely different from Mike Smith's who was meticulous in preparation and coaching. Mike England brought with him a more laid-back attitude, a few free-kicks and lots of five-a-side, which suited me down to the ground; it was just like Liverpool. Mike England was a determined enthusiastic manager, who'd die for his country. Like Mike Smith, he took us close to qualification in European Championships and World Cups so many times, but somehow we always managed to miss out at the final moment.

Still, what a start to a managerial career he had: we had given England a good hiding, 4-1, at the Racecourse. I was marking Peter Barnes that day and, although he got their goal, he's told me since I kicked him all over the pitch.

We made a great start to the World Cup campaign too. We'd been drawn in Group Three, along with Iceland, Russia, Czechoslovakia and Turkey, and took eight points from a possible eight in our first four matches. We 'defrosted' Iceland 4-0 in Reykjavik in June 1980; we 'stuffed' Turkey 4-0 and Czechoslovakia 1-0 in Cardiff and then went to Ankara to beat Turkey 1-0 away with a Carl Harris goal.

We'd made a brilliant start, but we always knew that Russia were going to be the side to beat, because they had so many world-class players. We met them at the Racecourse in May 1981, just after our domestic season had finished and their starting line-up read like a *Who's Who* of world football. They had Dasayev in goal, Chivadze and Baltacha at the back with Bessonov and Kipiani in midfield. I played right-back that afternoon and was marking arguably the trickiest and speediest of all, Oleg Blokhin, who had been European Footballer of the Year in 1975.

Thirty thousand packed into the Racecourse on a warm summer's afternoon and, although it finished scoreless, there was some lovely football on show. I always had the feeling they could have stepped up a gear if they'd wanted to; they had so much class, but we really battled and certainly deserved the point. I got in a couple of really solid tackles on Kipiani in the early stages and, later on, we crashed heads and both of us went down. I got up before the count of ten, but he was pole-axed! Eventually he got up but was staggering all over the place and had to go off. Don't mess with the Jones head! I also played Blokhin quite well, but, now and again, I got a taste of his amazing pace and, just when you thought you had him, he'd suddenly zip past you.

Mike England wasn't unhappy with the 0-0 score-line and the former Everton centre-half Tommy Jones chose me as the Man of the Match for

Wales along with Rinat Dasayev for them. We were both awarded a Russian samovar (tea-urn to you and me), which had been provided by a Soviet newspaper. I told the press I'd stick a few pints of bitter in mine. Actually, I've never figured out how to use it because the instructions are in Russian too!

We'd dropped our first point and then dropped two more when the Czechs beat us 2-0 in Prague. Already it looked as if the Russians would be going to Spain and it would be between us and the Czechs for the second qualifying spot. So far so good – that was until October 1981 when Iceland came to Swansea and we blew it. We didn't have the best of luck admittedly, but we blew it, no question: drawing 2-2, having been 2-0 up.

Robbie James and Alan Curtis had scored early on and I thought we'd cruise it until the floodlights failed and the teams were taken off for 45 minutes. It was a break that cost us our concentration and rhythm and, although we were professionals, it was hard to keep our minds tuned in when the body was stiffening up. Once the lights came back on, they scored twice to grab a point and end our chances of going to Spain.

It was a sickener. You don't mind getting hammered by Germany or Brazil, or someone of that calibre, but to throw away a two-goal lead at home to Iceland was terrible. Our goal difference was worse than the Czechs and it meant we needed a point away to Russia in the final game to have any chance of going through.

Looking back now, I wish we hadn't bothered going over. It was a nightmare from start to finish. It's never an easy place to travel to at the best of times and as we were playing in Tblisi – which is now Georgia – we had to change planes three times to get there. We flew Aeroflot from Stansted to Riga, which is now the capital of Latvia, on the Monday morning and, having touched down, waited an hour before jumping on another plane from Riga to Moscow. At Moscow, we sat around for three hours. Eventually we took off for Tblisi and, by the time we got there, we were all knackered. I went straight to bed and slept most of Tuesday afternoon in preparation for the match on Wednesday.

As I said before, we'd played well against the Russians at the Racecourse, but I always felt they had a little up their sleeves. I was right because they murdered us and, from a personal point of view I was given the biggest run-around of my international career. In my defence, I was marking Oleg Blokhin again, but they just kept dinking the ball over my head into space and he took off like the roadrunner. I couldn't have caught him if I'd been on a motorbike he was that quick and, although I was trying to go with him, I couldn't get within ten yards.

It was an amazing night with 80,000 screaming Russians watching our thrashing and, when Mike England subbed me in the second half, I came off, turned to him and said, 'You bastard.'

'What do you mean, "You bastard"?' he replied.

'Well, you could have taken me off earlier!'

Seriously though, when I came off, I felt like sprinting to the touchline and kissing him. You could almost see Blokhin winding me up, to punish me for having the nerve to play well against him at home. He was determined to show just how good and how quick he was and I had a nightmare.

It finished 3-0; he scored one and we were lucky. After the match, some reporters came over to ask me what I'd made of it all. I asked them if they had a picture of Blokhin because I'd only seen the back of him on the pitch! One reporter enquired, 'Did you know, Joe, that his mother and father are former Russian sprinters?'

I stared back blankly. 'Oh, yeah. Well, my dad's a hospital porter and my mam's a cleaner; what bloody chance did I have of catching him?'

Next morning we started the long haul back, but fog at Tblisi Airport meant we had to return to our hotel and come back later to wait for a flight. After that, it was the same route and the same hassle as before: Tblisi to Moscow; Moscow to Riga; Riga to England. I was sitting next to Mickey Thomas when the captain announced we were flying over southern England and, as we got near the runway, I turned to Mickey for reassurance. 'Hey, Mickey, Stansted wasn't this big when we left.' Just at that moment the captain came on the tannoy to tell us we'd been diverted to Gatwick.

I was a wreck when I got back to Wrexham, but still played against Barnsley away on the Saturday; I remember going in for a tackle after 20 minutes and going down injured. I couldn't move. I didn't want to move. I think I had a kip in the end. I know I was substituted. From Russia with love!

The Russians qualified outright and, although we got ten points like the Czechs, they had a better goal difference, so, while they packed their bags for Spain, we had to make do with a friendly against the host country in Valencia as part of their warm-up for the World Cup. It might have been the final itself the way they approached it and, with a partisan crowd screaming for goals if not blood, it was one hell of a game.

As usual, we met up at a hotel in Maidenhead on the Sunday night before flying out to Spain the following day and it was great to see everyone.

We flew out on the Monday and trained in the afternoon. It was a good job too, because the Spaniards were taking it seriously with players looking to gain places in their World Cup squad. You could feel the tension in the changing rooms and, before we ran out, Mike England gave one of his by now legendary team talks when he kept getting the names mixed up. He ended in immaculate fashion. 'Right, lads, I've nothing left to say. Let's get out there and get stuck into those bloody Italians!'

I was playing sweeper in a five-man defence and we drew 1-1 when we really should have won. Robbie James got our goal and the fans were really revved up. It was an unbelievable atmosphere for a friendly and even I found it a bit intimidating. At one point, I edged up for a corner and got a flick on for Gordon Davies to poach a winner, but the referee disallowed it for some reason.

At full-time, the fans went mad and started hurling bottles and cans down on to the pitch. I think Mickey Thomas was hit and I was just glad to get off. I did manage to swap shirts with Alesanco before we got into the dressing rooms, hoping they might mistake him for me. He was the famous hard man of Spanish football in those days.

After the Home Internationals that season, we rounded off things with a match against France in Toulouse. They'd been scheduled to play Brazil who had pulled out, leaving us to step in. Ta, lads! What a great game that was and, even though it was a friendly, it was one of the most memorable matches I played for Wales. They had the big names out that night – Platini, Tresor, Giresse, Bossis, the lot – and we beat them 1-0 with a goal from Rushie. Once again, Mike England laid the foundations in the dressing room.

'Now, listen, you've got to watch that feller in midfield, what's his name, Michael something, Michael er er...'

'Michel Platini.'

'That's him. Make sure you watch for him.'

It was safe to say the Welsh team went out sniggering to face Michael What'shisname. He was only the European Footballer of the Year, after all!

When the final whistle blew, we all started celebrating and I went over to swap shirts with Bossis. I had an eye on Platini, I must admit, but he was too far away. As I was taking my shirt off, I could see Leighton James sprinting over to the star midfielder to make sure he got his shirt. It didn't really register with me until we got into the changing rooms afterwards, when Leighton told the lads the story behind it. 'Did you see Michel Platini come over to swap shirts with me?'

All the lads had already seen Leighton dash 30 yards to get Platini's shirt; we just started laughing!

In a way, Mike England's arrival coincided with a new era for Welsh football, with the likes of Neville Southall, Kevin Ratcliffe and Rushie making names for themselves alongside the old crocks like Mickey, Brian Flynn, Alan Curtis and myself. Suddenly the future was so bright we had to wear shades!

You could tell Rushie was going to be a star as soon as he made his debut for Wales against Scotland. He was quick, clever, lethal in the box and with that natural goalscorer's touch. His only weakness was his heading! The first time I met him was just before he signed for Liverpool and we were both doing a question and answer evening in Deeside. I remember saying to him then that he was going to the best club in the world. Little did I know that he would become one of the world's great players.

But that's the great thing about Rushie; he's the same now as he was then. I don't think he's changed one bit despite all the success he's had. His family are down to earth and so is he, a real home-loving bloke who enjoys a pint down at the local with his mates. His wife Tracey's the same, down to earth and really friendly. I've got to say good things about him, because down the years he's always managed to get me the odd pair of boots!

In many ways, I think that's why it didn't work out for him in Italy at Juventus – simply because he's such a homely bloke. I'd often speak to him on the phone.

'Where are you ringing from, Rushie, Flint?'

'No, I'm in Turin.'

'Don't need a left-back, do they?'

I don't think it was so much that he was lonely, just that he missed being with his mates. 'The Italians never go out for a pint and you know what, Joe? There's no dartboard in the local!'

That's Rushie all over – not at all a big-time Charlie, just a normal bloke who's never forgotten where he comes from. I never played against him or Kevin Ratcliffe in a proper match, but when we were with Wales I'd warn them that, if I ever got the chance, I'd kick them all over the pitch. They'd laugh at me, probably knowing I'd never get close enough to catch them. Mickey, Rushie and me would wind Kevin up because in the early days we'd all played at Wembley and he hadn't, so whenever he was within earshot the three of us would start off.

'And did you see that little slope just down at the end of the tunnel?'

'See it? I fell down it.'

'And what about the little patch which cuts up in the corner?'

'Oh yeah. Got to be careful you don't get the foot caught.'

We'd keep it up for ages until he cracked. 'Ahh, will you lot give it a rest.'

Kev has played at Wembley more times than we've had hot dinners since then and went on to prove himself at the very highest level. When he first came into the Welsh team, he played at full-back, but without doubt his best position was centre-half. He had great pace and was a good header. He went through a period where he took stick off the Everton fans, but, if you look at the all-time great Everton teams that are picked from time to time, then the name of Kevin Ratcliffe is nearly always included.

In my later years with Wales, I played alongside Kev at centre-back and in most games we did well together. I had one of my best games with him against Scotland at Hampden, when we won 1-0 in the World Cup-qualifying match of 1985.

Neville Southall is a lot quieter than Kev and Rushie, but he loves a laugh and a joke with the best of them. I've known Nev since we were both kids on the estate and, like Rushie, he's down to earth. Nev's very much his own man, always has been, always will be and he's one of the hardest trainers I've ever seen. No wonder he's so good. He's a perfectionist who often stayed behind for more training, or went out by himself to practise or correct things. The routines he went through in training were incredible. Everton fans probably know that he often got to the ground earlier than anyone else to get on to the pitch to practise goal-kicks and get himself loosened up.

He was that good that managers and coaches just let him get on with it, so, while everyone else turned up in a suit and tie for a match, you often found Nev in a tracksuit. He was also one of the bravest players I've ever come across, a great organiser in the box and, like Pat Jennings before him, he's got massive hands. I felt sorry for the likes of Eddie Niedzwiecki, Tony Norman and Andy Dibble who were good 'keepers in their own right, but they had the misfortune to be around when Nev was playing.

It's because the likes of Rushie and Neville never forgot themselves and became bigheaded that the Welsh side did so well over the years on limited resources. When Nev first came into the squad, he couldn't even drive. He'd meet up with the rest at my house, having scrounged a lift off Kev or Rushie. As I say, he always did his own thing and, as he was a teetotaller, the only thing you had to watch with him was when he mixed his drinks. Dandelion and Burdock with Orangeade was always a potent combination. A couple of those and he was anyone's!

Mark Hughes joined the set-up a little later and he can rightly be classed alongside the likes of Rushie, Kev and Neville as one of the very best. Mark's a Wrexham lad, though I didn't know him until he came into the squad. He's another great bloke, who mixed in with everyone, though he was a lot quieter off the pitch than he was on it. He just had to cross the white touchline and he turned into a bull. He was like the Incredible Hulk; in fact, I'm sure he turned green when rattled, but what a player. Imagine having to face him and Rushie!

Mark had a completely different style to Rushie, but in his own way he was just as good. He was strong, brilliant at holding the ball up and bringing other players into the game. He was criticised at Manchester United for not scoring regularly enough, but, when he did, they were some of the most spectacular goals you'll ever see. Mark Hughes was a class player. He was also a really good lad. When I was in hospital with my broken ankle, one of the first people to pop in and say hello was Mark Hughes.

Back in 1982, the disappointment of missing out on the World Cup was eased, knowing we had such great players coming into the side for the European Championship, due to be held in France in 1984. For the first time in ages, we'd been given a decent draw alongside Yugoslavia, Bulgaria and our old friends Norway. I fancied our chances even though a 1-0 win over Norway at Swansea wasn't exactly a flying start.

After that, it was off to Titograd and Yugoslavia in December, a match that saw my one and only goal for Wales.

It was a great trip all round, although when we arrived at Zagreb Airport my kit had gone to Frankfurt. I went to Customs and explained the situation and they asked me to make a list of the items I'd lost. I was as fair as I could be. 'Three sheepskin coats, fourteen suits, four diamond rings and twenty-seven pairs of snakeskin shoes!' I was lucky I had my boots with me, but my bag turned up quite quickly once the Customs blokes had rung through – an eventful start.

We flew from Zagreb to Titograd and the weather was awful. The Under-21s were with us and they had played the day before, which certainly didn't help the pitch. Mark Hughes was actually playing for the Under-21s and I think it was one of his first trips. When we kicked off, it took me 20 seconds to go into the book. Their two strikers kicked it to each other and then knocked it out to the right-winger. By the time the ball reached him, I'd clattered him on to the running track and was in the book. I'd seen the ball coming and set off on a massive slide tackle. It was so wet that I slid about 30 yards, covering myself in mud from head to toe.

They murdered us from set-pieces, but we looked as good as they did in open play. Every time they got a corner or free-kick, they seemed to score and, when we went in at half-time, they were 3-2 up. Then came the magic moment; as usual I took up a position on the near post as Brian Flynn teed up the corner. It came over and dropped in the six-yard box. Rushie went for it and I went for it, and it finally broke at the near post and I whacked it with every ounce of strength I had. A magnificent 25-inch drive and the 'keeper even got a hand to that!

I was off up the pitch with my arm in the air and I think they caught up with me somewhere near Dubrovnik! It finished 4-4; we'd got a point, but what a match.

In April 1983, we beat Bulgaria 1-0 at the Racecourse to put ourselves top of Group Four with five points from three games, but in September we blew it again by only drawing 0-0 with Norway in Oslo. Although we took some stick in the press, I honestly believe that by this time there really were no easy international matches. Norway had some good players, most of whom were playing in Germany and Italy.

A month later, we travelled to Sofia in Bulgaria and, if Yugoslavia was relaxed and enjoyable, then Bulgaria was cold and dismal. We arrived on the Monday, trained and then had a quiet evening at the hotel. I was sharing with Mickey Thomas as usual and, when I woke up in the morning and looked out of the window, there was thick snow everywhere. By thick, I mean at least a foot deep and there was no way the game would be on. Tommo was in bed.

'Mickey, it's covered in snow; we've got no chance of playing.'

'Shut up and get the kettle on.'

It was only when he finally saw the snow for himself that he believed my warning. It had been fine the night before.

The game did go ahead, though, and when we ran out it was still freezing, with the snow piled high along the side of the pitch. I was frozen but gave the usual salute to the Welsh fans who had made the trip with us. Sure enough, there they were singing and chanting, wearing nothing but T-shirts. Tough lads, I'm telling you – all the Holyhead boys, Kelly and the gang. They still follow Wales everywhere and a temperature of minus seven wasn't any problem at all.

The game was a joke and we lost 1-0. Throughout it, the winger I was marking kept spitting at me. Every time he came anywhere near, he'd spit right in my face and, as I've said before, there's nothing worse than a player who can do that to another player. Other than smack him a good one, which I didn't fancy doing, I thought I'd better spit back, so when the chance came I let go a beauty; unfortunately it just dribbled down my face and froze to my shirt! I was trying to wipe it away quickly to save embarrassment and didn't try again. It was like an icicle hanging from my chin!

We were all bitterly disappointed. We hadn't played badly, which made it even more disappointing but conditions had really made it a lottery.

Mike England told us to stay in the hotel at night and not go into town, but in fairness it was absolutely brilliant. The hotel had clothes shops, a Japanese restaurant and a casino. Soon everyone was having a drink and putting the game behind them. I couldn't get into it that night; I was fed up about the result and went to bed early, only to be woken by Mickey bursting in at three in the morning and telling me how much money he and Rushie had won at the casino. 'And, Joe, you want to see Gordon Davies. He's dancing by himself at the disco, really giving it the John Travolta.' Even in my half-awake, half-asleep state, this registered because Gordon was always one of the quieter lads who rarely went berserk.

The next morning we were all on the bus at eight in the morning ready to go, but there was no sign of Gordon. The whisper went round among the lads and Mike England was getting edgy.

'Gordon Davies isn't here. Has anyone seen him?'

'No.'

'Well, where is he then?'

Next thing, the hotel doors opened and Doug Livermore and the team doctor, Graham Jones, came staggering towards the coach, each with an arm around Gordon. The toes of his shoes were scuffing across the floor as his legs trailed behind him. He was literally dragged on to the bus with all of us pissing ourselves laughing.

Mike England was furious. 'That's an absolute disgrace,' he said.

Obviously, Mike thought Gordon had been overdoing the drinking, but it turned out he'd eaten some Japanese food and he'd got terrible food poisoning. What a sight he was. They dumped him in the front seat and he looked like a scarecrow because he couldn't move his arms or legs. The team doctor had to sit with him and, when they got him to the airport, they put him in a wheelchair and started giving him injections, presumably painkillers.

They got him on the plane and stuck him at the front in a different part from the rest of us, still in his wheelchair.

'Hey,' I said. 'What if we take off quickly and Gordon comes flying down the aisle in his wheelchair, out of the back door?'

We all started laughing. He didn't get any sympathy at all until we landed in Manchester and they whisked him off to hospital straight away. Even after that, he got stick because, if ever we wandered into an airport and someone saw the wheelchairs they often have there, everyone would be off. 'See Gordon's in the squad again!'

The defeat in Bulgaria meant we had to beat Yugoslavia at Ninian Park in December to have any chance of reaching the finals. There was a terrible build-up to the game for me because I did a little piece with Bryan Cooney from the *Daily Star* for his regular column and it got a little bit out of hand. We were talking about my early life with the 'Parrots' and, when we moved on to discuss the way I played, I said jokingly that, even if I was playing against my own family, I'd tackle them because that was just the way I approached football. It was only a passing comment, but when the piece went out on the day of the game, it said I'd mug my own mother!

I was furious and demanded they retract this straight away, mainly because I was worried that it would upset my mam. I went to see Ken Gorman from the *Daily Star*, who's my mate, to ask for something to be done and in the meantime I rang my mam and Dad to tell them what had happened. Eventually the paper agreed to print an apology, which appeared the following week. I was satisfied with that and happy the comments had been taken back.

It hadn't helped my preparations, but, by the time we kicked off, I was concentrating 100 per cent. I've always been like that, able to chat and relax right up until kick-off, but then, when the warm-up finishes and we're preparing to start, I'm right into it.

I get tired of saying it but once again we missed out, only drawing 1-1 in front of a crowd of 25,000. Robbie James got our goal and Bazdarevic scored for them. It was bitterly disappointing and I really felt for Mike England who'd worked so hard. Yugoslavia went on to beat Bulgaria in Split a week later to overtake us and go through.

Looking back, 1983 hadn't been all bad for me with Wales. In June, I won my 50th cap and Mike England had asked me to captain the side against the Brazilians at Cardiff. It meant leading the side out next to Socrates, their legendary captain, and in the dressing room beforehand Mike England ran through each player, telling the lads what to do and what not to do.

'Neville, command your area. Joey, stick tight, don't give them space.' He eventually got to Brian Flynn. 'Flynnie.'

'Yeah, boss.'

'Penalties ...'

'Sure.'

'Don't give any!'

We fell about. Brian thought he was being asked to take them. He'd given one away in the Home Internationals and we slaughtered him!

Eventually the two sides lined up in the tunnel and we walked out on to the pitch. It was a beautiful sunny day and there was live TV coverage. I was scared stiff the lads might stop at the end of the tunnel and leave me to walk out by myself like a prat, but luckily they didn't. I shook hands with Socrates in the centre of the pitch and was in half a mind to ask him then if he would swap shirts with me at the end. I thought it might sound a bit naff and tossed the coin instead. Careca and Eder were up front for them, but we did well and drew 1-1. Their goal was a bit scrappy because Jeremy Charles was fouled and everyone stopped waiting for the whistle that never came. One of their lads played it over my head and Isidoro put it in. Brian Flynn scored our goal. It wasn't a penalty, but a diving header, which is a real collector's item when you're just 5ft 4in!

Sure enough, at the final whistle, I looked round for Socrates, but our sub, Dudley Lewis, sprinted across and swapped shirts. I didn't mind, but it would have been nice to say I'd swapped shirts with the great Socrates. After all, I almost had the thing off his back during the game. At one point, the ball was cleared and Socrates and I suddenly found ourselves face to face, nose to nose. There was a little scuffle, but my Portuguese was about as good as his Welsh and it quickly petered out.

CHAPTER EIGHTEEN

WALES ON TOUR

I hope you're keeping count, because I've just about lost it. The 1978 World Cup Finals had been missed narrowly, by the wave of Joe Jordan's hand. The 1980 European Championship had been missed, so too the 1982 World Cup and now the 1984 European Championships, when once again we'd looked favourites to qualify.

The 1986 World Cup-qualifying group threw up Spain, Scotland and our old friends, Iceland – I knew this was my last chance of making it to a major finals. It had been relatively quiet on the international front in the early part of 1984 and we'd been to Norway and Israel for an end-of-season tour after the Home Internationals.

As I said before, Norway loved us going there because they always beat us. It was almost a foregone conclusion because we never seemed to get going at all in that country. Sure enough, we lost the friendly 1-0 in Trondheim and I had a nightmare. It was probably my worst game for Wales – the Blokhin debacle apart – and I knew things were looking bad when Neville Southall rolled the ball out to me for an early touch. I looked up confidently and it ran under my foot and out of play. It sort of summed up my performance.

At the end of the game as we trudged back into the dressing room, Mike England really went for me. He started ranting and raving and giving us some stick, until I'd had enough and had a go back.

'I know I was crap – stop going on.'

He kept at it though and gave us a right bollocking until the dressing room went quiet for the first time. We all sat there staring at the floor, no one really knowing where to look or what to say. In the end Mickey started up again. 'Anyway, lads. I've got a few tickets to a party, anyone like to come?' We cracked up laughing.

Typical Wales! Our next stop was Israel, just a stone's throw from Norway of course, but I'm glad we went because that was another one of the best trips I've ever been on with the national side. Gordon Davies had knackered his ankle in Norway, tripping over the hotel steps, so big Andy Holden from Wigan was called up in his place and joined up as we headed for Tel Aviv.

We arrived on the Monday and weren't playing until the Wednesday, so one of the tour guides organised a trip to the Holy Land, Bethlehem and all that. Being a Catholic, I couldn't wait to see the places that Jesus was said to have been to, but Andy Holden and Peter Nicholas decided they'd stay behind at the hotel to sunbathe by the pool. It was boiling hot, but they assured us they never burned, and so the rest of us took off on the coach.

I can honestly say this trip was one of the most fantastic experiences of my life. On the way there, I was trying to imagine what it must have been like all those years ago, when events in the Bible took place. I was with Ken Gorman from the *Daily Star*, who was covering the tour and both of us were genuinely moved as soon as we set foot in the old walled town. First of all, they took us to the exact spot where Jesus was supposed to have been born. We walked down some rickety steps, past three ancient churches and I was beside myself with excitement. It was too much to take in. All around there were pilgrims from different countries, people singing, and even the likes of Kenny Jackett in our party, who isn't religious at all, was fascinated like the rest of us.

Nobody really knows if this was the exact birthplace, but it didn't matter one bit to me. We stood and looked ... and I just let my mind wander. There's such an atmosphere about the place that you can't fail to be caught up in it. The next stop was Calvary where Jesus was crucified. We retraced his steps when he was carrying the cross and, on one of the walls, there's an imprint of a hand, which is supposed to be his after he'd fallen under the weight of the cross. All the lads put their hands in one by one.

'Big hands, hey?'

'Massive.'

'Would have made a great 'keeper!'

I was just staggered by everything about the place. We moved on to the site where the cross was actually set up and on to the tomb where Jesus was resurrected. You actually walk down into it – it was an incredible feeling.

We stayed for a while and then moved on to the Wailing Wall, which just about capped everything. There were loads of people kneeling and literally wailing: it was as simple as that. We all had little hats on because it is such a sacred place and there seemed to be thousands of people weeping, praying and crying out. It was an unforgettable sight. There were so many people dressed in long black coats, all looking the same. It was hot and steamy, but they were all fully clothed, singing and calling out.

When we arrived back at the hotel, we set about looking for Andy Holden and Peter Nicholas, but they were nowhere to be seen. In the end, they were found in Nico's room lying side by side on the beds with the curtains shut. Apparently, they'd both fallen asleep in the sun and had been burned to bits! They were in agony and the hotel manager had suggested putting yoghurt all over them. We were slaughtering them as they lay there moaning, covered from head to toe in yoghurt.

We played the match in sweltering heat and drew 0-0. It was quite funny because Andy Holden actually came on as sub just before a corner. Straight away he went up for it and, when it came across, he just flattened the goalie – absolutely battered him. What a great way to begin an international career!

It was back to the serious stuff again in September of 1984, away to Iceland in Reykjavik for the first World Cup qualifier. That was yet another disappointment because we lost 1-0 and didn't play well. Once again it was the supposedly weaker side in the group that we slipped up against …

That was the downside. The trip itself was one of the funniest I'd been on. It was the usual stuff in the hotel lobby; someone had tied an Icelandic bank note to a piece of string and a group of us sat hidden, leaving the note lying in the middle of the floor. Loads of people would see it and bend down to pick it up, then we'd pull it away and they'd get the shock of their lives. One bloke followed it and followed it, until he cracked his head on a glass table.

We never performed in the game itself, but poor Mickey Thomas had a nightmare. He was just coming back from injury and wasn't quite100 per cent, but in the warm-up, and during the national anthems, the Icelanders were slagging him. I couldn't understand it. As we lined up for the anthems, I was standing next to Mickey and in the crowd there were loads of banners saying, 'GO HOME MONKEY THOMAS'.

'Hey, Mickey, they can't spell your name.'

'Shut up and sing.'

'No, look. There's another: MONKEY THOMAS GO HOME.'

We couldn't work it out at all and, every time he touched the ball, the crowd went mad, booing and whistling.

It was scoreless at half-time and, when we went back into the changing room, Mike England was going mad. 'Have you punched one of their players?'

'No, I've not done a thing. Honest.'

'Well, you must have done something because they bloody hate you.'

We ran out for the second half and the same thing happened. Every time he went near the ball, the fans went mad. When they scored, it capped everything and, at full-time, Mike England was fuming. 'I'm not going to say anything about the game now ... but you,' he said turning on Mickey, 'you upset everyone and had everyone on at us.'

Afterwards we went for a few drinks and eventually ended up in a club. It was only then that we realised what had gone on. The locals were still giving Mickey stick.

'Where's your monkey mask now, Thomas?'

Mickey and I turned to each other straight away and laughed. Apparently, years earlier when we'd played Iceland at Swansea and the lights had gone out, Mickey and I had done a piece for the *Daily Star* wearing monkey masks. The headline had said, 'WE'LL MAKE MONKEYS OUT OF ICELAND.'

The article had quoted Mickey and not me, thank God, and obviously it was something that struck a chord with them – 'Go home, Monkey Thomas.' No wonder they couldn't spell his name!

Mickey left the club early because he was getting too much stick, but the rest of us stayed on. When we eventually left, it was early in the morning, but it was still light. It was a weird experience, walking home from a club in broad daylight. Apparently it's always that way during the Icelandic summer. It was a bit like having a lunchtime session in the Fairfield pub in Wrexham on a Sunday, coming out half pissed and weaving my way home with my two dogs to watch football in the afternoon!

We were off to a terrible start, which got worse after Spain battered us 3-0 in Seville in October 1984. The only consolation was that I missed that game, as well as the return with Iceland the following month, through suspension. We managed to scrape a 2-1 win over Iceland at Ninian Park, with Mickey and Mark Hughes scoring. By the time we went to Scotland, I was back in at centre-half.

I've been lucky in many ways during my career and with Wales I know I've had my disappointments, but I've also had my fair share of tremendous moments. I'd been in the Wales team that became the first ever to beat England at Wembley in 1977 (apart from a wartime international) and I was also a member of the first Welsh side to beat Scotland at Hampden Park since 1951. That was the match that kept our hopes of qualifying for Mexico alive because we won 1-0 and we deserved it, no question. We played brilliantly in front of 62,000 and Rushie rattled in the winner after Mark Hughes had once again led Alex McLeish and Willie Miller a merry dance. As a centre-half, I felt sorry for those two that night because Rushie and Mark took them to the cleaners.

I was playing in the middle alongside Kevin Ratcliffe and had one of my best games for Wales, marking Kenny Dalglish and Mo Johnston. They weren't a bad partnership, were they? Kenny had given me the slip when they beat us to get through to Argentina in the 1978 World Cup, but this time I felt I'd got my own back.

I tackled Mo Johnston one time and, as he got up, he started smiling over at me. 'Are you going out tonight?' I just laughed back because I'd been out with Mo after a Home International match in Glasgow before. And I don't know how I ended up with him – I think the Welsh lads had left the nightclub – but I was left with Mo and his mate. We had a good laugh and they put me in a taxi at the end of the night, a smashing feller.

Mike England was delighted with the performance and no wonder. He'd told us to go out and die for Wales and we'd come up with a great win. We were back in with a chance of making the finals.

We beat Scotland in March 1985 and then played superbly against Spain to win 3-0 at the Racecourse the following match. I wasn't playing because I was injured, but it was the night Mark Hughes scored that amazing volley, which became the Goal of the Season. It was another tremendous performance, which meant we had to beat Scotland in the last group match of the tournament to make the play-offs for the finals.

It was Anfield all over again, except this time it was Cardiff in front of a packed 40,000 crowd. I had to play right-back, although I'd have preferred to play centre-half. Pat Van den Hauwe was chosen there, but at least I was playing. We felt we could do it. We'd beaten them up there and the Joe Jordan incident was still in the mind of every Welshman. When Mark Hughes put us 1-0 up, I was convinced we were on our way.

I was marking Gordon Strachan and, although he was always involved in the game, I felt I coped quite well. In the second half, Jock Stein took him off and sent on Davie Cooper, who was an out-and-out winger with a silky left foot. He began to cause problems, but we were looking safe enough at the back.

Suddenly every terrible memory of 1978 came back when the ball bounced awkwardly in the box and sort of hit David Phillips. The ref pointed to the spot. Davie Cooper tucked away the penalty and my last chance of making the finals of a major championship had gone. I was sick to the pit of my stomach.

More than that, I remember walking up the tunnel and straight away there were rumours that Jock Stein had been taken ill. I saw him in the medical room and, soon afterwards, we found out he had died. What a terrible night! Football no longer mattered. My thoughts were with Jock Stein's family. It put everything into perspective and it was a while before I got over it all.

It was a month later that we returned to something like normality with a friendly at home to Hungary in Cardiff. They whacked us 3-0 and I went straight out and put a bet on them to do well in the World Cup. They didn't as it turned out, but then what do I know? I was playing right-back again and, in the second half, I saw the numbers go up on the sidelines and Alan Curtis and I were substituted. We sat there watching the rest of the game and I could sense he was feeling what I was feeling.

'Well, Curt,' I said, 'that's the end of our international careers.'

We laughed and shrugged, but I think we both knew it was time for Mike England to look to the future.

The following year, I wasn't included in the squad that toured Saudi Arabia and, when Mike England rang me up to explain, I told him that I'd been thinking of retiring from international football anyway. Long before the squad was announced, I'd discussed it with Janice and my dad and, although he was keen for me to carry on, I felt I'd had my share of great matches and great times; it was time someone else was given their chance. It wasn't a decision I took lightly. I loved every minute of every match I played for Wales and I'm as patriotic as the next person. I just felt I was coming to the end at the very top and I've always been a person who likes to go before I'm told to leave.

I thanked Mike and he thanked me for the service I'd given and I told him that, if he was ever struggling, then I'd come back and help out. He said that he would bear that in mind. I was 30 years old and, with 68 caps tucked away, I decided to call it a day.

I was just one short of Ivor Allchurch's Welsh appearance record and I had thought about trying to beat it, I must admit. I would have loved to have played on and on if it had been possible. However, it wasn't to end there because, in March 1986, Mike England phoned to tell me that he was struggling for players through injury and asked if I'd help out.

I jumped at the chance to play and equal Ivor Allchurch's record. The game was against the Republic of Ireland and, as it happened, it was Jack Charlton's first game in charge. Mike England made me captain for the match, which was gratifying since Liam Brady was captain of the Irish side. It was the third time I'd played against them and it proved a lucky third win as well. Ian Rush scored the only goal to give us victory.

I did enough in that game to have people asking why I'd decided to pack up international football. I gave them the same answer that I gave Mike England – I felt it was time to bring on the younger players.

A month later I was to pass Ivor Allchurch's record when we played Uruguay at the Racecourse. I was captain of the side for that game, which was fitting really as I'd made my debut at Wrexham against Austria. I was also presented with a silver tray from the Welsh FA and one from the Wrexham Supporters' Association. It was a proud moment for me and my family.

I remember conditions for the game were absolutely terrible and I'm sure it would have been called off if Uruguay hadn't travelled so far for what was a friendly. They had qualified for the World Cup that summer in Mexico and, as South American champions, were regarded as third-favourites behind Brazil and Argentina. They had star players like Enzo Francescoli, Miguel Bossio and Venancio Ramos in the side and we earned a creditable 0-0 draw, which was a great result for Wales.

At the end of that season, the Welsh FA had arranged a tour to Canada, who had also qualified for the World Cup. They were grouped with France, Hungary and Russia and had invited Wales to play two warm-up games against them.

It was a trip and a half to say the least; we were there for two weeks. The first game was played in Toronto and, as soon as we arrived there, I was sharing a room with Robbie James, who sadly died a few years back while playing in the League of Wales for Llanelli. We ended up going for a couple of pints in downtown Toronto and we actually got caught in the middle of a film shoot. We were drinking Newcastle Brown Ale inside a bar when they cordoned off the whole area outside to film a police series. Unfortunately, I never got round to seeing Robbie and myself on TV looking out of the bar window!

The game was about four days later and it was live on TV, but we lost 2-0, though I was voted the best defensive player on view. The second game was played in Vancouver, which meant a flight almost as long as the one to Toronto in the first place. However, in the meantime, it came out that the Canadians weren't happy with the fact that Neville Southall, Kevin Ratcliffe, Pat van den Hauwe and Ian Rush hadn't travelled over for the game in Vancouver, following the first ever all-Merseyside FA Cup Final.

Understandably they weren't very happy about this, but then they took it too far by saying that we were a poor outfit and a disgrace. Mike England got the squad together and collectively we decided to give them something to remember us by.

When we arrived in Vancouver, we put our bags in our hotel and went training at the stadium where the game was to be played. It was going to be played indoors on Astroturf, but as soon as we turned up to train they turned the lights out! Mike England lost his head with Tony Waiters and after a while we were allowed to train in the arena. From then on, we treated that game as a World Cup Final.

The game kicked off and some of the tackles that were going in were the best you'll ever see; we had players bouncing off the Astroturf! The Canadians began to stand back and complain about our physical approach, but we put them right by telling them that they shouldn't have slated Wales! In the end, we easily won the game 3-0 with a couple of goals from Dean Saunders and one from Malcolm Allen.

As it turned out, that was to be my last game for Wales, so it's pleasing to say that I won my first game and my last! What an amazing career! I never expected to play for Llandudno Swifts, let alone Wales, and never mind against Rummenigge, Beckenbauer, Platini and Socrates.

Joey Jones from Llandudno had done all that and captained his country too. I haven't a single regret and I feel privileged to be able to say I represented my country. I've also seen half of the world playing for Wales, alongside good lads who all shared the same passion for our country. Amazing!

CHAPTER NINETEEN
RETURNING HOME

In all, I had played 68 games for Huddersfield, but the move to Wrexham meant returning home. I still lived in the town and had always hoped I'd finish my playing career at the Racecourse because the club means so much to me. I was only 32, which in this day and age is still quite young in footballing terms.

The season held forth the prospect of exciting times ahead since Dixie McNeil had signed a mix of youth and experience that summer, including Joe Hinnigan, Mike Carter, Geoff Hunter, Jon Bowden and a youngster called Kevin Russell, who went on to have a smashing career in league football and is now assistant-manager at Wrexham.

As usual, my debut was an absolute disaster. We played down at Torquay in front of just a handful of our fans, since Torquay had banned all away fans. I recall that not only was the weather red hot but it was also one of the hottest games I'd ever played in. The team had travelled down the day before and stayed overnight in a hotel. We were all full of hope for the new season and it couldn't have started better when Mike Carter gave us an early lead.

That was about the only thing we did right that day, as things went from bad to worse and we lost 6-1! The whole team had an off day. To be fair to Torquay, though, they absolutely hammered us and to be honest it could have been ten!

It made the journey home from Torquay feel like four days rather than four hours! It was a murderous journey. When we stopped for a cup of tea, the players wanted to thrash it out there and then, but Dixie told us to wait until Monday.

I had played at centre-half at Torquay, but the next game at home to Hartlepool saw me switched to left-back, with Roger Preece coming in at right-back and Jon Bowden making his debut. We went on to win 2-1.

Despite that early set-back, we recovered to finish the campaign in 11th position, just four points off a play-off place. If we had shown a bit more consistency early on, we could have attained a play-off place, but all in all it had been a season for getting to know each other.

One game I particularly remember that season was against Scarborough at home. Neil Warnock was in charge of them at the time and playing against me was a lad by the name of Colin Russell, who I'd played with in the reserves at Liverpool. He was a good player and a good goalscorer, but during the game he elbowed me in the face off the ball and fractured my cheekbone, which also broke my eye socket.

I had headed the ball clear and the next thing I knew I had this elbow in the side of my face. I rolled over on the ground and saw Colin Russell running off. I jumped up and ran after him, with the aim of knocking him out! But for the first time in my life, I remembered we were winning this game and that, if I got sent off it, it would cost me a lot of money again – and a suspension! So I told him I would see him after the game. He then told me that it was for all the kicks I'd given him over the years.

I didn't have any treatment on the injury and carried on playing, but by the end of the game my eye was almost shut. I remember Mike Salmon saying to me in the dressing room that my cheekbone looked broken. I went in to see our trainer, George Showell, and he told me to get myself to the hospital for an X-ray.

I left the ground and got in my car, but, as I was about to drive off, I spotted Colin Russell walking through the car park. I drove my car at him and blocked his way out of the car park. I got out and began giving him verbal. Again, he repeated that the elbow had been for all the kicks I had given him over the years. I told him I'd never even kicked him and that I would catch up with him. With hand on heart, I can honestly say that, during my playing career, I had never ever elbowed anybody on purpose. I might have punched a few people and head-butted them, but I'd never used my elbow!

I went to the hospital where they X-rayed me and they confirmed that I had fractured both my cheekbone and eye socket. They told me they would have to wait until the swelling had gone down before they could operate on it, so I went home.

I eventually had the operation; they had to insert a wire into my eye socket to keep it all together, which is still there to this day. Looking back though, I could have caused it more damage since I carried on and finished the game. The injury put me out of the team for almost three months, but all I could think of was going back to Scarborough for the return.

That game arrived in March. I was still not happy with what Colin Russell had done to me and I wanted revenge. I don't advocate that now, but it was the way I was at the time. When we arrived at the ground, I put my kit in the dressing room and went looking for him. However, I couldn't find him.

As we took to the pitch, I spotted him and could see him trying to make contact, but I ignored him. I was playing left-back and, if the chance came, I was going to have him. That chance soon came. The ball was played to him and I was running full pelt at him. I actually stopped and he jumped in the air as if I was going to cut him in two.

All through the match, he tried to keep away from me and then, midway through the second half, I was coming out of the box with the ball and he kicked my ankles. I stood up and punched him in the face. In fairness, Russell pleaded with the ref not to book me, although I should have been sent off, never mind booked! It made me feel a little bit better, especially as we went on to win the game 2-0. From that day to this, I've never really seen Colin Russell again. What I would say is that, when we were at Liverpool, I got on all right with him, but that incident soured it for me.

Because of the players that Dixie had brought in, the following season should have been a time when those players began to gel for a push to get out of that division. A couple more signings came in the close season of 1988, with Graham Cooper arriving from Huddersfield. I'd played with him and he was a player who would definitely get people off their seats – it was just unfortunate that they got off their seats and went home!

Seriously though, Graham was a great character to have in the dressing room and a real crowd-pleaser. He had long, black flowing hair and lightning pace. He drank in the same pub as me for a while and would get up and do a Tom Jones impersonation on the pool table, which would have the pub in raptures. He became well liked at Wrexham.

That 1988/89 season began with an away win at Exeter, with Coops and Kevin Russell scoring. By Christmas, we were top of the league, but a run of just one win in nine saw us scrape into the final play-off place in seventh position. That season was to be memorable for me as it was my best season for scoring goals. I scored eight league goals and, at one stage, was leading scorer! I also made my 500th league appearance, ironically at the same ground where I had made my league debut – Millmoor, Rotherham. To cap it all, I scored in a 2-2 draw to make it a double celebration, quite different to the time I made my debut there as a raw 17-year-old.

On two occasions that season, I came very close to netting my first-ever hat-trick. At Rochdale where we drew 3-3, I'd scored two and, in the last minute, I was just running in to head a Jon Bowden corner, when Roger Preece nipped in front of me to head home and deny me my moment of glory. I also came close when we played Carlisle at home after I'd scored both our goals in a 2-1 win. However, it was still to be the best season I ever had in terms of goalscoring and that showed at the end of the season when Kevin Russell and I were chosen in the PFA team for Division Four, which I took as a great honour since it was chosen by the players who I'd played against week in, week out. I had previously been included once before in a PFA team when I was at Chelsea.

One major low point for me that season was being beaten by non-league Runcorn in the FA Cup. We had travelled to Runcorn, where the pitch is on a big slope and earned a 2-2 draw in what was a very physical cup-tie. In the replay four days later, they deservedly scored near the end to beat us 3-2. Embarrassingly for us, it was the first time that any

Wrexham side had been beaten at home in that competition by a non-league side, which is not something to be proud of.

However, we put that defeat behind us and went on to reach the play-offs where we met Scunthorpe United in a two-legged encounter. We beat them quite comfortably at home, 3-1, and travelled to Glanford Park expecting an onslaught, but it never happened and we won 2-0 to go through 5-1 on aggregate.

In the final we met Leyton Orient, but unfortunately for us it was a two-legged final as Wembley wasn't used for play-off finals until the year after. We were drawn at home and the score was 0-0. It left everything to play for in the second leg, but the game was a lunchtime kick-off, which made it difficult for our fans to travel down. However, there were still almost 2,000 of them there in a crowd of over 12,000.

Shortly before half-time, we went a goal down, but Jon Bowden equalised for us just after the break. However, Mark Cooper, who I had been sent off with in a league game earlier that season, was to score the winner. It was a sickener. Orient were up, while we remained a Fourth Division club. To be fair to Orient though, I would say that on the day they deserved to win.

You can imagine how miserable our trip home was. That was, until we began to reflect on how we'd done: after all, we'd had a decent season and we'd reached the play-off final. Dixie decided to stop in Whitchurch for a few drinks. When we got back to Wrexham, I went out on the town and got legless. It was one way to see out a season!

After reaching the play-offs, everyone had high hopes for the new season, but it turned out to be a disappointment! Dixie signed experienced goalkeeper Vince O'Keefe from Blackburn, Sean Reck from Oxford for £35,000 and Gary Worthington, who always used to score against Wrexham, from Darlington. Gary was the nephew of Frank!

The season started badly since we won just three of our opening 13 games, which led to Dixie McNeil resigning as manager. The final straw for Dixie came when we played Maidstone away. Most clubs would have travelled overnight, but we drove in cars to Crewe Station and then went by train to Euston before travelling across London on the underground carrying our kit bags!

Our pre-match meal consisted of butties we'd bought at Euston Station and, when we finally arrived at Dartford where Maidstone played at that time, we had to jump into taxis to get to the ground. We quickly got changed, warmed up and played the match. Not surprisingly, we lost 2-0.

Straight after the final whistle, we rushed off to change. We never had time to have a team talk because we had to get back to Euston to catch our connection for Crewe. It was utterly demoralising to travel like that, but that's the way it was at the time. The club was skint.

It was the final act for Dixie. We played Torquay at home on the Tuesday night, but he wasn't there. George Showell and Brian Prandle took charge for the night and we were told that Dixie had gone away scouting, which wasn't surprising really as we needed 11 new players the way we were playing!

It wasn't until the next day that the news broke that he'd actually left the club, which came as a big shock to everyone. Dixie had been a great servant to Wrexham Football Club. All the lads were sad that he'd gone.

Fortunately for us, Brian Flynn was in the squad – he'd always talked about one day becoming a manager. I phoned him up to suggest he applied for the job, but the chairman, Pryce Griffiths, had already approached him to take over in a caretaker capacity with a view to the job becoming permanent.

His first game in charge was at Hartlepool. We lost 3-0, but the one thing that came out of that game was that he gave a young player by the name of Chris Armstrong his first taste of league football. He later went on to play for Millwall, Crystal Palace, Tottenham and Bolton before returning to Wrexham in the summer of 2003.

In Brian's first week as manager, we had a midweek reserve game up at Carlisle. When he had previously talked about taking over a club, he told me that he would want to work in a threesome. This meant he wanted an assistant-manager, plus a coach, so the management team could bounce their ideas off one another. He didn't want an assistant-manager who was just going to agree with everything the manager said.

It was then that he informed me that Kevin Reeves was going to meet him at the reserve game and have a chat about the assistant-manager's job. I didn't have a problem with that. Brian had played with Kevin at Burnley and he had also worked with him for the PFA. I didn't know Kevin back then, apart from having played against him.

Brian asked me if I wanted to be player-coach, which was great. At that particular time, I had only qualified for my UEFA 'C' licence. However, I wasn't too keen on taking any further coaching badges and I told Brian that. He said not to worry, as I could just use my experience. Anyway, I soon completed my 'B' licence and later attained 'A'.

When Brian took over at Wrexham, he said one of his main aims was to get the youth policy up and running again. Dixie had started to put it in place with the signing of Cliff Sear, but it really took off when Brian took charge. He had come through the youth policy at Burnley and he knew it was the lifeblood of a selling club like Wrexham.

He was quite happy to throw a lot of the youngsters into the side that season. If we did finish bottom, at least it would give the youngsters the experience of playing league football. It was quite pleasing for me because, along with Cliff, I'd been helping train youngsters on Monday nights on the club car park for the past couple of years. That season, quite a few played in the first team.

It was up to us to try and get youngsters to play with the right attitude. My job was to try and motivate the players for every game.

However, it was a struggle as there was no money available to bring in new players and Brian was forced to blood youngsters before their time, players like Chris Armstrong, Phil Hardy, Gareth Owen and Waynne Phillips. I missed the final run-in to the season because I damaged my ankle ligaments at Lincoln in February and it was then that Brian brought in Eddie Youds from Everton on loan, while the directors gambled and let Brian spend £30,000 on Mark Sertori from Lincoln City. It was a gamble that paid off.

We met Mick Mills's Colchester side in March 1990. The game was billed as the big showdown: whoever won stayed up; whoever lost would go down to the Conference. Although we were struggling at the time, we did have a great set of lads and they went out and won the game 3-2. It was played in all weather – sun, rain, sleet and snow – but Gary Worthington scored twice and Andy Thackeray netted as well to ensure victory.

With our fight against relegation over, I recovered in time to play our last match of the season at Grimsby, who had won promotion. However, it turned out to be a disaster for me in more ways than one. We lost 5-1, but the score was actually 0-0 when I went to clear a ball upfield with my heavily strapped right foot. Strangely, it was my left ankle that rolled over and snapped. Not only did it snap, but it also ripped away the ligaments – a bit of meat off the bone, as they say!

I remember Neil Salathiel running over to me and saying, 'Get up, Joe, he's given us a free-kick.'

I couldn't move. I looked up at him and said, 'I think it's broke.'

George Showell came running on and I was stretchered off. They took me into our dressing room and laid me on the floor. The doctor came in and actually started to take my boot off, at which point the pain became excruciating. He actually told me, 'I don't think it's too serious. I think you've just done your ligaments, but we'll send you to the hospital for an X-ray.'

By now, the ankle had begun to swell right up. We went to the local hospital and the first thing they said was that it was broken. They told me I would need an operation as it was going to have to be pinned and screwed, while the ligaments would have to be sewn back on. I asked how long that would take and the doctor said that I'd be in for at least a week. I said, 'There's no way I'm staying here for a week!'

They then advised me to stay, but I was adamant I was going back to Wrexham and that I did!

During my time in the hospital in Grimsby, I was lying on a trolley and there was a chap next to me who kept repeating, 'Grimsby are winning.' Then he said, 'That Joey Jones has been carried off; he's in hospital somewhere.'

I was sat there on the trolley in my kit talking to him! He must have thought I'd been playing in a local park game!

Brian Prandle had been with me all this time and someone gave me some painkillers, which he took for his headache! Eventually they told me that Wrexham Hospital would accept me. The team bus turned up to take me home. They pushed me on in a wheelchair and I hobbled on one foot to the back of the bus to put my leg up on the back seat. There I sat all the way home to Wrexham.

I was dropped off at the Maelor Hospital, but by that time Janice had heard what had happened and met me there. The doctor took a look at my X-rays and said, 'Oh yes, it needs operating on. We'll do it next Wednesday!'

George Showell almost had a fit. 'You can't do that; it's his job.' George then contacted another doctor, Gwyn Evans, and in the end I had the operation the next day.

That injury saw me miss out on playing in the first-ever Welsh Cup Final to be played at the National Stadium in Cardiff. Unfortunately, we lost 2-1 to Hereford, but, as they were an English club, it still gave us the opportunity to represent Wales in the European Cup-Winners' Cup.

CHAPTER TWENTY

THE END OF MY PLAYING DAYS

I recuperated most of the summer, before beginning the slow process of getting back to full fitness. That finally came in November when I was picked at Northampton, but it was too late for me to play in the European games against Lyngby and Manchester United, as well as against Everton in a two-legged Rumbelows Cup tie.

In Europe we'd been drawn against a side called Lyngby from Denmark in the first round of the European Cup-Winners' Cup, with the first leg to be played at the Racecourse. To be honest, I'd never even heard of Lyngby.

The Lyngby manager and his assistant had arranged to travel over to watch us play Aldershot on the Saturday before the tie and Brian asked me to go to Manchester Airport to pick them up. I put a suit on for the day, representing the club and all that, but I was really embarrassed that I had to hold up a sign with 'LYNGBY' written on it, so they could recognise me.

On the way to the airport I was caught up in traffic and, when I'd parked, I had to dash down to Arrivals with my sign hidden under my jacket. I looked around to see if anyone was looking and then sneakily held it up for the Lyngby people to see. Luckily, they were the first two off the plane and

I quickly stuffed it in the bin. They were called Rick 'Somebodyorother', the manager, and Eric 'Somebodyorother', his assistant. I asked them to follow me back to the car.

Then I realised I didn't have a bloody clue where I'd left my car! I'd been in such a rush that I'd forgotten to check what level I'd left it on. I was up and down the stairs about ten times and in and out of lifts like I don't know what. I couldn't find it anywhere.

These poor blokes had to cart their cases wherever I went. They'd been speaking in English and had been really friendly at first, but then they began talking in Danish and I felt their mood changing. They must have been saying, 'We've got a right prat here. If his team is as well organised as he is, we've got no problem.'

We must have walked round the multi-storey for 45 minutes. I've never felt such an idiot. In the end I turned to them completely at a loss. 'It must have been nicked.'

Eventually I found it. What a relief. They smiled sympathetically. On the way back to Wrexham, I chatted with them about football. Rick spoke great English, but Eric didn't, so I chatted to him! No, we all had a little natter and they asked if they could borrow one of our balls to practise with because Rick said the balls they used on the continent were lighter than ours and swerved more. He said he'd send us one to try. When we got to the Racecourse, they thought it was magnificent. 'A real football stadium,' as they put it, and when I saw theirs I realised what they meant.

We beat Aldershot 4-2 the next day and they were very impressed. It was our first home win of the season; Graham Cooper scored two, Gary Worthington and Andy Thackeray got the others. When Kevin Reeves took Rick and Eric back to the airport, they said they were surprised by the speed of the game and its physical side.

It was unfortunate that we played the Lyngby home game in the middle of the two-legged Rumbelows Cup tie with Everton because only three and a half thousand turned up which was disappointing. We also had to contend with the new UEFA ruling that allowed us to field only four non-national players in the side. This meant the English lads who were regulars had to miss out and our younger Welsh lads, most of whom were 16 or 17 and on YTS, had to come in. Brian, Kevin and I had spent hours trying to come up with our best side. Andy Preece, Gary Worthington, Mark Sertori and Nigel Beaumont were the English lads included, but it was Mark Morris our 'keeper who kept us in it with a couple of vital saves when they broke clear later on.

We played quite well and had a couple of chances of our own. They looked a fair side with four full internationals and six Under-21s in the starting line-up. When it finished scoreless, the local press said we'd blown it. But we knew that, if it had to be a draw, then 0-0 suited us because they'd have to come at us in the second leg, which would give us the opportunity to catch them on the break.

Before the return, we had Everton in the Rumbelows Cup. It was Wrexham's biggest game for years. We thought we had a fair chance.

I arrived at the Racecourse at about five o'clock and already Neville Southall was out on the pitch practising his goal-kicks – that's how dedicated he was. The rest of the Everton side hadn't arrived, but Nev only lived up the road in Llandudno, so he'd driven himself. It had been a troublesome couple of weeks for Nev, as he'd been criticised in the press for sitting down by his posts at half-time during the Everton versus Leeds game when the Toffees were losing 2-0.

I walked out of the tunnel to see him and started winding him up by shouting, 'I hope you sit by your posts tonight, Southall.'

He laughed and we had a good chat. He said the whole thing had been blown out of all proportion. He gave me a pair of boots though after I'd asked him if he'd got any and he gave me the keys to his car and I went out to get them. Like Rushie, Nev's often given me the odd pair. Ta, Nev!

I've known Nev since we were on the estate in Llandudno together. Nev wasn't that big when he was on the estate, but he's massive now. When he worked on the building sites he didn't need to use a spade, he'd use his hands – they're like shovels. I've had some laughs with Nev – he's a great lad.

Unfortunately for us, he was the main difference between the two sides on the night. He was unbelievable. I've always said he was the best in the world at that time and he certainly showed it with save after save. We lost 5-0, but we honestly played really well. Nine and a half thousand were in the crowd which produced an atmosphere like the old days. I told our lads that, if we played like that in the league, no one could live with us. We drew 1-1 with Chesterfield on the Saturday.

A week after the Everton game, we played the second leg against Lyngby. Their ground was on the outskirts of Copenhagen and the local press were convinced we would be annihilated. However, we took an early lead after Brian Flynn's well-rehearsed free-kick. He found the head of Jon Bowden, who knocked it back across the goal for Chris Armstrong to run in and head past their 'keeper. It was a great goal for us because it had never once worked in training! Then it was backs-to-the-wall heroics as we held out to go through to the next stage, which was a great achievement for a club like us.

The draw for the next round brought us Manchester United, which meant we went the full length of the Football League from one United to another in the space of four days. On the Saturday, we'd drawn 2-2 at Hartlepool United and, on the Tuesday, we were at Old Trafford for the first leg of our second-round European Cup-Winners' Cup tie with Manchester United.

UEFA rulings meant we had to travel to Manchester on the Monday morning – a visiting team had to be in the country of the side it was playing 24 hours before the game. It was novel for us, being just ten miles down the road from the English border. BSB and Granada television came down to film us leaving Wales and crossing the border.

We went straight to Old Trafford to train and meet up with Brian, Kevin and the rest of the other lads who'd made their own way there. Just walking out on to the pitch was an experience. I told the YTS lads it was nothing compared to when it was full, but like me they were just delighted to be there. Once again, we'd been forced to include them because of the rules allowing only four foreigners in the starting line-up.

I was getting wound up just banging the ball into the empty net. Everyone loves doing that – whack! belting the ball into the onion bag! – whether it's on a council pitch or at Old Trafford. I took 'keeper Mark Morris for some training and was telling him about the tussles I used to have with Steve Coppell when I was playing for Liverpool against United. Happy days! Brian announced the squad afterwards and there were some disappointed faces, especially Gary Worthington who had been a youngster with United. He'd never made the first team and had been desperate to play this time round. To be honest, I was well pissed off because I'd not been included as one of the subs. I'd been given the impression I was on the bench and told Brian I wasn't happy when he left me out. He was right though. If I'd had to go on early, I wouldn't have lasted and I knew it. A bit selfish of me really.

After training, we checked in at our hotel in Altrincham and then Kevin Reeves drove me to Liverpool where I'd been invited to attend Ronnie Whelan's testimonial dinner. Ronnie had decided to get all the lads from the 1977 European Cup-winning team together on the top table and it was a brilliant night.

I was about the first there and had a chat with Ronnie and a couple of the lads. Then Ray Clemence and Jimmy Case came in, followed by Tommy Smith and Ian Callaghan. It was great chatting away about the old times. I'd gone there thinking I'd be a sub the next day and had asked our physio, Steve Wade, to come and pick me up at half-ten. When I found out I wasn't playing, I decided to get stuck into a few beers and left about half-one in the end. Tommy wanted me to stay longer!

Ronnie had asked the players if they'd walk in individually in front of the guests before sitting at the top table. All the lads got big cheers. Jim Watt, the boxer, was the guest speaker and he came straight over to Tommy and me and said, 'I thought I was the only fighter here.' I tell you, he looked unmarked. He must have been bloody good!

They showed the goals from the European Cup Final and there was a little tribute to Ronnie. Then Clive Tyldesley from Granada stood up to say a few words about each player. When he came to me, everyone started singing my name which really touched me. I think, if you ask anyone who played in the '77 side, they'll always mention the stars like the Keegans and the Heighways and would probably forget I was in the team. But I think Liverpool fans knew I was a Kopite and that my heart and soul was Liverpool out on the pitch. I hope they did anyway.

I was sitting next to Tommy and Cally, with Phil Neal and Ray Clemence alongside. It was a bit awkward because none of the lads really wanted to sit next to Emlyn Hughes! For one reason or another, he was not the most popular and it's well known that Tommy wasn't his biggest fan. After the speeches, I had a good chat with the fans. They were all coming up and telling me to 'stuff the Mancs tomorrow!'

I was training the next morning and didn't feel too bad considering the amount I'd drunk. Brian named the side and we ran through some set-pieces. Kev Reeves and myself went down to Old Trafford to lay the kit out and, when we got back to the hotel, we read that United's Mike Phelan was out with flu, which meant we had to change our tactics.

Jon Bowden had been earmarked to keep an eye on Phelan, but with Danny Wallace coming in instead, we rang Bowie up to discuss the switch. He came up to Brian's room and Brian said, 'Bowie, Phelan's not playing.'

'So you're not!' I quickly added. We all fell about laughing. I'm just no good when it comes to anything serious like that. In the end it was decided he'd play in front of the back four, which worked pretty well even though we lost 3-0.

We got to the ground and everyone was very relaxed – at least they looked relaxed. Twenty minutes before kick-off, the subs started asking where their tracksuits were. I'd left them on the bus! All that preparation in the afternoon and I'd forgotten the tracksuits. I had to get the tannoy announcer to contact the bus driver to go and get them. I asked the United kit man if we could borrow some of theirs.

I'd still got my filthy tracksuit on from training in the morning and there was mud everywhere. The lads were slaughtering me, saying what a scruff I was. Brian asked me to go and check if we had to run out together, so I stuck my head round the door and saw Alex Ferguson. He looked immaculate in his suit and I shouted over to him, 'Are we walking out together?'

'I think so, Joe.'

I could swear he was thinking what a scruffy bastard I was!

The bell went and we got up to leave. Mark Hughes and Clayton Blackmore nodded on the way past and Kev and I had a little chat with Nobby Stiles and Brian Kidd in the tunnel. I said to Nobby, 'Got any polish for my boots?' And he laughed.

I can get a bit wound up on the bench, particularly if the other managers are having a go. Alex Ferguson's number two, Archie Knox, flew out of his seat shouting at the referee after one tackle and I stood up and had a few words.

We played well and could have had a couple. The way the game was going, the Stretford End were beginning to whistle at United, but then just before half-time Brian McClair got free from a corner to make it 1-0 with a header and, a couple of minutes later, Steve Bruce made it 2-0 from a penalty. At half-time, we told the lads to keep going because we had looked dangerous, but in the second half Gary Pallister hit a third.

Afterwards, we told the lads they'd done really well against a First Division side.

Privately Brian said he thought we were in with a chance, albeit a slim one, if we could get an early goal – it'd have to be in the warm-up! – but I suppose United wouldn't fancy coming to the Racecourse even if they were 3-0 up.

Next day I was training in the morning and playing in the afternoon against Tranmere Reserves. It was the best yet as far as the ankle was concerned. We won 4-3 and I really enjoyed it. I got stuck in for the first time with a couple of thumping tackles, including one on Dave Martindale just outside the box. He was coming towards me and I thought it's got to be him or the ball and dived in. It was a two-footed tackle, but I played the ball cleanly and Dave went flying. He got up and started shouting at the referee. 'Hey, ref, what about the two-footed tackle?'

'Hey, Dave,' I said, 'I'm too old to change now!' And he ran off laughing.

Having recovered from my injury at Grimsby, I came back for the Northampton game in November, but it wasn't right, though I did make a further 20 appearances that campaign, but I never really felt comfortable because of the ankle.

That season saw the side finish 92nd in the Football League, which highlighted for me the fact that I'd won the First Division title with Liverpool and had now finished bottom of the Football League with Wrexham. So I can honestly say that I've experienced football at the top and at the very bottom as well!

Scunthorpe away was our second-to-last game of the season and, as usual, I was in charge of making sure we had the kit plus a full complement of personnel before we set off in the coach from the Racecourse. It was half-past one and we had to pick up Kev Reeves and physio Steve Wade. Brian Flynn was going straight there.

First we stopped off at the Lord Daresbury Hotel just outside Warrington to pick up Wadey. 'No directors travelling with us today?' he said jumping on to the coach.

'Not that I know of. Why?'

'Cos David Rhodes told me yesterday that he was travelling with us.'

David Rhodes at the time was club secretary and vice-chairman. 'Where is he then? Cos he's not on here.'

'He definitely said he'd be getting on the bus with us.'

'Well, he never told me!'

I was just beginning to panic when we saw his red Datsun flash past in the outside lane. 'Shit! I've forgotten our vice-chairman!'

I thought he would have seen the coach and pulled in at the next services to wait for us, but, when we turned off at Birch Services to pick up Kevin Reeves, there was no sign of him. The lads started wading in with the stick. 'Better look for another job then!'

I got the driver to stop at Hartshead Moor to see if he was waiting there, but he wasn't, so we carried on to Scunthorpe. By the time we got to the ground, they were calling me 'Frank Spencer' again, but I didn't give a shit! Brian Flynn walked towards us. 'Where's David Rhodes?'

'I've left him.'

'But he's got the tickets...'

After that, Kev Reeves and Wadey really began steaming in. 'Van driver next week, or maybe a milkman?'

I'd had enough. 'Look. If David Rhodes gets here and starts on me, I'm going to tell him to piss off. OK.'

'Maybe you could get a job as a travel agent.'

'Fuck off!'

Eventually David Rhodes arrived and, with me poised to go on the attack, he never said anything at all. I was ready and waiting to get stuck in, but he never said a word. I couldn't wait any longer. 'Where've you been?'

'You bloody left me, didn't you?'

That was it. Never mentioned again.

It is difficult checking everyone's aboard because I never know who's coming with us or not. Once I get the lads on, that's it as far as I'm concerned but my track record for remembering anyone else isn't very good. A couple of seasons ago, I left the chairman, Pryce Griffiths. We were on our way to Chester by the time he caught up with us and flagged down the coach. He was all right about it too.

We lost at Scunthorpe and finished bottom of Division Four. League tables don't lie, but I think we deserved better than that. It hurt me. It hurt all of us who'd put so much work and effort into the club. Our only chance to salvage pride came the following week against Swansea in the Welsh Cup Final at Cardiff Arms Park, with the winners picking up a place in

Europe. It's not the FA Cup Final and never will be, but, if you're there, you want to make sure you win. There's prestige, pride and cash for the winners. A plum tie in Europe meant money which the club didn't have a lot of.

Because it was Swansea, the *Wrexham Evening Leader* asked me to do some publicity shots down at the local pond next to some swans. I didn't mind until one of the birds bit my finger! It nearly took the end off and was pissing with blood. Not the best of omens!

In the meantime, I heard from a former team mate that the Secretary of the Welsh FA, Alun Evans, had had a go at Wrexham when he was speaking at a dinner. Apparently, he had said that our faces should match the colour of our shirts after we finished bottom of the league. That annoyed me because in his position he shouldn't have made comments like that, even in jest.

I've always got on with Alun Evans, although I've known players who weren't so keen on him. But, even in Wales, there is such a thing as the North-South divide, with us in the North feeling the South always get better treatment from the Welsh FA. I was determined to have a go back at him at the first opportunity, which just happened to be when he was being introduced to the two teams shortly before kick-off.

Evans and the rest of the dignitaries met the Swansea players first and then they walked down the line to shake hands with the Wrexham lads. He offered me his hand and I shook it, saying, 'You're out of order, you are.'

'What are you on about?'

'What you said about Wrexham ... you're always having a go at us.'

He hurried along, saying it was only a joke. I left it at that. Things like that don't bother me and it certainly didn't affect the way I played. Unfortunately, that wasn't very well as we lost 2-0!

Afterwards I went upstairs for a drink and Alun Evans came straight over to me. 'I'm not happy with what you said.'

'Oh aye. Why?'

'You shouldn't have picked that moment; you should have been concentrating on the match.'

'Listen. It doesn't affect the way I play and I can say what I like. You've made your share of outrageous statements in the past because I've heard them.'

He started saying he hadn't made any comments about Wrexham, which made me worse. 'The source who told me about this is very reliable. A person I trust and admire.'

He just kept on saying I was a disgrace for picking up on it before the match. 'You're the disgrace. Not me.'

We were like two kids really. People in the bar had been listening and began chipping in. One bloke shouted over, 'You won't get any more caps now.'

'No, he won't,' said Alun Evans.

'I don't want any more; I've got enough.'

It was a right old row, but in the end we got talking about other things and it all calmed down.

I go back a long way with the Welsh FA. I've been hauled up in front of them enough times during my career. The committee have had more than their fair share of stick down the years, some of it deserved, but most of it when players have thought they've been tight-fisted, short-sighted or just plain stupid. I know a lot of fans, too, who've not been able to understand some of the decisions they've made. But when all's said and done, on the whole I've been on good terms with most of them.

That doesn't mean to say I haven't been in trouble. Alun Evans once rang me at home and asked me to appear in front of the committee after Ian Rush told a story about me in his autobiography.

It was at the time when the Welsh FA offices were still in Wrexham. I had been training with Wales down at Bisham Abbey during the build-up to a Home International match with England. Rushie and I had been laughing because our training gear was absolutely crap. We had grey tops and some had 'WALES' on them, but others had 'ALES' because the 'W' had fallen off. Some of the lads had blue shorts on; some had orange. The socks were in different colours and we had bags down as goalposts.

In the meantime, England turned up on their team coach looking immaculate in matching tracksuits. Sammy Lee, Ray Clemence and Terry McDermott were there and I could see them laughing at us. We looked like a Sunday League team. In the end I shouted over to Rushie, 'We look like Rag Arse Rovers!' We didn't mind because it was part and parcel of playing for Wales, but we did look a right state.

Anyway, Rushie put it in his book and I got called up in front of Alun

Evans and the national committee. 'Why did you say that Wales looked like Rag Arse Rovers?'

'Because we did look like Rag Arse Rovers! I'd be lying to you if I said I hadn't said it; you'd have said the same thing yourselves if you'd seen us. The training kit's a disgrace and has been so for donkey's years.'

They told me they'd consider what action to take against Rushie, which made me smile because they couldn't ban him. He was the only world-class player they had!

Even before I became involved in the Welsh set-up, I'd heard stories and rumours about the committee and, in fairness, it does seem as if they have improved over the years. Mike England once told us all about a selection meeting he'd been to when he was the national manager. For some reason the committee met in Birmingham, I've no idea why, but they did. Mike had to hand in the squads for a forthcoming international. All through the meeting, Mike was interrupted by Mr Ivor Percy, who was a lovely bloke. He kept shaking his head, scratching his chin and muttering to himself, 'It's just not fair. No, it's not fair at all.'

Mike said he ignored him at first and carried on talking, but he was worried something was wrong with the team selection. In the end, he pulled up the meeting, 'Excuse me, gentlemen, but Mr Percy obviously wants to make a point. What is it, Mr Percy? What exactly isn't fair?'

'Well, I don't think it's fair that the team should travel in tracksuits and we don't.' Mike said he just had to laugh. He was about eighty then!

There was always someone on the committee you could have a chat and a laugh with. In my case, it was Elfed Ellis, a real dyed-in-the-wool Welshman, who loved his football. All the lads loved Elfed because he was so enthusiastic for the game. He was the man who first took Mike England to Blackburn to begin his career. He lived for his footy and he also liked a drink.

I remember lining up for Wales at Ninian Park during one of the Home Internationals when Elfed struck. People often ask me what is going through your mind during the national anthems. Not being Welsh-speaking, in the early days I'd just be trying to remember the words and hum the bits I didn't know.

At Ninian Park, you always faced the directors' box and the national anthems gave you a great chance to see who was there. If you were on the transfer list, it was time to check which managers were watching!

As the national anthem was being played this particular afternoon, Elfed appeared above the tunnel at the front of the directors' box; his tie was all over the place and his shirt was unbuttoned. He was singing away as loud as he could. All the lads saw him. They were whispering and nudging each other.

All of a sudden, bam, Elfed fell backwards down the steps. We were all standing to attention trying not to laugh during what was left of the anthem. When we broke and ran to kick in, all the lads were laughing. 'Did you see Elfed?'

Sod the game, all the talk was of Elfed!

CHAPTER TWENTY ONE

RED MIST

The 1991/92 season got off to a hell of a start. The opening game against Hereford on the Racecourse and I was sent off before half-time! I'd told everybody I was as fit as ever and wanted to play in every game. It was only a bit of a scuffle and I was trying to calm things down, but the ref still whipped out the red card. Some things never change. Off we go again!

There'd been the usual buzz around the ground for the first home league game and we'd brought in a couple of new faces. That's not strictly true because they were a couple of well-worn faces really: former Wales international Gordon Davies, a mere strip of a lad at 35, and my mate Mickey Thomas, as youthful as ever at 37. I'd just been made captain again and slotted in nicely between them at 36! Cunningly, we'd been moaning about lack of experience the whole of the previous season!

Anyway, it was what we needed with so many young lads in the side. Mickey and I were twice the age of most of them. Brian Flynn had told me to lead by example and, for the 30 minutes I was on the pitch, I made sure I did. It was as bad a sending-off as I've had, not because I smacked anyone or scythed them down but because I was completely innocent and the ref read the situation wrongly.

In my excitement to get out and play, I'd forgotten to strap my ankle up and it was killing me. Tackles were flying in thick and fast which was no real surprise. Games against Hereford always felt like a local derby. I was marking one of their new lads, Paul Robinson, a big centre-forward, and I went to close him down right in front of the dugouts. I was just shielding him when his elbow whizzed past my ear. I don't know if it was intentional or not, but I carried on trying to get the ball.

A few other lads saw it and stepped in. I grabbed him by the shirt and threw him off. That's all I did and I got ready to make my point when the ref, Brian Coddington, who was refereeing his first-ever league match, came over and said, 'I'm not having this.'

'Quite right, ref, you don't want that kind of thing at all.'

I was looking at him and suddenly got the feeling he was about to book me. I began to complain, but as he pulled his hand out of his top pocket I realised it contained the red card. 'Get off!'

'You what?'

'Off.'

'But I haven't done anything.'

I really lost my rag after that. What a disgraceful decision. I slaughtered him, calling him everything I could think of. As he stood there waving the red card in front of my face, a thought flashed through my mind and I'm glad now it flashed out again just as quickly. For a split second, I wanted to grab the card out of his hand and rip it up. I was that mad. Luckily, I just walked or that would have been me finished I'm sure of it.

Some of the press lads asked Mickey what it was like being back at Wrexham playing with me again and he told them he didn't know because I hadn't been on long enough! A three-match ban, what a start to the season that was!

In all, I've been sent off quite a few times in my career. The first time was for Liverpool up at Middlesbrough, which I've already told you about. And then there was the one on my debut with Chelsea and my first for Huddersfield down at Brighton, followed by the rest in my three spells at Wrexham.

Some sendings-off have been more deserved than others, including the

Liverpool one. Others have been unfair and, in my opinion, petty like the one against Hereford. It depends on the referee. It depends on what you do and the circumstances of the game. My first sending-off for Wrexham came during the relegation season of 1981/82 when we went down to play Tottenham in the League Cup. No complaints, I punched Steve Archibald and I deserved that one.

It was the third round and, before the game, I remember chatting with some of the radio lads who'd come down to cover the game. Spurs were having a new stand built and it meant we had to change in a Portakabin in one corner of the ground. We were all laughing because it was one hell of a walk if you got sent off - famous last words!

I was marking Tony Galvin who was a pretty good winger on his day and I was playing him well. In the middle, Steve Archibald was giving Wayne Cegielski a rough time and twice caught him with his elbow. It was beginning to annoy me and I was screaming at Ceggsy to dig him back.

In the second half, I came in behind Archibald to close him down and, as he laid the ball off, he whacked me on the side of the head with another elbow. That was that, I'd had enough. The ball had gone and, out of the corner of my eye, I saw him standing next to me looking at me, so I let him have it. CRACK! A right hook. It was stupid, I know, but he'd been dishing it out all night. A few of their players came rushing towards me and by then I was ready to take on everyone. I remember Garth Crooks dashing up and, as I set myself, he started shouting, 'No, no, I'm trying to stop you getting sent off.'

That calmed things down a bit, but the ref had no alternative. 'Off!' I began the long, slow walk from one corner of the pitch to the other and Ray Clemence, who was in goal for Tottenham, came out to have a go at me for being stupid, so I had a go back at him. Their trainer who'd come on to treat Archibald also said something, so I told him to fuck off or he would get it!

The Tottenham fans were going mad. I walked as slowly as I could towards the Portakabins and one or two objects were thrown at me. When I finally got there, they were locked! Nightmare. The fans were calling me for everything and I was freezing my bollocks off standing outside in my kit. It must have been ten minutes before someone arrived to let me in. After the game, I went into the players' lounge and a couple of their lads quietly snuck up to me and said they were glad I'd belted him, but I'm not saying which ones. It didn't really matter to me because we'd lost 2-0, which was the most important thing and my stupidity had probably cost us. That's what really counts.

My second sending-off for Wrexham came in another big game, down at Ninian Park, Cardiff, and was for a second bookable offence. The ball came across and I went to play it down the line when one of their lads, Tarki Michalev, came in to challenge. I completely missed the ball and caught Tarki, bouncing him down the line instead of the ball. I was walking before the ref got to me and Tarki was making the most of it, rolling around on the floor, so I had a few words before departing.

'You cheating git, get up.'

'Off!'

'I'm going, I'm going.'

Years later, I was sent off twice in consecutive seasons for Wrexham down at Peterborough during my third spell with the club. The first one came in 1988, when I slid into Noel Luke. It was a hard tackle, but I've seen worse - a second bookable offence! A year later, I came on as sub after returning from injury and, as I was warming up, their fans were winding me up. 'How long this time, Jones? Twenty minutes? Half an hour?'

I came on in the first half and, when play resumed with a throw-in, one of their blokes collected the ball, took it past me and fell over my outstretched leg. Booked! I couldn't have been on more than fifteen seconds. I hadn't touched the ball.

'Name?'

'I've only just come on.'

'Name?'

The game went on without any further incident until they scored in the dying seconds to make it 3-1. It was miles offside ... honestly, miles and miles offside, so our centre-half, Nigel Beaumont, went running after the ref to complain. I went running after him to calm him down and, as I got near, I shouted to the linesman, 'You don't give a toss, do you?'

That was the only thing I said and the ref told me to get off.

'What?'

'Off!'

I hadn't even reached the tunnel by the time he blew the final whistle.

The Peterborough fans couldn't believe their luck: 3-1 winners, a last-minute goal and me sent off again! I began arguing with everyone in sight and wouldn't get off the pitch; I was waiting to have another go at the ref. Next minute, a policeman grabbed me. 'Get down the tunnel.' That was that. I thought I was back in Llandudno!

The next one was at home to Orient when Wrexham were running neck and neck with them for the Fourth Division promotion play-offs in 1989. Their centre-forward, Mark Cooper, kept catching me with his elbow whenever I went near him. I don't know if it was intentional or not, but in the end I shouted for the ref to get a grip.

'Can't you get a hold of this feller?'

'Get on with the game.'

'Well, if you're not going to do anything about it, then I am.' That was my first booking.

Later on, we jumped for a ball and I felt the wind as his fist flew past my nose. I've seen it twice on video. We landed and I whacked him one back, a glancing right which really didn't connect hard. He started shouting at the ref that I'd belted him. The ref stopped the game and sent me off. Cooper got sent off too.

My one and only sending-off with Huddersfield was at Brighton and it was a real nothing affair – handbags at 20 paces between Mick Ferguson and me, with both of us getting the bullet. I'd gone for a ball with him and, when we both landed, he flicked my leg, nothing more, so I flicked him back. We then went nose to nose and the ref ran straight over.

'Get off!'

'You're joking, aren't you?'

'Get off!'

'I'm not going unless he's going.'

We were like two kids. Sure enough Mick went too and we both walked off together towards the tunnel. Someone threw a cup of coffee that hit me and, when we got to the dressing rooms, I began wondering whether to belt him properly because no one would have seen it. I reckoned I could whack him and then nip into the safety of the away dressing room before he could respond. Funny really, because I've chatted to Mick Ferguson since up at Hartlepool where he was watching the reserves and it appears he was thinking exactly the same thing!

I don't know if it was because I was getting slower or more bad-tempered, but I honestly believe the standard of refereeing has changed beyond belief during my time in the game. I don't mean that it's got better or worse; it's just that now you get booked if you sneeze. Nat Lofthouse wouldn't have lasted ten seconds these days, charging the 'keeper and all that. I don't think Tommy Smith, Ron Harris, Norman Hunter, Denis Smith and all the players like them would have survived in today's game.

I've seen players booked for nudges and petty fouls – little pushes that don't even deserve to be called challenges. It's sad to say that great players have become great divers because they know the ref is going to give them free-kicks and book defenders. From the defenders' point of view, bookings mean disciplinary points which end up in suspensions. You might as well smack someone and get sent off as tap them and get sent off – two petty fouls and you're gone. I look at the old footage shown on television and think back to the likes of Tommy. Tackling is such a major part of the game and now I honestly believe it's dying out.

In fairness, good referees don't let situations develop during a match. They can tell if two players are giving each other stick and clamp down straight away. Refs that talk to you and have a joke with you during the game are refs that players respect. Usually they don't have to resort to red and yellow cards to keep order. It's the ones who come waving the things in your face who are ruining things. If players are treated like kids, they'll act like kids.

Neil Midgely, Clive Thomas, Keith Cooper, John Lloyd and George Courtney – love them or loathe them, they were refs who I always felt listened to players and talked to them. Neil Midgely was as good as any, as far as I'm concerned, because he had a laugh and a joke and would talk you through the game. Sadly, he is no longer with us.

The professional foul has made the situation worse in my view. Defenders are now scared to make tackles because they know the consequences. Tackling is as much part of the game as passing or goalscoring, but if you're afraid to make a challenge then, in my opinion, one of the game's great arts is being destroyed.

I certainly wouldn't continue to watch football if tackling was outlawed. The crowd love nothing more than a crunching tackle, but I'm seeing defenders today trying to get out of the way of a forward when he's coming through. As soon as defenders make contact, they're booked.

I agree that a defender should be sent off if he does haul the forward down when he's in on goal, but even down the flanks players are being sent off for so-called professional fouls. Tommy Smith, Norman Hunter and the like became heroes because of their toughness and strength; tackles in their day were much harder than today's. Everyone accepted it. Now they don't and football's worse off as a result.

I don't think I was a dirty player – if I'd been more sneaky I could have got away with a lot more, but that's never been my style. I modelled myself on Tommy Smith who wasn't a dirty player, but a hard player instead. I never got near to Tommy's level of skill and ability, but I knew I was on the right track because he was a tremendous inspiration to those around him.

Football's a hard game and it has its share of hard men. I know I've done things I shouldn't have, like butting John Hickton and belting Steve Archibald, but it's very rare that incidents like that occur without good reason. If you dish it out, you've got to be able to accept the knocks back. I've given out my fair share and taken a lot in return. That's football; it's a man's game – as simple as that.

That 1991/92 season had seen us make a reasonable start, but the ankle that I broke at Grimsby was beginning to play up and the game which stands out for me was when we played Cardiff at Ninian Park. This was a derby game despite being 150 miles from Wrexham, but it was North v South and there was always an edge. In this particular game, we lost 5-0! The lad that Nigel Beaumont and I were up against was Chris Pike and he scored a hat-trick. On the bus radio on the way home, I heard him say that he hadn't scored an easier hat-trick because the two centre-halves were fairly slow. I immediately thought that the writing was on the wall for me!

Obviously after a 5-0 defeat, we were all subdued and Flynny, Kev and I were asking how we were going to lift the players for the next game. It was then I suggested that we stop off in Monmouth and buy a few beers for the bus. That way we'd get the result out of our system, then have a hard week's training for the Burnley home game.

So that's what we did. We chatted with the players and had an in-depth discussion as to what went wrong. We trained hard all week and everyone was ready for Saturday. However, within the first three minutes we were 2-

1 down and we went on to lose 6-2! It apparently equalled Wrexham's biggest-ever home defeat in the Football League.

I remember running back past an oncoming Vince O'Keefe for the sixth goal and trying to scoop the shot away, but I tripped and rolled into the net where my foot got stuck. I remember Joe Jakub coming into the goal to collect the ball and I looked at him and said, 'Joe, what the hell am I doing here?!' He just turned away laughing.

At the end of the game, we were coming off and, quite rightly, the fans weren't happy, but as we came close to the tunnel there was one fan in particular who gave us a barrage of venomous abuse. Believe me, I wasn't happy with what had happened but I just snapped. I ran and jumped up on the paddock fence and was hanging over the top, throwing punches at him. Mickey had hold of my ankles trying to stop me from going over and saying, 'Joe, he's not worth it.'

However, if the chap's reading this book now, then I apologise as it wasn't the right thing to do, but it was the way I was. I was just as disappointed as everyone else.

From then on, I played just a handful more games for the first team. As it happened, my last game was a 1-0 home defeat by Chesterfield in November, but I went off injured. The specialist had another look at the ankle and advised me it wasn't getting any better, so on my 37th birthday I finally decided to call it a day. I knew I'd begun to get caught and my ankle wasn't the same any more. I had to be perfectly honest with myself and certainly didn't want to let anybody else down, especially the fans.

It was obviously a sad occasion for me because playing football was all I'd done since leaving school, but I had the consolation of knowing that I would be able to carry on coaching and playing reserve-team football to help the kids along. In fact, I continued to play reserve-team football with the youngsters until I was 44, which in my eyes was an achievement since I wanted to keep playing as long as I could.

CHAPTER TWENTY TWO
MY MATE MICKEY

Mickey and I met up again when he re-signed for Wrexham in the summer of 1991 and it wasn't long before it seemed just like old times. We'd both been asked to speak to youngsters about the dangers of fire up in Llandudno. Mickey wouldn't speak in public, so I had to get up and say a few words. Afterwards, we got chatting to some firemen who'd come up to help out and, by the time we left, both of us quite fancied taking up fire-fighting as a career after football.

The following week, when Brian Flynn was giving us a pre-match team talk in the dressing room, saying how well we'd been doing, everyone was silent apart from Mickey who kept whispering quietly in my ear, 'He says we're doing well, Joe.' I was trying not to laugh.

'We might not need to become firemen after all. He says we're doing just fine.'

I was doubled up trying my hardest not to laugh as Brian was getting the lads keyed up. Mickey just kept on and on. I burst out laughing and Brian stared at the pair of us. I was supposed to be setting an example as a coach, but how could I with him around?

Throughout his playing career, he's had a history of going missing – disappearing completely the night before a game, then reappearing fresh as a daisy in the morning, having been out all night. After he joined Chelsea, he was at it again.

In the third to last game of the Second Division Championship season, we went up to play Manchester City at Maine Road. We had to win to maintain any hopes of winning the title and they had to win to have any chance of getting promotion. It was a massive game for both sides and it was live on television. Mickey and I travelled from Wrexham together and met up with the rest of the lads at a posh hotel just outside Manchester. As always, I was sharing a room with him, and I was lying on the bed watching telly when in he came. 'Right, I'm off then.'

'What d'ya mean you're off?'

'I'm off.'

'Off where?'

'Home. I'm not staying here tonight.'

'You can't go. What if John Neal finds out?'

'So what? I'm not staying here; I've got a bit of business on. If anybody asks, tell them I've gone for a walk.'

That was that. Off he went. There was no point in arguing with him, but sure enough at half past-seven the next morning, there he was knocking on my door. 'All right, Joe. Lovely morning.' He had all the papers under his arm and settled down in the chair for a read and a cup of tea.

We had light training on the Friday morning and played the match in the evening, but I had to come off with a hamstring pull at half-time. It didn't matter because Mickey was the best man on the pitch by a mile and we won 2-0, with goals from Pat Nevin and Kerry Dixon. He could have been up all night for all I knew; it didn't affect him.

He did the same thing before a Wales v Norway game at the Racecourse in February 1985. We'd been staying at the Bryn Howell Hotel in Llangollen in the build-up to the match, but the night before Mickey suddenly got one of his rushes of blood. Once again, I was sitting watching the telly when he walked in and started getting his coat on.

'I'm off then. See you in the morning.'

'We're playing tomorrow, you can't.'

'Don't worry, I'll be back in the morning.'

Off he went and, sure enough, at half-past seven he was knocking on the door with the papers. Mike England never found out and probably still doesn't know, but there was no point in me talking to Tommo because, once he had it in his mind, that was that.

I worried like hell because I knew the trouble he'd get into if someone found out. What if he had a crash or got stopped by the police. Anything could have happened.

It happened at a number of clubs over the years, even at Manchester United and Everton. I'd get phone calls at weird times of the day and night from him, telling me what had happened.

'Joe?'

'Yeah.'

'I've legged it.'

When he was at United, the club organised a friendly match in the Far East and the first-team squad and officials were due to fly out from London. Mickey told everyone he wasn't going, so Lou Macari bet him he didn't have the bottle to stay behind. Sure enough, the players' luggage was flown down to London with the party and then shifted on to the charter flight out of the country. Mickey's luggage went on tour, but he didn't! He took the money off Lou Macari and caught the shuttle straight back to Manchester as the others boarded the plane east! I think the club fined him heavily.

At Everton, he fell out with Howard Kendall when he refused to go with the reserves to Newcastle. He'd been out injured and wanted to play for the first team, but Howard Kendall wanted him to play in a reserve game because the Merseyside derby was a few days away and he wanted to make sure Mickey was fit for that.

Mickey told him he wasn't going on the coach and Howard Kendall told him he had better be on it. Sure enough, Mickey didn't turn up and Kendall called him into his office and sold him to Brighton. Straight away, Mickey caught the plane to meet the manager, Mike Bailey, and after he'd put pen to paper he gave me a ring.

'Joe?'

'Yeah.'

'It's Mickey. I didn't realise it was this bloody far!' I think he thought he was signing for New Brighton!

Down at Chelsea it wasn't too bad, but Mickey and I led a lonely life travelling up and down the motorways each morning. At training one time, John Hollins came over to announce that the club were taking us all on a mid-season break to Spain.

'Right, lads, we're off on holiday.'

Mickey and I just looked at each other. 'We're not. We're off home to Wales.'

We started laughing, but we both kept our word and, while they all went off on the trip, we went back home.

If we went for a night out in London, it was usually just the two of us, but with Mickey you were always guaranteed a good time. The most bizarre evening came in London's Soho when we went to meet our mate Ken Gorman from the *Daily Star* who was doing an interview with Mickey. We had a couple of beers and wandered outside to see all kinds of goings on at the Xenon nightclub. It turned out it was a massive bash for George Michael's birthday and we stayed around to watch.

Mickey and I were in jeans and trainers and Ken in a tatty jacket. Naturally, we were refused entry. As we stood there watching the stars going in, we noticed a limousine driving round to the back of the club, so we followed it and saw George Michael dash out of a back alley and into the car.

After George Michael had driven off, we could hear music coming from the door he'd come out of. There were two doormen there, but we decided to try and get in. Ken Gorman took out his press pass and we just followed him in, saying we were the press as well! Once inside, it was like a *Who's Who* of British rock with Paul Young, Spandau Ballet, Duran Duran, Nick Kershaw, Joey Jones and Mickey Thomas! Talk about the rich and famous. We looked like a couple of cleaners, but who cared? There was free ale all night or, more precisely, free champagne. Some people recognised us and came up to chat; at first we were careful to avoid the cameras because we were training the next day. After the tenth buck's fizz slipped down our necks, we were throwing ourselves in front of them, trying to get our pictures taken with Andrew Ridgely. We got Bill Wyman's autograph and had a chat with a few of the stars. It was one of the best nights I've ever had and, by the time we got out, it was well into the early hours.

John Neal let us get on with it because we always gave everything on the pitch. And, in fairness, so did Ken Bates, even though he had a reputation for being difficult. So many people have different opinions about Ken Bates that it's difficult to know where to start. There's no question he's outspoken, meaning the press pick up on things he says and give him a hard time. I think most people have the wrong impression of him. I had my rows with him and he had his goes at me, but he was always very straight – you always knew where you stood. Personally, I like people to do business that way. He had a great sense of humour and you could always have a joke. If he called me 'Jonesie', I'd call him 'Batesie'. He was always willing to talk to you even if he didn't agree with you and he rarely missed a match home or away. He always came in the dressing room beforehand to wish the lads luck, and have his say.

One time I was warming up in the corridor outside the changing rooms at Stamford Bridge, kicking a ball against the wall. He came walking towards me, pretending to tackle me and, when the ball broke between us, I went straight over the top with my studs – right down his shin, scuffing his suit.

'Yesssssss!'

I was laughing with some of the apprentices who'd been standing watching.

'I hope you do that at three o'clock,' he said.

I think he was a frustrated footballer because he loves the game and gets involved as much as he can. I remember him coming out to play penalties with Mickey Thomas and me one Friday afternoon. As always, Mickey and I were hanging round with nowhere to go and he joined in, wearing his suit and taking shots at us both. He wasn't bad. I couldn't imagine many other chairmen doing that.

After the ones I'd known at Liverpool and Wrexham, I had the impression of chairmen as being quiet, reserved, behind-the-scenes men but Ken Bates was completely different. He once walked into the changing room before a match wearing the biggest fur coat you've ever seen – massive it was, right down to his ankles – and when he burst through the door, all the lads were laughing, 'Fuck me, it's King Kong!' This coat really tickled me and I had visions of him walking into the boardroom at Anfield wearing it. They wouldn't have known what to make of it.

As I say, he did have a sense of humour and, after one game, the lads threw him into the bath fully clothed. Someone shouted, 'Get his wallet first!'

Big Derek Johnstone, who'd joined Chelsea from Glasgow Rangers chipped in too. 'Sod his wallet. Someone stick their foot on his head and keep him under!'

You can't keep Ken Bates out of the news for long. He's always going to make headlines because he's not afraid to say what he thinks, even if it means upsetting people. A couple of years after I'd left Chelsea – March 1987, to be precise – he had a little dig at me and Mickey in his programme notes before the home game with West Ham and the papers were on to me straight away to have a go back.

Basically, he was explaining that John Hollins had changed the style of management from the days of John Neal, who'd operated a 'laid-back' form of leadership. 'How could he John Hollins punish Paul Canoville for being late for training when Mickey Thomas and Joey Jones never turned up?' he wrote.

Anyone who knows me will tell you just how hard I train, even on days off, and I didn't like the idea of the Chelsea fans thinking Mickey and I had been cheating them. In the *Daily Star*, I replied, 'He's talking a load of rubbish. When it came to doing it on the pitch, Mickey Thomas and I never let Chelsea down and that's where it counts. I'm not the type of player not to train and never have been. I don't understand why he had to have a go at us.'

Those were my feelings and, as far as I was concerned, that was it. My quotes appeared in the paper on 21 March and, three days later, Ken Bates wrote to me saying he'd been misrepresented. 'At no time have I ever suggested that you or Mickey Thomas have ever given less than 100 per cent on the pitch. I was sorry at the time and in fact still am that you left the club because you were unable to move to London.' He went on, 'You are and will always be an honoured guest at Stamford Bridge.'

As I say, I've no axe to grind with Ken Bates. He was entitled to say what he wanted and I respect him for that, even though I didn't agree with him. I've never been one to back down either and I think he respected me for that too. No one could have given more effort when they played for Chelsea than Mickey and I did. There's no question of that.

My retirement from football didn't come about until after Wrexham had played and beaten Arsenal in the FA Cup third round, when Mickey scored one of the most memorable goals in FA Cup history. I'd played in the first-round match against Winsford United and we won 5-2 at home. It turned out to be a good cup-tie and we later signed one of their players, Dave Esdaille, who was a Ruud Gullit look-alike.

The next round saw us meet Telford United, which I missed because of my ankle injury, but we managed to scrape through 1-0 to earn a dream tie at home to the mighty Arsenal. Because of the small squad and the fact we had a number of injuries, I was on the subs' bench for the game with James Kelly. Nobody gave us a cat in hell's chance of winning; they were the reigning league champions and we were the reigning bargain-basement boys!

The most inspiring words before the game came from our chairman, Pryce Griffiths. He came into the dressing room prior to kick-off and wished us all the best, adding that, if we could earn a replay, the money would be helpful to buy some better players! I don't think he realised what he'd said!

We held them to a solitary Alan Smith goal at half-time, but they'd been well on top. We were still holding our own in the second half when we were fortunate to be awarded a free-kick on the edge of the box. Mickey placed the ball and, bang, it went in. The whole place went berserk. Mickey had never hit a better ball than that. He came running over to the dugout and we were all hugging each other. What a goal!

Everyone still talks about that goal and it's always on TV when the FA Cup programmes come round, but it was Steve Watkin who scored the winning goal. When Steve beat Tony Adams to steer the ball past David Seaman, you haven't seen anything like it in your life. Everyone went completely mad. The fans were brilliant. It's a game that will never be forgotten by anyone who was there.

After beating Arsenal, we were drawn to play another First Division side in West Ham away from home. Again we were given no chance, but we shocked them by thoroughly deserving a 2-2 draw.

We brought them back to a packed Racecourse and I felt we were unlucky to lose. Colin Foster scored for West Ham, but the talking point of the game was Tim Breacker tripping Karl Connolly on the way to goal. The ref only booked him when we felt strongly that he should have been sent off as Karl was through. However, it had been a brilliant and unforgettable cup run.

It was following the Arsenal game and during the build-up towards the fourth-round match with West Ham that Mickey hit the headlines again. I'd just finished training when I got a phone call off Flynny to say that Mickey had been arrested for allegedly distributing dud £10 and £20 notes. I was shocked to say the least, but I didn't know the full extent of what he was being charged with until later.

He was accused of selling the notes off to some of the YTS lads. One of the trainees had been caught spending them in the Tivoli nightclub in Buckley and the police later arrested several trainees. During interviews, Mickey's name came up and further investigation led to the police charging him with passing forged notes.

Looking back though, if someone had been selling dodgy notes when I was on the groundstaff, then I would probably have bought some myself! Obviously, I know that it's not right, but as a youngster when you're skint, the temptation is there.

Despite being charged, Mickey continued playing. He would get banter from the opposition fans, but he would make a joke of it in his usual way. The West Ham game at Upton Park saw their fans throwing what we thought was confetti – it was like being in Argentina in the World Cup – but it wasn't confetti they were throwing, it was fake £10 notes with Mickey's head on them in place of the Queen's! Mickey took it all in good part, but when I asked him what he'd done, he said, 'Joe, I haven't done anything; I haven't done a thing.' Being close to Mickey, I believed him.

In August 1992, while waiting for the trial, I again received a phone call from him at about four or five o'clock in the morning. Like most people, I hated the phone going that time of the morning as it usually meant bad news.

When I answered, I thought at first it was some dirty phone call because all I could here was someone whispering, 'Joe-e-e … Joe-e-e.'

I asked who it was and the person on the other end said, 'It's Mickey.'

I asked what he wanted. 'Joe-e-e, I've been stabbed with a screwdriver and hit with a hammer.'

'Who did it, a couple of joiners?'

'Don't make me laugh; they've broken my jaw as well!'

I asked him where he was phoning from. 'Bodelwyddan Hospital.'

Apparently, the injuries he received would have killed a lot of people, but fortunately, as he was so fit, he was OK.

I later found out what had happened: he'd been parked up in a car in a lane between St Asaph and Dyserth with the wife, the only problem was ... it wasn't his wife! It turned out that she knew the two men who had attacked Mickey, while also threatening to cut off his genitals and break his legs! To be fair to Mickey, he made light of the attack and just got on with it, while the fellers who did the attack later received prison sentences.

The trial for the counterfeit money took place at Knutsford Crown Court in July and I went along. I sat in the public area and could see Mickey in the dock; he was looking his usual twitchy self. I sat there with Janice and I could see him looking around until he spotted me. He then began to call out in a quiet voice, 'Joe.'

He called out again, 'Joe.'

So I leaned over and said, 'What?'

'This screw next to me knows your Frank!'

I was thinking, What's that got to do with the trial? Then I noticed the judge looking over the top of his glasses and picking up the counterfeit money to pass round the jury. He said, 'This is a very very good copy.'

With that, Mickey shouted out, 'Yeah, it was a very good machine!'

I knew he was very nervous, but those in court who didn't know him didn't know what he was like: he's funny and likes to make a joke of things, whatever the circumstances.

It was then said that none of the counterfeit notes were found on Mr Thomas, in his house or in his car. But Mickey shouted out, 'I know, because I'd spent them!'

I just couldn't believe it. I was thinking, You're digging a big hole for yourself here. Thankfully it was soon time for lunch.

During the adjournment, Mickey wasn't allowed out of the court area, so I went out to get him a sandwich. When I came back, his barrister came running down the corridor and asked Mickey, 'Who's your best mate?'

'Joe is,' he replied.

'Come with me.'

He then asked Mickey and me to follow him into a private room, where he asked me, 'How do you think it's going?'

'To be honest, not too good, as he keeps opening his mouth!'

I then suggested to his barrister that he should call me into the witness box to give him a character reference. Mickey looked at me and said, 'You're not going in that box?'

'Well, you're going to go, aren't you?' I suggested.

'I'm not going in the box.'

With that, his barrister got up and walked out. When I asked Mickey what he was doing, he said, 'I haven't done anything, Joe, and I know I haven't done anything, so why should I go in the box?' He never did give evidence and I wasn't called for either.

The jury took more than two hours to reach a verdict. He was up on four charges of selling £800 worth of fake notes: on the first, he was found not guilty, but on the next three he was found guilty. He was given bail for pre-sentence reports to be made.

It was about three weeks later that he was finally sentenced. I was in the Isle of Man with Wrexham when the news came through that he'd been sentenced to 18 months in prison. My first thoughts were for him as I knew he couldn't keep still at the best of times, so how was he going to cope with being locked up in a cell? Thankfully, he got through his prison term and has since carved out a good career for himself.

He went to Walton Prison in Liverpool first and then on to Kirkham Open Prison near Preston. While he was there, he asked me to get a team together to play a charity match to raise funds for a disabled girl who lived in the local village. So along with my cousin, Mike Berry, we got a few celebrities together for a Kirkham Anonymous XI against a Stan Boardman XI, who included Flynny, Kev Reeves, Alan Kennedy, Tim Vincent, Derek Hatton and one or two from *Brookside*, including Louis Emerick and Paul Byatt, as well as some other ex-players. I drove the Wrexham mini-bus and we wore the Wrexham kit. The inmates stood around the pitch watching the game, with Mickey's side winning 5-3!

After the match, we went back to the dressing room, but found it had been broken into! They'd rifled through lots of items and I found a pair of boots I'd just bought were gone. I told Mickey and some of his mates, who told a screw. In the meantime, I had to walk over to the officers' mess for a cup of tea in my stockinged feet! Some of the inmates were laughing at me and I said, 'Robbing bastards!'

One piped up, 'What do you expect? You're in prison!' And they all started laughing!

However, within five minutes, a knock came on the mess door and a prisoner came in and asked me, 'Are these your boots?'

I told him they were. I went to put them on and I found a watch in one of them. It wasn't even mine!

It wasn't long after that Mickey made the front page of the *News of the World*, with a picture of him in prison drinking out of a champagne bottle. They were having a crack-down on prisons and the story was about prisoners having an easy life. Mickey was moved to Sudbury Open Prison in Derbyshire and then later across the road to Foston Hall. I visited him and again he asked me to get a team together for a charity game. Alan Hudson (ex-Stoke & England), David Fairclough (ex-Liverpool), Jim Beglin (ex-Liverpool & Eire) and Rob Palmer (ex-Derby and now works for Sky) all played and the game was kicked off by Miss England, Alison Hobson. We won 5-4.

While I was there, Mickey asked me if I'd turn out for the prison side against a police team, which I agreed to. The game was played at Burton Albion's ground and I took the Wrexham kit for us to play in. Our team consisted of a prison officer in goal, three lifers and me in defence; in midfield, there was another officer, Mickey and an armed robber; while up front we had a second armed robber and two lifers. We kicked off and some of the challenges were beginning to get a little bit tasty. I was thinking that, if it kicked off, there was going to be murder! Thankfully, the game went OK, though we lost 3-2. After the match, we were presented with a trophy and the prisoners were allowed a drink before they went back to prison.

During his time inside, Mickey often asked me what he could do when he was released. We'd chatted about this before it all happened, wondering what we would do when our playing careers were over. We'd thought about taking our heavy goods licence. I told him I would contact the PFA as they help ex-players with funding for courses.

Mickey told me he'd received a number of letters in prison from people asking if he would go and do question-and-answer sessions for their clubs when he was released. He asked if I would go with him. I said, 'I'll come with you to support you, but I don't fancy talking in front of people.'

Following his release, I went with him to a couple of these question-and-answer functions. A lot of people would ask Mickey about his career and he was very funny and very good at answering the questions. Obviously as I was sitting there with him, people began to ask me about my career and I would reluctantly tell them some of the experiences that I have mentioned in this book.

Gradually, we began to do these sessions together and it led us to doing after-dinner speaking as well. It was something I thought I could never do. Not that we've done it all that regularly, because standing up in front of a hundred or so people is more nerve-wracking than playing in front of 100,000 fans at Wembley. Anyway, that's what we did when he came out and it helped Mickey get back into some kind of normality, which eventually gave him the confidence to land a job as a sports radio presenter with Century FM who are based in Manchester.

I was in the Isle of Man with Wrexham when I received a call from Mickey, saying that he had been invited to Century FM with the prospect of hosting a football phone-in show which Jan Molby had run before going into management. He asked what I thought and I told him to go for it. He did a pilot show and, within days, they wrote back offering him the job – I'm pleased to say it's since gone from strength to strength for him. I've heard him on the radio and I'm not being biased when I say that he is very, very good. He has also done a lot of TV work with the Manchester United TV channel, MUTV, and also with BBC Wales.

People have called Mickey the 'Welsh George Best' and there are similarities. For a start, George Best served a prison sentence and they both played for Manchester United and had long black hair, though Mickey looks more like the Welsh Yul Brynner or Alf Garnett now! When I first saw his picture in the paper, it was one of the strangest things I'd ever seen. He always had long hair before, but now his is right down to the wood.

I was pleased when I heard that Wrexham were going to allow Mickey a testimonial in 1995. After all, he was skint. However, I knew that one or two of the club's directors were not happy about it because of what had gone on at the club. I didn't agree with them. He had given good service to Wrexham and will forever be known for that goal he scored against Arsenal, when he put Wrexham back on the map and helped turn the club's fortunes around at a time when it was struggling financially.

Wolves were the opposition for the testimonial. Colin Lee, who we'd both played alongside at Chelsea, managed them. Vinnie Jones turned out for Wrexham that night and, as well as Wolves and Wrexham supporters, a number made the trip over from Stoke where Mickey was a crowd favourite.

I still chat to Mickey most days; he's what I call a true friend. When I had my heart operation, he took Janice to visit me in hospital in Liverpool every day. He'd come from Colwyn Bay to Wrexham and then take her back; then he'd go on to Manchester for his radio show. I can't thank him enough for that.

It was also good to see him when he visited because we both have the same sense of humour and like a laugh about the past. I'd say to him, 'Bloody hell, Mickey, I used to get into trouble when I was younger, but you get into trouble when you're older. It should be the other way around. People make mistakes when they're young.'

I can honestly say that I have not met anyone who actually knows Mickey who dislikes him. A lot of people who had a go at him didn't know him. He is a very generous man; he'd give anybody as much counterfeit money as they wanted! Seriously though, he can be too generous for his own good.

CHAPTER TWENTY THREE

GOING UP!

In the summer of 1992, Brian Flynn was looking for a striker to partner Steve Watkin up front. We heard that Chester had released Gary Bennett, so Brian, Kev Reeves, Cliff Sear and myself were talking and I said I'd phone him to find out what he was planning.

When I spoke to Gary Bennett, he was keen to join us. At first, his signing didn't go down too well with Wrexham or Chester fans. Chester fans were pissed off about losing him and Wrexham fans looked on him as Public Enemy Number One. However, he soon won fans over with his goalscoring exploits. Before he joined us, he had a reputation as being a bit of a 'Psycho' – his nickname from Chester fans after his unfortunate clash with Sheffield Wednesday's Ian Knight. However, that reputation soon disappeared at Wrexham; even though he played with enthusiasm and aggression, deep down he was just a big pussycat!

His first season with Wrexham saw us get off to a good start, that was until November when we failed to win and were knocked out of the FA Cup by Crewe. We were absolutely battered 6-1. Not only was it Mickey's last game for Wrexham, but it was also one in which he was sent off. Mickey told me that Craig Hignett had a go at him about being past his best and, with the side getting beaten, he took it out on the next person he saw, which happened to be Tony Naylor.

At that time there was a lot of rivalry with Crewe, who were managed by Dario Gradi. He has worked miracles in terms of bringing young players on and playing good football, but I didn't always see eye to eye with him. Over the years, I have had more than one or two arguments with him on the touchline.

One incident, which stands out, was when I pulled him up about what he'd said to one or two people in the game that I knew. He'd allegedly told them I needed counselling. He was probably right but I wasn't going to have him saying it! So I had it out face to face with him. He categorically denied he'd said anything and asked me to shake hands with him. I did, but to be honest I haven't really spoken to him since. I know I'm not one of his favourite people, but then he's not really one of mine either.

With the loss of Mickey, Brian and Kevin decided to bring in a midfield player on loan. We signed Mike Lake from Sheffield United and he turned out to be a great signing. He was a good passer of the ball, he could tackle and he could head the ball too. From then on, we went on a decent run, losing just three of our last 27 league games, which culminated in promotion as runners-up to Cardiff City – a Welsh promotion double!

With four games to go, we met Cardiff at the Racecourse in front of our biggest crowd of the season, 10,852. It was a great game, which Cardiff won 2-0, but it was tarnished by accusations of racial abuse towards Cardiff's black players, Cohen Griffith and Nathan Blake, who both scored. I can honestly say that I never heard or witnessed any racial abuse – nor would I condone it if it did happen. There is no way that Wrexham FC or their supporters are racially motivated. If you look at the club since, we have had our fair share of black players.

What did tarnish the club that day was the stick that Cardiff manager Eddie May received. (Remember, I'd made my league debut alongside Eddie for Wrexham.) One or two things had been said in the press prior to the game and I do remember a Wrexham fan spitting at Eddie. Whoever spat at him doesn't realise how lucky he was because, if Eddie had got hold of him, he'd have ripped his head off! I was disgusted that Eddie came back to the Racecourse and received that kind of treatment.

We then beat Carlisle 3-1 at the Racecourse and, with York losing at Rochdale, we had to win at Northampton Town to gain promotion. On the way down, we passed hundreds of fans and I put on the theme from *Rocky*, 'The Eye of the Tiger' – as all the lads were trooping off the bus, I had it blaring out. I don't know about the lads, but I felt like Muhammad Ali coming off that bus! In the dressing room, we were really up for it. We knew what was needed...

Over half of the crowd were from Wrexham; it was a brilliant turn-out and I knew there was no way we were going to lose. Gary Bennett scored two goals, one a penalty, and the scenes at the end were unforgettable. I was really pleased for everyone at the club, the fans especially, but also for Brian and Kevin. It had been a constant struggle and we'd nearly gone out of the league, but this was what we'd aimed for and had now achieved. It was a great drive back to Wrexham and quite a lot of alcohol was consumed on board the bus.

On the Saturday, we met Colchester and it was a real promotion party. Almost 10,000 were there to celebrate. I don't remember much about the match, apart from the fact we won 4-3 to clinch the runners-up position, but we had a great celebration after the game with fans flocking on the pitch to cheer the players and staff in the directors' box.

After the game, my mind moved on to my testimonial match. Graeme Souness had kindly agreed to bring along the full Liverpool side to play Wrexham and we had a terrific night. My cousin, Mike Berry, who had done a lot of the organising, along with the rest of my testimonial committee which included Richard Hallows, Kerry Wycherley, Graham Jones, Ron Morris, Geoff Renton and Dave Lovett, arranged for a celebrity game to be played prior to the match.

That game included a number of celebrities and former team-mates of mine, including Alan Hansen, Phil Thompson, Mike Peters, Stan Boardman, Derek Hatton, Rob McCaffrey, Mick Vinter, David Fairclough, Steve Heighway and my brother Frank. We also had Ronald McDonald on the pitch, while the RAF Falcons parachute team provided us with the funniest moment. The Racecourse was a three-sided ground at the time because the Mold Road side was closed. The plane flew over and the parachutists began to fall one by one. It looked fantastic as they came down with coloured smoke pouring out of the canisters strapped to their ankles. However, one of them missed the pitch and went over the hoarding on the Mold Road side of the ground to land on the old terracing! Then we saw a pair of hands on the boarding and the parachutist appeared to what was probably the biggest cheer of the night!

Liverpool brought a very strong side that night. There were also around 2,000 Liverpool fans there, which made me really choked because they didn't have to come over. Along with the Wrexham fans, they made it a real night to remember. The game finished 2-2 and it wasn't like most testimonial games because there were tackles going in. A certain young player by the name of Robbie Fowler came on and scored for Liverpool with more or less his first touch, so I tell people now that I more or less set Robbie out on his career! John Barnes played in that match, while David James came on to play for Wrexham after Mark Morris got injured. I can remember the Kop chanting, 'Sign him on' after he made his first save!

Mark Hughes pulled on a Wrexham shirt for his one and only time that night. He scored in front of the Liverpool fans and was given merciless stick by them as he was a Manchester United player at the time. Jimmy Case also scored a thunderbolt for Wrexham. It was a good night all round. After the game, we had a party in Peppers nightclub, with a host of celebrities, Warrior from *Gladiators*, Denzil from *Only Fools and Horses* and The Farm pop group who had a number-one hit at the time with 'All Together Now' – they had us all singing along with them to it. Brilliant!

That night was followed by a trip to Magaluf for all the Wrexham players as a thank you for winning promotion. It was a great way to end the season! The summer of 1993 saw Brian look to strengthen the side in time for the new season in a new division and it was during the Isle of Man tournament that we spotted a big, strapping centre-half playing for the Northern Irish side Crusaders, Barry Hunter. We watched him playing against Stockport and he was marking Kevin Francis who was about 12 foot! Barry played him very well, as well as anyone we'd seen. Brian eventually signed him for £60,000 and he went on to captain Northern Ireland.

He also proved to be a good signing for Wrexham, a wholehearted player with aggression. He probably overstepped the mark a few times, but who am I to comment on that? Three years later, we sold him to Reading for £400,000, which was a healthy profit. Though we didn't want to see him go, we couldn't stand in the lad's way.

Another influential signing that season was goalkeeper Andy Marriott from Nottingham Forest. We initially signed him on loan, but a couple of months later the club paid out £200,000 to sign him permanently, which still left me as the club's costliest player – apparently I cost £10,000 more!

Unfortunately, Marriott left after he fell out with Brian over the transfer of a promising youngster named Neil Wainwright to Sunderland. We felt Wally, as we called him, should have stayed at Wrexham for another season to get a few more games under his belt, but as a free agent we couldn't stop him and the club received a paltry £100,000 for him.

As for Andy Marriott, Sunderland also paid out £275,000 for him. It was a shame really that he never stayed at Wrexham that little bit longer and the way he left the Racecourse left a sour taste – but these things happen in football.

That season, it was nice to see youngsters who had come through the youth system beginning to get games under their belts. I've already mentioned Wally Wainwright, but also the likes of Johnny Cross, Dave Brammer, Phil Hardy, Scott Williams, Gareth Owen, Waynne Phillips, Steve Watkin, James Kelly, Kevin Jones, Bryan Hughes and Kieron Durkan were all improving with the experience of playing regular first-team football.

Overall, the season was one of consolidation in the league. Having just won promotion, the only real high spot was playing Nottingham Forest in the Coca-Cola Cup. They had future England international Stan Collymore in their side and he scored a hat-trick in a cracking 3-3 home draw, before we lost 3-1 at the City Ground.

In March, Welsh team manager Mike Smith asked Brian Flynn if he would manage the Under-21s side. Brian came and asked me if I would like to help him. I jumped at the chance as it wouldn't clash too much with my job at Wrexham – Kevin Reeves was left to take training while Brian and I were away. It was great to be involved with the up-and-coming youngsters of Welsh football, players of the calibre of Robbie Savage, John Hartson, Lee Jones, Rob Edwards, Danny Coyne, Deryn Brace, Robert Page and Gareth Taylor, most of whom went on to play for the full national side. There was a certain player who was eligible to play for us, but unfortunately we couldn't have him, and that was Ryan Giggs.

We had a good basis for the Under-21s squad and, when we got together, we tried to introduce more of a club atmosphere like when we used to play.

Brian would allow them to have a drink if they wanted one, but we trained them hard at the right time and laughed at the right time.

The first game that Brian and myself took charge of was a friendly in Austria, which we drew 1-1. We then went on to play the 1996 European Championship-qualifying games; we were in a group with Moldova, Georgia, Bulgaria and Germany. We had quite a good record, our best results being a 5-1 home win over Georgia, a 1-0 home win over Moldova and a very good performance in a 1-0 defeat in Germany.

After eight games coaching the Under-21s, Brian and myself were asked to go and see the new Welsh manager, Bobby Gould. Brian had been interviewed for the main job, but it had been given to Bobby. I had a feeling what was going to happen next and told Brian we were going to be sacked. I refused to go and, when Brian phoned me that night, he said, 'Joe, you're right. He's sacked me, but he wants you to stay on.'

Straight away I replied, 'No way. If you're going, I'm not staying.'

Brian added, 'Well, he said he's going to ring you soon.' I'm still waiting for that call!

CHAPTER TWENTY FOUR
CUP SUCCESSES

Back at Wrexham, we were continuing to show improvement on and off the pitch. A mid-table position of 12th was followed in 1994/95 by a similar mid-table position of 13th, but we were one point better off. The highlights came in the cup competitions, the first being the two games with Premier League side Coventry City in the Coca-Cola Cup. We were unfortunate to lose 2-1 at home, but went to Highfield Road and put up a battling performance that eventually saw us lose 3-2, with Jonathan Cross scoring a stunning 20-yard goal.

In the FA Cup we knocked out Stockport and Rotherham in the early rounds and then drew Premier League side Ipswich Town at home. True to tradition, it was another giant-killing act, with goals from Kieron Durkan and a Gary Bennett penalty earning us a 2-1 win. The fourth round saw us drawn away to Manchester United. We were averaging crowds of just over 4,000, but it certainly lifted the town and our allocation of 7,000 tickets was snapped up. It was great for our lads to go and play at a stadium like Old Trafford in front of a full house. We never disgraced ourselves; the worst thing we did was to take the lead early on through Kieron Durkan, which really upset them. They eventually beat us 5-2, with Johnny Cross scoring a cracker late on.

At the end of the season, Wrexham also reached the Welsh Cup Final, which was the last time the club were to play in the competition. In the final, we met Cardiff City at the old National Stadium at Cardiff Arms Park and it proved to be a great day since we won 2-1. Gary Bennett scored both goals. The win meant that we'd qualified for Europe, where Wrexham had a great tradition. As a Third Division club, they had reached the quarter-finals of the European Cup-Winners' Cup in 1976 when John Neal was the manager, but I'd missed out on that run, having left the summer before.

When the draw was made for the Cup-Winners' Cup, nobody had heard of our opponents, Romanian side Petrolul Ploiesti, but I had. The name took me back to my boyhood days when I followed Liverpool who had played them in the European Cup in 1966. The first leg saw us draw 0-0 at home in early August and, when we went over there, I remember staying in a great hotel, but the training pitch was a mud bath. We were also hampered by the UEFA ruling which meant just four 'foreign' players could be used. It forced Brian Flynn to leave out the likes of Peter Ward, Kevin Russell, Tony Humes, Craig Skinner and Bryan Hughes. Paradoxically, that leads me on to the fact that I feel that there are too many foreign players in the game today. Each club should be limited to five foreign players, possibly six, because it's got to the stage where it's stopping many promising youngsters from coming through.

In Romania, we stayed in Bucharest prior to the game and travelled about 45 miles to the industrial city of Ploiesti. We had our final training session on the pitch, during which our full-back Deryn Brace broke his collarbone in a training accident. We were that short, I thought I would get a game, but Brian opted for a young YTS lad, Andy Thomas, who was only 17.

It was a red-hot day and young Thomas did well. We did everything to stay in the game, but they scored on the hour and went through 1-0 on aggregate. It certainly wasn't a disgrace to lose to them, because they were a decent team. It was to be Wrexham's last game in Europe and the only way we're going to get back into Europe now is if the Welsh FA brings us back into the cup, otherwise we're going to have to enter the Eurovision Song Contest!

Back to the bread and butter of league football and we had begun to show we were a team capable of holding our own in the Second Division. The 1995/96 season was no different and we finished in our best position (8th) since returning to the league, missing out on a play-off place by just three points. That season had also seen the return of Kevin Russell to the Racecourse. He had been a great success in his first spell at the club, but he'd probably played for another 90 clubs before he came back to us!

Peter Ward was also a major signing that season from Stockport. He had a great left foot, was very aggressive and great at set-pieces – he was also a winner. He is coaching at Stockport's centre of excellence now and I wouldn't be surprised to see him go into management as he's got all the qualities.

Wrexham once again shocked the football world with yet another successful FA Cup run in 1996/97, which put the town back on the map. However, the cup run almost ended embarrassingly in the first round when we only beat local rivals Colwyn Bay after a replay. We then went on to beat Scunthorpe United, again after a replay, before being drawn to play West Ham at home.

The first game caused a rumpus after Harry Redknapp complained it shouldn't have been played because of the amount of ice and snow on the pitch. Bryan Hughes put us ahead, but they equalised through a Portuguese player by the name of Hugo Profirio who apparently hadn't seen snow before! After the match Harry Redknapp, who I have a lot of respect for, said we'll see how they play when we get them on a decent pitch.

Prior to the replay, the TV show *Blue Peter* invited me and Tony Humes, Bryan Hughes and Karl Connolly to appear as a surprise for the presenter, Wrexham fan Tim Vincent, who was leaving. They wanted us to take penalties. When I took my penalty, I hit the dog on the head, which thankfully wasn't shown on TV! We also presented Tim with a signed Wrexham shirt.

In the replay at Upton Park, we played some good football, before Kevin Russell scored a spectacular goal in the last minute. We held on to win on what was a very decent pitch. In football, you should always be careful what you say since words have a habit of coming back to haunt you!

It was great to see a young lad by the name of Mark McGregor starting to make his name in the side by this time. Cliff Sear and I had had him training with us on Monday nights on the club car park. In fact, there were a lot of youngsters in the team who had come through the youth policy, players like Phil Hardy, Bryan Hughes, Gareth Owen, Steve Watkin and Karl Connolly who'd come from non-league.

The next round saw us drawn away to Peterborough United, which everyone thought would be a formality after victory over West Ham. It proved to be a tough game, but we were to knock them out 4-2 after twice coming from behind.

That was enough to earn a tie with Birmingham City at St Andrews. Birmingham were in Division One, but were still a big club. Twenty-two thousand were in the crowd, including a large following from Wrexham. Steve Bruce headed them in front, but we hit back with goals from Bryan Hughes, Tony Humes and Karl Connolly. A lot of people still say that this was one of the best cup-ties Wrexham had ever played away from home. After the win over Birmingham, Brian Flynn splashed out £100,000 to bring Gary Bennett back to the Racecourse.

It was great for the club to be in the quarter-final draw for the third time in our history, but it proved to be a bit of an anti-climax when we were drawn against fellow Second Division side Chesterfield. Everybody had high expectations: after all, a side from Division Two was certain to reach the semi-finals. But Saltergate isn't the biggest of grounds and everyone wanted tickets. On the day, what made it worse for us was that it was to be a dinnertime kick-off owing to the game being televised live. Players' body clocks are geared for three o'clock kick-offs and it certainly had an effect.

For the Chesterfield game, I travelled across with Brian Prandle, now chief scout at the club. We arrived at the ground early and went into the dressing rooms. They really were drab – basically, after playing at the likes of Birmingham and West Ham, we were hoping that it didn't all go wrong at a place like this. Sadly for us, that's what happened. The lads just never produced a performance to match previous rounds.

Unfortunately, we lost to a terrible goal following a mix-up between Deryn Brace and Andy Marriott, with Chris Beaumont nipping in to score. From then on, we never came back. To be fair, they thoroughly deserved their win on the day.

Chesterfield went on to meet Middlesbrough in the semi-finals at Old Trafford and they were very unfortunate indeed not to have reached the final. I honestly believe that, if we'd met Middlesbrough the way they played that day, we would have beaten them. Chesterfield were unlucky to lose because they had a perfectly good goal disallowed by ref David Elleray, who should have kept to being a school teacher!

With the cup run over, Wrexham picked up on their mid-table league position and went on to finish once again in 8th place – with one point less than the previous season which at least showed we were consistent!

The summer of 1997 saw the opening of Colliers Park, Wrexham's new training ground. It cost in the region of £500,000 and it was one of the best bits of business the football club had done in years. It was something Brian Flynn had pushed for with the directors. They bought a piece of land on the outskirts of Wrexham, near Gresford, which was transformed into a state-of-the-art training ground as good as anything in the Premier League. Over the years, we have had the likes of England, Wales, Barcelona, Rangers and West Ham, to name a few, use the facilities for training prior to big games and they have all been impressed with them.

It was a massive change for us because over the years we had trained at the likes of Stansty, Lindisfarne, Wrexham Rugby Club and even on the club car park! It was absolutely brilliant for the club to have their own training ground once again. We did train at Stansty during my first two spells at the club, but due to the club's financial difficulties it had to be sold off. The new facilities mean we can attract more youngsters to the club, just like when I first joined the club during the John Neal era.

It was to be a rather mediocre season until around February; the only highlight until then had been the FA Cup tie with our biggest rivals Chester in front of the Sky TV cameras at the Deva Stadium in December. Almost half of the 5,000 crowd were from Wrexham. The game had an added edge to it because Gary Bennett was playing for them, having returned in the summer. Thankfully, he failed to score, but he received a great reception from the Wrexham fans, which was a miracle in itself. However, on the night we ran out 2-0 winners with two goals from Karl Connolly.

The next round saw us play Premier League side Wimbledon at Selhurst Park where we deservedly earned a scoreless draw. However, in the replay we were unlucky to lose 3-2 and it was shortly afterwards that we managed to push ourselves into the play-off reckoning in the league and took it right down to the wire. We went into the last game of the season at Southend, knowing we had to win and that both Gillingham and Bristol Rovers had to drop points.

With a tremendous following behind us, we won the game 3-1 and, at the end of the game, our fans were telling us that both Gillingham and Bristol Rovers had drawn. Just when we were on the verge of celebration, we heard that Rovers had scored six minutes from time to clinch the last play-off place. Their game had been late in kicking off. Unfortunately, we finished 7th on goal difference which was nonetheless a great tribute to the club.

That season had also seen the emergence of another one of the youngsters that Cliff and I had brought through from our Monday night coaching sessions – Neil Roberts. I took a lot of satisfaction from the fact that he had broken into the first team and he has since gone on to play for the full Welsh national side. He was one of the best youngsters I have coached in terms of attitude.

At the end of that season I had asked Brian and Kevin to let him train with me through the summer. Every day, we were out training along with a great mate of mine, Mal Purchase, who trains the local boxers in Wrexham and is a fitness fanatic. I knew Mal would put Neil through it and get him super-fit.

It certainly paid off as we eventually sold Neil on to Wigan Athletic for £450,000. So, if anyone wants an example of perseverance and attitude, they needn't look any further than Neil Roberts. People were undecided about his abilities but he never let his head go down and came back because he stuck at it with the right attitude.

CHAPTER TWENTY FIVE

IN A RUSH!

Everyone at the club was looking forward to the new campaign but, after last season, the only improvement we could make was a play-off or promotion place. Life had also been made more exciting by the fact that Brian had persuaded Ian Rush to join us.

Following his release by Newcastle, he had been training with us and Brian persuaded him to play in the pre-season Isle of Man tournament. That caused a lot of interest and, from talking to the fans over there, they all wanted him to join up. Rushie was probably the biggest signing that Brian could have attracted to the club.

As well as playing for Wrexham, Ian was also looking to get more involved in the coaching side of the game, so one of the conditions in his contract was that he would help me run the reserve side, like I used to help Cliff. His debut came against Reading at home in the opening game of the season and a crowd of almost 7,000 turned up to see us win 3-0. Ian never got on the score sheet in that match which was to be the story of his season with us – amazingly he never scored a single first-team goal!

That wasn't because Ian Rush had suddenly become a bad footballer.

Without being disrespectful, he was playing with a different type of team-mate at Wrexham. Rushie was making runs that our lads couldn't see and, when he did get through, he never seemed to get the rub of the green to score.

Some people thought he was a flop. I didn't think he was a flop. A flop is when people don't do anything. Ian contributed a lot to the club. He gave a lot in terms of training, where the likes of Neil Roberts, Karl Connolly, Andy Morrell and the young lads looked up to him. They could all learn off him in the way he presented himself and how he had looked after himself to play at the highest level as long as he did.

Rushie was getting more involved in the coaching side of the game, helping me with the reserves. I remember his first game away at Sheffield United where I said to him, 'I'll do the talking and you can have your say after.'

He told me that he didn't want that yet; he wanted to listen and pick up the experience. We worked well as a pair and well before the end of the season he was giving team talks like a seasoned pro. The lads would hang on to every word he said because they respected the fact that he knew what he was on about. The only goal he scored for Wrexham came in a reserve game at Lincoln. After scoring, he looked over to the bench and I promptly took him off!

By now, Wrexham were struggling just below halfway and overall it proved to be a disheartening season for both Ian Rush and Wrexham as the club dropped to a lowly 17th position, just three points above the dreaded drop. It therefore gave us something to put right next season. We felt that the team and the squad had begun to show cracks and, with hindsight, I believe that we should have changed things. However, we stuck at it.

Following Mark Hughes's appointment as Welsh manager in December 1999, I was given the opportunity by Mark to leave Wrexham and become part of the new Welsh set-up. I was flattered, but I felt I had a job to do at Wrexham and turned the offer down. It might sound daft, but I really didn't want to give the job up. I enjoy seeing the youngsters come through and, if I'd gone with Wales, I feel I'd have been letting Wrexham down. It's a decision I haven't regretted and Wales have been absolutely brilliant under Mark.

That season, we had made one or two changes; we brought in Kevin

Dearden from Brentford, Ian Stevens from Carlisle, David Lowe from Wigan and Craig Faulconbridge from Coventry who earned himself a contract. One major signing was made in September, namely Darren Ferguson, who had been playing in Holland.

Darren is the son of Alex Ferguson and he had won a Premier League medal with Manchester United before leaving to join Wolves. It must have been difficult for him playing for his father, but he has been a tremendous asset at Wrexham. Darren's got a great attitude: he wants to win every game as well as every five-a-side in training.

He's a player who wants to go that extra yard and, if he upsets people on the way, so be it. I'd much rather have people like that in my side who you know are going to get the best out of themselves and their team-mates. He makes an ideal captain, but I think it's fair to say that, when he first came to Wrexham, we had a little bit of a run-in. He was taken off in one of the games and came and sat in the dugout. He'd made it clear he wasn't happy. He then said something to me, so I turned round and told him straight that, if he wasn't happy, I'd see him in the dressing room where I'd knock his head off! We both have a very similar temperament. He's fiery and so am I.

I told him that he had been taken off for the good of the team and that he had to accept that decision. To Darren's credit, he came to me the following day and apologised, saying he was out of order in what he did. To me, that is a sign of the man. We've had a few more disagreements since, but he's still the type of player I'd pick in my side. I think that, if he'd had that yard more pace, he would still be playing in the Premiership.

Wrexham were in the news again after beating Kettering Town in an FA Cup replay, which was screened live on Sky. A win over Rochdale at home saw us drawn against Premiership side Middlesbrough at home in the third round, which brought memories of Wrexham's win over Boro in 1973/74 flooding back to me. There was a great crowd of almost 12,000 to see the likes of Christian Ziege, Festa, Gary Pallister, Paul Gascoigne and Juninho playing at the Racecourse. Brian Deane put Boro in front, but we hit back to win with goals from Robin Gibson and Darren Ferguson. The atmosphere was electric and it was a great win by us that day. Unfortunately, we were deservedly knocked out in the fourth round at home to Cambridge when our fans' expectations were high, but we could have no complaints about the 2-1 defeat.

Back to the league and we'd shown improvement from the previous year, though we finished in a mid-table position of 11th.

The summer of 2000 was overshadowed by news of the death of a great friend and working colleague of mine, Cliff Sear. Dixie McNeil had been in charge when he made what was his best-ever signing – bringing Cliff Sear to Wrexham Football Club. The club's youth policy at the time was very poor, so, when Dixie heard that Cliff had fallen out with Harry McNally at Chester, he offered him the chance to join his home-town club. Cliff was well respected in the game and is known to have discovered Ian Rush for Chester, but he was also first on the scene to sign up Michael Owen for Wrexham at a young age, which quite a lot of people don't know.

One of the first players Cliff picked up came after a tip-off from one of the coaches at the club, Idris Pryce, who had done great work with youngsters over the years. He recommended a young lad by the name of Chris Armstrong who went on to play at the top with Tottenham Hotspur. I went along with Cliff to see Armstrong playing for Llay Welfare in the Welsh National League. We soon found out that he was too good for that level and Cliff invited him in.

As I gradually came to the end of my playing career, I began to help Cliff more and more with the reserves and eventually became his assistant. I learned a hell of a lot from working with him. He wasn't one of these stop-start FA coaches; he would do it in his own way. Kids don't like coaching to be too complicated and Cliff believed in doing it the man-management way and in passing on his experience, which he did.

For me, Cliff Sear was one of the reasons Wrexham brought through so many youngsters because, when Flynny took over, he would just ask Cliff which ones were ready and Flynny would trust his judgement by playing them in the first team. He had good judgement of young players.

Gradually I began to take over the reserve team and I started to implement my own brand of coaching which I had partly learned from experiences throughout my career, but mostly from working alongside Cliff. Hopefully Wrexham have seen the benefits of what I picked up alongside such a great coach.

On the playing side, the summer period was an important time for Wrexham as we lost the services of Karl Connolly on a Bosman move to QPR, while we signed our first overseas players, Hector Sam and Carlos

Edwards, who arrived from Trinidad. It was my cousin, Mike Berry, a football agent, who had brought them over the previous season for us to look at. Brian, Kevin and I had seen a tape of them playing and had been impressed with what we saw.

Hector Sam had also interested Crewe, but I pulled a few strings with my cousin and suggested he brought them both to us so they could keep each other company. Anyway, they came over, trained with us and played a reserve game at Shrewsbury. They did look a bit out of place at first, but you could see they had something.

Brian brought them back over and eventually, after lots of red tape, they signed for us. There is no doubt they have both improved since they've been here. Hector, we know, can be a little erratic, but he can also be a top-class player. I feel he could be as good as Dwight Yorke if he would just knuckle down and work that little bit harder. He twists and turns brilliantly and needs to believe in himself a bit more.

Carlos Edwards, I believe, could play in the top flight now. He has pace, he can run inside and outside, he can strike a ball, but he will be the first to admit he can improve a bit on his crossing. There again, everyone can improve no matter what level they are at. But I do believe that he is good enough to play at the highest level now.

A year later, we brought in another Trinidadian in Dennis Lawrence. When people first saw him, they thought he'd never be a good centre-half; first of all he was ten foot tall! Secondly, he was built like a floodlight; people thought he was cumbersome and played a bit like Bambi, but he's proved everyone wrong. We knew he had something. Both Dennis and Carlos were in the Trinidad Army, so they were disciplined and never let things get them down. They are mentally tough and, whereas Dennis was getting a bit of stick early on for some of his performances, he stuck at it and won the fans over. He has become one of the first names on the team sheet.

That summer also saw us sign Michael Blackwood, a left-winger from Aston Villa, and Lee Roche on a 12-month loan from Manchester United. The latter was signed through Brian's connections with Alex Ferguson and he proved to be an excellent signing for the club and won an England Under-21s cap while with us.

Another interesting signing that summer was a French-Moroccan by the name of Emad Bounane. We were told he was a left-back by his agent and we played him against Manchester United in Brian and Kevin's testimonial match during the close season. He played very well in the game; he had the size, he had the pace, and we signed him on a year's contract. He never spoke very good English, but he was a character. I got on very well with him; he used to call me 'The Crazy Man'. I would take him in for weight sessions, which he would do anything to get out of. He would also rub me up the wrong way by trying to play himself out of tricky situations. He became a crowd favourite very quickly, but as a former defender myself I used to do my head in! If he went upfield on an overlap, he'd want a taxi to bring him back. He'd just stroll back.

We found out later – after he was getting criticised within the club for the way he defended – that he was actually a left-winger. I remember one incident in the reserves at West Brom; we were winning the game and at half-time I'd been telling him not to take any chances. At the start of the second half, he had the ball on the goal-line close to the corner flag and he tried to dribble his way out. He lost the ball, they crossed and equalised. I went absolutely berserk with him. I began shouting at him, but he turned a deaf ear and said he didn't understand. Despite the reserves winning 2-1, I was still fuming in the dressing room over the goal we'd conceded. I told him that, in that situation, he had to get rid of the ball. Then he said, 'Oh no, I look for solution.'

I told him, 'No, the solution is you hoof the ball over the halfway line because it could end up in the back of our net as has just happened.'

By this time, the rest of the lads had started smiling and laughing. I told them to get changed and be on that bus in ten minutes. All the kit was put on the bus, all the lads got on, but there was no Emad. I returned to the dressing room and there he was still in the bath shampooing his hair. I told him he had two minutes or the bus would be gone and he thought I was joking. I went and sat on the bus and the next thing we saw was Emad running out with shampoo still in his hair and soap still in his eyes, half-wet and half-dressed in his tracksuit. From that time on, he was never late for the bus again.

However, I had a lot of time for Emad. He was a nice lad, but he was never going to be a defender, though I do believe that he would have fitted into the system that Denis Smith later introduced at Wrexham with two wing-backs. He was quick, six foot tall and a natural left-footer. I liked him a lot and I'd like to think he respected me. Even after he left, he would ring me up asking for advice as he went for trials in Belgium, or with QPR, Hartlepool and Swindon. If I wasn't in, he would leave a message: 'This is a message for you, Crazy Guy...'

During that season, we also signed Lee Trundle from Rhyl. I'd gone to watch him four or five times before we actually signed him. I couldn't make up my mind about him. He would come out with his collar up, a bit of a tan and plenty of oil on him. He had all the tricks; he was taking throw-ins, taking corners and taking free-kicks but I just couldn't make my mind up. Brian and Kevin watched him and thought the same. Brian then arranged a friendly with Rhyl at Belle Vue and he scored a hat-trick, including two beautiful chips. Brian said to me, 'Get him in.' The following week, he joined us on trial and played in a reserve game against West Brom.

It was during that game that I remember the ball being knocked out from the left-back position to just over the halfway line. In one swift movement, Lee brought the ball down with his left foot and, before the ball hit the floor, he'd smacked it against the post. If that had been a Brazilian, you'd have read about it. Gary Shelton was in the dugout next to us and he turned to me straight away and said, 'Who's that?'

I quickly replied, 'Oh, he's only a lad we've signed on a two-year contract.' He was only on trial!

Lee turned out to be a good signing for us. He was at Wrexham for just over two years. He was a crowd-pleaser, had some great tricks and he could score goals. When he first got into the team, he was scoring for fun. They weren't just tap-ins; they were spectacular. It was unfortunate how it ended up for him at Wrexham: he upset a lot of fans when he said that he'd wanted to play at a higher level and he dropped a division to join Swansea, but the lad did really well with Brian and Kevin.

The partnership Lee Trundle had the following season with Andy Morrell was exceptional. Rob McCaffrey, who I'd known as a young TV reporter from my Liverpool days, had recommended Andy to me. He asked me to have a look at a lad who wanted to break into football. He was playing for Newcastle Blue Star in the Northern League at the time and worked in a health club in Leeds.

I suggested sending him to us and, to be fair, Brian would let anyone come in and train with us. He did well and we then played him in a friendly against Connah's Quay. Robin Gibson, our own player, came running in to head the ball and headed Andy in the face, fracturing his cheekbone which put Andy out for at least six weeks. Brian and Kevin told him to go away, get himself fit and come back in.

He came back at his own expense, started playing for the reserves and did very well. He scored an awful lot of goals for me in the reserves and I thought he deserved his chance in the first team long before he got it. He was never a regular until the arrival of Lee Trundle and the pair of them hit it off in their first game together in a 3-2 win at Walsall in February that season.

Andy later moved to Coventry City and he deserves every success he gets. He is a great clubman, a great goalscorer and a player who always gives 110 per cent. When he left the club, he sent me a nice card thanking me for helping him at Wrexham. Again, I always like to think that, if you treat players the right way, they'll respect you.

We finished that season in a mid-table position of 10th, which wasn't too bad considering the amount of movement in and out of the club that season.

CHAPTER TWENTY SIX

THE END OF AN ERA

The season hadn't started brilliantly since there were one or two problems behind the scenes. You could tell something was not right. Brian had been trying to get money to bring in one or two players, but he was blocked in his attempts to sign Jim Whitley despite having arranged for him to come in.

Results-wise, the season hadn't started well and, a week or two before he eventually left, Brian again tried to bring in players to try and change things around. With a year left on his contract, he told the board that, if they weren't going to back him now, he might as well leave at the end of his contract. He wanted to find out if the board were prepared to back him.

The final nail in the coffin came when we lost 5-0 at Tranmere, completing a run of one win in eight games since the start of the season. That was on the Friday night and, on the Saturday, Brian phoned me to tell me that he'd received a call from the club and that he thought we were about to be sacked. I was going to Port Vale for a scouting trip with Brian Prandle since we were playing them on the Tuesday night. I told Brian I might as well go and do the report anyway because someone would need it, to which he agreed. He told me we were required at the ground at 9am on Monday morning. In the meantime, Brian rang me a couple of times that day, as well as on the Sunday, to confirm what he'd been told. He categorically said, 'The three of us are going.'

To which I replied, 'OK then.' After all, we were a team.

On the Monday, we reported to the Racecourse and were met by a chap named David Hughes, who had been doing some work at the club on behalf of the chairman, Pryce Griffiths. His first reaction was to say, 'What are you doing here?'

We went into director David Rhodes's office and David Hughes told Kev and me, 'You're not getting sacked; we just want to see Brian. I don't know what you two are doing here...'

Brian then answered, 'Hold on. The three of us have been told to come here.'

He replied, 'Well, not to my knowledge.'

Kev and I said we'd hang around anyway. Brian went upstairs to the directors' room and, after about 20 minutes, came down and said, 'I'm gone. They want to speak to you now, Kev.'

Kevin went up, came back down and said, 'I'm on my way too; they want to see you now, Joey.'

So I went up fully expecting the same treatment. David Rhodes said to me, 'Brian and Kevin have gone. You can have the same deal as them, but we haven't got anyone to look after the team for tomorrow night. We were hoping that you could manage the team tomorrow to help us out.'

Obviously, I love the club, so I told them I would have a word with Brian, but before I left the room, I again asked if I was going on the same deal. David Rhodes replied, 'Oh yes, you can go on the same deal.'

I went down and had a word with Brian and Kev and told them what had been said. Brian replied, 'Yeah, you go on and do it, Joe, that's OK.'

So I went back up and told them that I would do the job tomorrow, but with the senior pros, Kev Russell, Darren Ferguson and Brian Carey. It was like the old joke really: the Englishman, the Scotsman, the Irishman and the Welshman! The board were quite happy with that. To be honest, I was very disappointed – gutted, really – that Brian and Kev had gone. After all, we'd been working together as a team at the club for almost 12 years since October 1989.

Despite my dispute with Brian, I'm glad to say that we are friendly again now, but, while Brian was at Wrexham, I felt he was unfairly criticised by a lot of people. I thought he was absolutely brilliant. He was the longest-serving manager the club had ever had; he got the youth policy up and running again to the extent that it was on a par with what John Neal achieved at the club; he was the inspiration behind the building of the training facilities at Colliers Park. I feel he was, and is, a top manager. I honestly do and I am very surprised that he hasn't managed a bigger club.

When we were players together at Wrexham, I always knew he would go into management because of how organised he was. We were invited over to Canada to do some coaching by Mike Povey, who was from Wrexham but also had something to do with the Canadian FA. We'd been asked to do soccer clinics with Derek Johnstone and Bob Wilson. We were chatting one day and Brian said he'd like to be a manager; I remember asking him, if he ever got the chance to take over at Wrexham, would he? And he said, if the option arose, he would.

A year later, when Dixie McNeil left the Racecourse, I phoned Brian to tell him. I thought he was the natural successor to Dixie. One or two people at the club had asked if I would be interested in doing it, but managing the first team is something I've never been interested in. It's never been my style – either you want to be a manager or you don't and I've never had the urge to do it. I was quite happy to back Brian for the job. As I said, he appointed Kevin Reeves as his assistant and me as his first-team coach and, to be fair, over the years the three of us worked well together. If Brian said he wanted something done and Kevin and I disagreed with him, he would listen and would sometimes change his mind. At other times, I would say something and Brian and Kev would say, 'No, that's not right,' but at the end of the day Brian had the final decision.

In terms of team selection and players he wanted to sign, he would always ask for our opinion and he would also take a two-to-one decision. As a threesome, we worked quite well together. Basically we knew what we wanted as a team and as a club. We had very similar ideas and that's a sign of any good partnership. One thing that bugged me was Brian being criticised for sitting up in the stand during matches, while Kev and I were in the dugout. I didn't agree with the criticism because people watch from different areas. Brian thought he would get a better view from the stand, while Kev and I were at ground level. We had no problem with that. At half-time, Brian would let us know about any changes he wanted during the second half.

Nobody complained when we won promotion; no one complained when we reached the FA Cup quarter-finals – but, as soon as things started going wrong, they would look for faults and the result was criticism that Brian should be in the dugout.

Another problem certain people had was the fact that, throughout his time with Wrexham, Brian lived in Burnley. Those people probably didn't know that he lived in Wrexham five days of the week. He used to stay in the Trefor Arms in Marford and, contrary to what people thought, the club never paid for that. He did!

Brian used to be at the ground, or the training ground, at eight o'clock in the morning. I lived two and a half miles down the road and I couldn't get to training for nine o'clock! That's how committed he was to his job and this club.

There was another side to Brian that not many people have seen outside the confines of the dressing room. Believe me, he could lose his temper with the best of them. I've seen him go berserk, shouting and raving, kicking buckets, throwing whatever he had in his hands. Kev and I then had to balance his performance out with a completely different act. But, of course, there were times when it worked the other way round and Brian would be the good guy. When he was manager at Wrexham, he had the chance to go to bigger clubs, something which was never made public. Because people understood how good a job they were doing at Wrexham, both Brian and Kev were widely respected in the football fraternity.

When Kevin joined Wrexham, he moved his family to the area. He had been one of the first-ever million-pound players and had played for England twice, though I'd wind him up by calling him the one-cap wonder! He was also on the substitutes' bench for England when Wales beat them 4-1 at the Racecourse.

He used to say, 'It's a good job I never came on.' But I used to answer back, 'Yeah, because it would have been double figures!'

He was a completely different character to Brian. I'd played alongside Brian at international level, but had only played against Kevin. He was very laid-back, but cared 110 per cent about football. He was passionate in every job he did; he would do it to the best of his ability. He was a very good player, but very underrated, I thought. He played in the 1981 FA Cup Final for Manchester City against Spurs, but he was to have his career terminated prematurely because of injury. He became a great coach and one of the nicest fellers you could meet in the game. He wouldn't have a bad word to say about anyone; I've got an awful lot of time for him.

He's got a great sense of humour and we had some great laughs together. I used to take the mickey out of him once I found out that, when he was coach at Birmingham under John Bond, he had Lee Sharpe, who later went on to play for Manchester United, Leeds and England, but Kevin released him! Well, it was the club who released him, but I used to say that it was him! So, whenever he recommended a player, I would wind him up by saying that I'd have to have a look at him as we couldn't rely on his recommendation!

At times, Kevin was very quiet and very inoffensive, which is why I think the three of us got on so well. We had just the right chemistry! For people who don't know me, I am quite shy if I don't know people, but on the other hand I can fly right off the handle, which happened numerous times in the dugout.

There were a number of occasions when this happened. A couple of managers I'd had run-ins with who spring to mind are Neil Warnock and Dario Gradi. I also had many a bust-up with opposition players in the tunnel which supporters never heard about purely because, if anyone attacked a Wrexham player verbally, we would stick up for the lads and the club ourselves. A lot of fans don't realise the number of flare-ups that take place in the tunnel at half-time or at the end of a game. I've had players by the throat and they've had me by the throat, but it's all part of the game as far as I'm concerned. To be honest, I quite enjoyed it!

In all the years that I have been in the dugout, I've only been sent to the dressing rooms once. It was during a relegation battle at Northampton in March 2002 and, in all honesty, it had nothing to do with me. It was a big important game for Wrexham and we were getting beaten. One of their players, Paul McGregor, was fouled by Kevin Sharp, which led to Sharpy being sent off. Just after that, McGregor went down again after another innocuous challenge in front of the dugout. I told him what I thought of him, but referee Rob Styles thought I'd said it to him and stopped the game.

He came across to me and ordered me out of the dugout. I then remonstrated with him because I'd not aimed the words at him. In the end, a policeman came over and grabbed me! I gave him a bit of verbal and he threatened to arrest me! I eventually went into the tunnel and booted the door open. It was then that the stewards arrived, wanting me arrested for booting the door. In his report, Rob Styles, reported me for calling him a 'f***ing c**t'. In all honesty, I never said that. I just don't use the 'C' word. He was totally out of order because I know I never said that.

I then wrote to the FA denying what was in the report and stating that, in all my years in the dugout, I had never once been in trouble. I have full respect for match officials, but after that my respect for Rob Styles went straight out of the window. He's not been out of the news since and I feel he's a ref who likes to make a name for himself at the expense of others. Despite that, I still had to pay my £500 fine!

Over the years, the three of us have had some great laughs. Kev and I had a very similar type of humour, and, though Brian can be quite serious at times, he does like a laugh too. Brian was very meticulous, but Kev and I would do things which would trigger each other off. Brian was very neat and tidy, but when he left the room, Kev and I would swap the phones over, put his books the wrong way round, stick crumbs on his desk and hide his pens. We'd then make a rapid retreat since we knew he would go berserk, but we'd be outside laughing!

In terms of management, I thought Brian was spot on. I honestly did. We had some great games at Wrexham under Brian. He led us to promotion to Division Two in 1993. He established Wrexham in that division and we came close on numerous occasions to reaching the play-offs. His record speaks for itself.

Unfortunately, at the beginning of the 2001/02 season, we struggled and that, combined with what went on behind the scenes, resulted in him leaving the Racecourse. People had been saying for a while that he'd taken us as far as he could, but I for one certainly didn't believe that.

He made some good signings for Wrexham and he also made the club a lot of money by selling at the right time. People should also not forget the cup runs that we had as well as our games in Europe. I felt Brian did everything right, especially taking into account the fact that he never had an awful lot of money to back up his efforts. He did spend £200,000 on

Andy Marriott, but, compared to other clubs Wrexham were playing at that time, it was nothing.

Look at the players Brian sold and the players who came through the youth policy that he and Cliff Sear had set up. For me, his record is fantastic. That's my opinion and nothing will change that because I know how he works. I had great times with Brian and I think what happened to him and Kevin after they had saved the club from relegation to the Conference was a disgrace.

Anyway, I stayed at Wrexham and I did the Port Vale game with the lads. We changed the system to play with two wingers, which we felt the fans wanted to see. We did our best, but lost 3-1. After the game, the directors asked if I would look after the side again on the Saturday against Peterborough United. The team had a two-week break before the next game, which would give them more time to appoint a new manager. Again I spoke to Brian and he said, 'Yeah, do it.' I told him that, after the game, that would be it. We changed the team for the Saturday, leaving out the two wingers, Robin Gibson and Michael Blackwood, as we had still only won once in nine games – we thought we would make it harder for them to beat us. We actually did quite well, but lost 2-1. We were obviously disappointed in not getting a result, but at least I was consistent. Two games in charge – lost them both!

After the game, I was asked if I would take the training until the new manager was appointed. Again I agreed to do so and, in the meantime, there were a number of names being mentioned of managers who might take over – people like Colin Lee, Barry Horne, Jimmy Mullen and Dixie McNeil, but it was the ex-York, Oxford, Sunderland, Bristol City and West Brom manager Denis Smith who actually got the job, and his name hadn't even been mentioned!

Following his appointment, Denis phoned me up and said he wanted me to be his assistant. I said straight away I didn't want to do the job. I told him I had been with Brian and Kev for years, which was why I would be leaving. He asked if I would give it a week until he saw how the club was run. I was in charge of the reserves and Denis's first game was a reserve game away to Preston. We were about three down after 20 minutes and lost the game, which ended up something like 7-4. After the game, Denis again asked if I'd stay on, but I said, 'No, I'm going.'

The chairman, Pryce Griffiths, who I get on very well with, then called me in for a meeting with himself, David Rhodes and Denis Smith. He immediately asked, 'What's all this about?'

'I think I'm going to go on the same agreement that Brian and Kev had.'

David Rhodes then said, 'We haven't got an agreement with you.'

I flew into a rage straight away and we had a heated argument.

Pryce told me, 'If you walk out the door, you won't get a penny.'

I couldn't afford to walk out and so I said that I would do the reserves until the end of the season – and then go. I refused to do the kit which caused more of a row. Most clubs have a kitman, we don't! Kev Reeves and I had done the kit between us ever since George Showell left. Though a lot of people might not think it's a big job, it is a responsible one, especially in this day and age when all the shirts are named and numbered on the back. Quite frankly, it can be a pain. You have to pack it all and make sure it all goes back in the skip at the end of each game. Then, when we get back, I have to throw it in the right piles for Marlene, the wash lady, to clean the next day. Anyway, I told them I'd do the reserves to the end of the season then I would be gone.

It was hurting me like hell because I love the club, but I also didn't want to fall out with Brian and Kevin because they could have got the impression I was staying on intentionally, which in effect led to a big bust-up between me and Brian. I'd been phoning Brian to inform him about what was going on and, for one reason or another, he said something down the phone which I reacted to.

The next morning, I wasn't just fuming, I was going berserk. I turned up at the training ground with steam coming out of my ears. I phoned Kevin up and asked him what was going on. I told him what had happened on the phone with Brian and added that, if I got hold of Brian, I'd paste him! I asked Kevin, 'What does he want me to do? I've informed him of what's happening. They won't pay me up, so what does he expect me to do? Walk out? I can't afford to walk out.'

I had been put in a distasteful situation where I was getting it from both sides. I love Wrexham Football Club and I also wanted to be loyal to Brian and Kevin, but the two sides were conflicting. A few months later, I found out that I needed a heart operation and all this aggro didn't help; Janice said I'd been getting very short-tempered. One thing is certain: I personally wasn't feeling at my best, which I'd put down to football at the time. Eventually, I decided to get my head down and do my job because I was still a professional and I'd always carry out my duties to the best of my ability. However, it was becoming widely known that there had been trouble between me and Brian – we'd been mates for years – and it was sad that it had come to this.

Denis Smith's first game in charge was at home to Queens Park Rangers and he asked me to join him on the bench, but I told him it was a new regime and I would take a back seat. By then, he had asked me my opinion on who he should appoint from within the club as his assistant and I put Kevin Russell forward straight away. I knew Kevin was completing his 'A' coaching licence and would be perfect for the job; he was also nearing the end of his playing career. I decided to stay in the background, though Denis would ask for my advice – I would sit and watch the game, taking notes for him and then having a chat at half-time.

Gradually, I'd begun to calm down over that telephone conversation with Brian, but when I've got something on my mind I have to get it off my chest – once that's happened, I'm all right as I don't hold grudges. I'd said to Kevin that I would catch up with Brian one day, but he was fortunate I didn't catch up with him until about four months later. I'd gone scouting to watch Everton playing Sunderland in a reserve game at Widnes. I walked up the stairs and there were Brian and Kevin, together with a number of other scouts, and I knew then that Brian couldn't avoid me. I approached him and said one or two things to the effect that he was lucky I wasn't knocking him all around the room! I expressed one or two home truths to him and Brian said one or two things to me, which showed, to be fair, that he didn't realise what had gone on. It cleared the air and, from that day on, I'm pleased to say we've been mates again.

I continued to train quite hard with the lads, but I was beginning to feel more and more tired every minute of the day; again I put it down to the job and everything that had been going on. After training, I would go out with my dogs for a walk around the park at Erddig and I found myself struggling to get up hills. I reasoned to myself that I must have been getting old and didn't think any more of it – that was, until one morning when I was driving to training. I was coming off the dual carriageway and, all of a sudden, I began to get this strange sensation which seemed to start in my stomach and then move up to my ribs. I felt myself being pushed further and further back into my car seat; it was like something was trying to break into my ribs with a hammer.

It only lasted a few seconds, but it was a really weird feeling. I am convinced that, if there had been stationary traffic around, I would have hit it as I couldn't see a thing. When I reached the training ground, I sat in my car for about ten minutes. My head was spinning, but I got myself together, went into the changing rooms and made myself a cup of tea. I then got changed and took the lads out training.

After training, I went home and told Janice what had happened, but I never thought any more about it. About three or four days later, I was in the car park and bumped into Keith Park, the club doctor. He asked if I was all right. I said yes, but told him about my funny turn and straight away (he has since told me) he knew that something was wrong.

A week later, Keith came up to me with an envelope and told me to take it to the hospital. I saw a Mr Cowell. He examined me, X-rayed my chest and, within ten minutes, told me I required a heart operation. I asked what he meant. He showed me the X-ray of my chest, which revealed that my heart was swollen. He told me that he was almost certain, without me having a scan, that I would need a valve replacement.

My first reaction was, 'Well, what if I don't have the operation?'

He replied, 'Within twelve months, you will have heart failure.'

When someone puts it like that, well, you have the operation! I had a scan the next day, which confirmed I needed the operation. I then had a monitor fitted to check out the heart and, later that day, I took charge of a reserve game at Tranmere!

I tried not to get too excited, which I found very difficult as we were being beaten. I had to wear the monitor for a week and, in the meantime, I had to go to Broad Green Hospital in Liverpool for an angiogram. That's when a doctor inserts a small tube into a blood vessel and then injects an X-ray dye which makes the vessels visible when the X-ray pictures are being taken. This allows the doctor to determine how well the blood is moving through the vessels of your heart.

Brian Prandle had driven me to the hospital and, when we went in, the nurse asked for my name, address and profession. She then looked up at me and BP and said to him, 'Can you go in that room there and get changed?'

He quickly replied, 'It's not me, it's him.'

When we were in the room waiting, I said to him that they must have thought that he looked ill!

Anyway, I went in and had the angiogram, but, true to form, like Frank Spencer, when they removed the wire from my groin, they couldn't stop the bleeding. The nurse said it usually took about ten minutes; I was there half an hour! I then had to go up to the ward where I had to lie flat on my back for between four and five hours to make sure the bleeding from my groin didn't start again before I could be discharged.

Before being released, I had to wait to see the surgeon who was going to tell me the results of the angiogram. But he was called into surgery, so I said I'd get them the following week because BP had returned to collect me. I'd been in the hospital for over 12 hours. I went back the following week and the surgeon told me that I would have to come in. He asked me when would be the best time and I said as soon as possible. I had the operation within a month.

This had all come as a bit of a shock since I had been fit all of my life – I was still only 47. It was a worry not just for me, but also for Janice and the rest of the family. It was like every operation; there was a risk with it, though thankfully the survival rate is high. I had the operation at Broad Green Hospital and beforehand, I had been told, I would be going into intensive care for 24 hours.

When I eventually came round, they took me back up to the ward. Janice and Mickey were there waiting for me, but I still felt half knocked out with the anaesthetic. Even so, I can remember Mickey looking at me and saying, 'Pity they didn't operate on your face because you're an ugly bastard!' which I had to laugh at.

The next day, I felt as good as possible in the circumstances. The nurses got me up to have a shower, but while I was in there I felt terrible. I felt as if I was going to collapse and fall over. I managed to get out, put a towel round me and sat there with sweat pouring off me. The nurses came in and took me over to my bed. They wired me back up to the monitors and saw that my heart had gone racing off, which meant they had to slow it down. After a couple of days, they got it back down.

I had been expecting to be out of hospital within four or five days, which I had been told would happen if everything had gone all right.

However, true to form, I ended up being in there for three weeks! After I had recovered from the operation, they had me walking up and down the corridor and going outside.

However, after a few days, I began getting dizzy and bouncing off the walls. I didn't want to say anything because basically I wanted to get out of the place. This happened again the next day and I told a male nurse who put me back on my bed. Then they ran some tests and found out that, after the operation, I must have had a slight infection, which had caused fluid to build up around my heart. That's why I was struggling. Mr Morrison, another heart surgeon, who had come to see me a few times, began talking about me having a pace-maker fitted, but he wanted to leave that option out as long as possible because of the job I was in. For the three weeks I was in hospital, the only thing that kept me sane was the fact that the 2002 World Cup was on.

I still didn't feel 100 per cent and they decided I needed another X-ray, which showed that fluid had built up. They said that they would have to drain it and I had to go back into the theatre. They drained a litre and a half of the stuff from around my heart! Apparently, when it was taken out, a theatre nurse said you could see the colour return to my face. I then had to stay in for a few more days to make sure my heart had gone back to normal. I asked what would have happened if I'd gone home and all this had occurred. I was told that it would have killed me! I was lucky therefore to be in hospital when it happened.

I finally got the OK to go home; I was so relieved. The nursing staff at Broad Green had been brilliant – I can't speak highly enough of them. I hadn't been the easiest of patients because I was so used to being active. I couldn't do all the things I wanted to do, like take the dogs out, and I used to upset Janice a lot with my moaning. One of my best mates, Mal Purchase, helped by taking my dogs out every morning before he went to work and George McGowan came around and cut the grass – great mates.

I'd had the operation in May 2002 and, by the time the lads had started back at training in July, I'd already begun visiting Wrexham's training ground at Colliers Park, as well as going to rehab at the Queensway Sports Centre. I was there with other patients and gradually got back into it. I'd gone from lifting these really heavy weights before my operation to lifting these very light dumb-bells after it. My mate Mal worked at Queensway and he'd be looking through the windows laughing at the weights I was picking up. I wasn't too bothered, though; after what I'd been through I was just glad to get hold of something and begin exercising again.

Denis Smith and the lads at the training ground also looked after me by making sure I didn't overdo things, since my first impulse was to rush straight back into my old routine. I eventually finished my rehab and got myself back in time to be in charge of the first reserve game of the season at Wigan. Mind you, I wasn't 100 per cent ... and neither was the team. We got stuffed 5-1! It was just good to be back.

CHAPTER TWENTY SEVEN
CURRENT AFFAIRS

Having recovered after my heart problem and returned to work at Colliers Park, I would be lying if I said that it hasn't affected my day-to-day routine. I do look at life differently now and one noticeable difference is that I don't worry about stupid things like I used to. I have always been a bit of a worrier, fretting over things like the team and whether we had been doing the right things. As a player, I would worry about everything, although most people took me for a happy-go-lucky type of person.

As far as coaching goes, it does mean I can't join in training sessions like I used to. When I first got back into helping out with training, I was tempted to join in. It was like coming off drugs really. I had always loved joining in training sessions with the first team and the kids and I definitely suffered withdrawal symptoms.

However, as I've passed my 50th birthday, I now stand back and, to be honest, it doesn't bother me that much. I still train but not as hard as I did before my operation. I have to take tablets every day and also visit the heart specialist, Mr Cowell, at the hospital every six months for a check-up.

Other than that, I have had no problems since my operation and I'm just happy to be here.

Looking back on my career though, I have a lot to thank my wife Janice for. If it hadn't been for her, I couldn't have been a footballer because basically it was Janice who kept me on the straight and narrow – with the help of my mam and dad of course. Off the field, she was the biggest influence that I could have asked for and she deserves more credit than anybody for what she has had to put up with over the years.

As a player – if we'd lost a game or I personally had had a bad game – I'd always take it home with me and, for a few days afterwards, I imagine that I was far from being a pleasure to live with. That's only because I cared about the game, but I really couldn't have gone through it all without her. I know that for a fact. She has been the biggest calming influence on me: a real diamond.

I have often been asked whether my son Darren was going to become a professional footballer, but I never ever pushed him into it. When he was a kid, I was always out kicking a ball around with him in the garden like most fathers do and when he got older, if he ever wanted to play football, I'd go on the field with him.

To be honest, he wasn't a bad player; he could kick with both feet, but he basically just wanted to play with his mates. He did play for the local Brickfield team in Wrexham and then for Druids and Hightown, but by the age of 15 or 16 he told me that he didn't want to play any more. I respected that.

But he still retains an interest in football and, like me, has a keen interest in both Wrexham and Liverpool. To be fair to him, he's been a great son in terms of the way he has behaved – he has never caused trouble like I used to! And most of that is down to Janice. He certainly wasn't spoiled, but he has always been polite and straightforward as a kid. He's a smashing lad and I couldn't have asked for a better son, and he has a lovely partner in Renay. Luckily, he's now a plumber, so I can always 'tap' him for a few bob!

Someone who has been spoiled, though, is my beautiful grand-daughter Mia Louise, who was born in August of last year. Apart from crying every time she sees me, she has given Janice and I a new lease of life; we cannot see enough of her and we look forward to watching her grow up.

Away from football, my dogs take up most of my leisure time. As a young kid, I always went on at my mam and dad about having a dog and, when I finally got one, I never did anything with it because all I wanted to do was go and play football. That first dog was a Terrier named Rex, which died from distemper.

When Janice and I got married, the first Christmas present I bought her was a Cocker Spaniel called Jake, which turned out to be a great pet despite Janice not liking him at first because he would hang on to her jeans! She would walk around the kitchen with the dog attached to her leg! He lived until the grand old age of 18. We then had another dog, a yellow Labrador called Brandon, which we bought for Darren really. However, he became a bit aggressive with other dogs, but still lived to be 12.

I have always loved walking my dogs and it was during these walks that I seemed to come across strays. I would usually hand them over to the police or the dog warden, but I actually kept one once. I found this dog and spent four or five hours walking around looking for her owner before heading for the police station. They put her into kennels and then, a few days later, Janice asked me about the dog, wondering if she was still in confinement. I phoned them up and the dog was still there. When she saw me, she began jumping around the pen as if she remembered me! We had to have her back, but it cost me £80 to get her out even though it was me who had put her in there! We named her Beauty and we've still got her now. She's been a great housedog.

I've since had a white Staffordshire bull terrier called Taff. I'd always wanted a 'Staff' and, like a lot of people over the years, I'd been put off by the reputation of the breed, but I wouldn't hesitate to recommend them. He is a smashing dog, a real character.

To me, dogs are very relaxing. If I ever feel stressed out, I take the dogs out for a walk and, while I'm out and about, I meet so many people. Fishing used to be my way of relaxing, but I don't go any more. I now think it's cruel to kill fish! I eat them, but I can't kill them! I've turned into the opposite of everything I used to be.

One other sport I enjoy is boxing. I am full of admiration for boxers and what they do. They have tremendous dedication in the way they train. It's a lot harder training like that than the way footballers train. Plus, when they get in the ring, they're on their own; they haven't got ten others to help them! If I hadn't been a footballer, I might have been a boxer, but I'm not sure I would have been any good! I had the aggression, but whether I would have had the skill for it, I don't know. One of my sister's boys, Joey Clarke, was a good amateur boxer and boxed for Wales. Mickey Thomas's lad, Aaron, is no slouch either. He is now a Welsh champion.

I have twin sisters, Sue and Kath. They are five years older than me and it was probably quite hard for them when I was a kid, since I was always on at my dad to buy me football boots. I remember Kath saying to him at one time, 'I don't know why you are buying him football boots; anyone would think he was going to be a footballer!'

Deep down, they were very supportive, despite not having much interest in football. They never came to watch me, but did come to the FA Cup Final at Wembley in 1977. Sue is the mother of my nephews, Joey, Shane and Little Frankie as we call him. Kath has two girls, Nicola and Lisa. I don't see them as much as I should, because in all honesty I haven't gone to Llandudno as much as I used to since my mam and dad passed away. But, like all families, if anything happens we're all there for each other and, when I went into hospital for my operation, they were very caring. I still keep in close touch with my brother Frank and his lad Josh has played for Llandudno in the Cymru Alliance.

I'm no different really from the many people who say that their mam and dad were the best in the world. My mam and dad always had to work and, with four kids, they never really had much. Many a time they would go without to look after us as kids, but there were always plenty of laughs in the house. However, they were both strict when they needed to be and they tried hard to keep us on the straight and narrow, which they mostly achieved, though I was the one who caused most of the problems for them. Whenever I did get into trouble, they were always there for me and would still back me up even though I was in the wrong – but boy would they let me know about it after!

If they had given out caps for playing bingo, then my mam would have been a record-breaker! When people used to ask what my mam did, I would tell them that she played bingo for Wales! She loved her bingo. My dad didn't venture out much – he wasn't a big drinker – but they would both go down to the local Legion or Labour club for the odd night out. They kept themselves to themselves really, but they looked after us as well as they could. We actually lived in a two-bedroom flat before moving to our house in Ffordd Las, which was a bit like moving into Buckingham Palace!

It was a big loss to all the family when we lost our mam in July 1994. She died of liver cancer and my dad died three years later. They were very sad times for all of us.

As I have already mentioned, Janice's mother, 'Ag', lived with us for many years after we'd got married. She had virtually brought up Janice and her sister Denise on her own, but she was like a second mum to me. I couldn't have asked for a better mother-in-law. We've had some great laughs. Denise has been like a sister to me as well over the years and her husband Graham gave Janice away at our wedding. When I lived in Moreton, they lived next door to us and he worked for Merseyside Police. He would come along to most of Liverpool's home games with me, but sadly he passed away in December 2001, leaving Denise and their two smashing daughters, Jane and Emma.

Since my playing days ended, I have received two very prestigious awards. The first came in September 1993, when, along with Neville Southall, I was awarded the Freedom of Llandudno and presented with a scroll, which is now framed in the hallway of our house. People don't ask me what it entails because in all honesty I don't know! I always thought I'd had the freedom of Llandudno when I was with the 'Parrots'!

I think in those days they would rather have locked me up than given me the run of the place! Joking aside, I must say that it was a great honour to be recognised by my home town for my achievements in football.

The other award I received came in December 2003, when I was presented with a 'Golden Cap' as one of only 22 players to have won 50 caps or more for the Welsh national side. Half of the players had been presented with their cap prior to the game with Serbia and Montenegro a month previously, but I was invited along to receive mine at the European Championship play-off with Russia at the Millennium Stadium in Cardiff. It was the first time I had visited the new stadium and it was a nice time to go, but unfortunately the result wasn't the best. I'd travelled down to the game with Darren and his partner Renay's dad, Neil, so we made a day of it.

Along with the likes of John Mahoney, Brian Flynn, Cliff Jones, Terry Yorath, Leighton James and Ivor Allchurch's widow, we were presented with the cap at half-time. It had my name on it, as well as the number of caps I'd won. However, I soon found out that it wasn't really made of solid gold; it was just gold in colour!

In all honesty, it was another great honour for me and, as I received the award, I couldn't help thinking back to all the memorable games I had played for Wales. It also made me think of my dad and the fact that it had been his dream for his lads to play professional football. This cap was for him.

Shortly after the Russian game, it was revealed that Yegor Titov had failed a drug test following the first leg; he was later found guilty of having taken a banned substance, which led the Welsh FA to seek the expulsion of the Russian team from Euro 2004.

I reckon several other members of the Russian team had been taking drugs because I remember standing in the players' tunnel awaiting the presentation of my 'Golden Cap' when the players came off at half-time. As they came walking past me, one of them sneezed and I felt great for a month after that!

That brings me up to today. As I come to the end of this book, Wrexham have been placed in administration and have consequently been docked ten points. It has been a very difficult time for all concerned at the club, with staff not being paid on time on several occasions, electricity being switched off (meaning cold showers after training) and phones being cut off too.

All this has come about following the sale of the club by ex-chairman Pryce Griffiths to former Chester City chairman Mark Guterman in April 2002. No one batted an eyelid when this deal went through – apart from the fact that he had previously been with Chester – but events have since proved we should have been more vigilant.

I knew something was wrong when, in the last league game of the 2003/04 season against Brighton & Hove Albion, the fans raised red cards in disapproval of Guterman. To be honest, I didn't have a clue what was going on, but it soon became apparent that something was wrong. First, it was rumoured that the players wee not being paid on time, then we found out that other things were not right too. To be honest, it was all rather confusing to me!

I tried to keep away from the politics of what was happening, but I could not fail to notice what happened in the first game of the 2004/05 season at home to Swindon Town. I was aware that the fans had marched through the town prior to the game in protest at Alex Hamilton, but at the start of the second half I noticed something happening in the middle of the Kop end of the ground. It soon became apparent that the club's owner and now chairman, Alex Hamilton, had walked in to that part of the ground. God knows what he was trying to do, but it certainly infuriated the fans.

Since then, Wrexham have been unable to pay their bills, which inevitably led to the Inland Revenue issuing a winding-up order against the club. To save the club going out of business altogether, it was placed in administration. This brought about an automatic ten-points deduction under the Football League's new administration rules.

What has happened at Wrexham I wouldn't wish on anyone in football. It seems the sole reason that these people came to Wrexham, a club with a proud 133-year history, was because they saw the ground as a potentially profitable property deal. They do not seem to care about the feelings of anyone concerned, the fans or those who work at the club.

By the time you are reading this book, I just hope that this chapter in the history of Wrexham FC will have come to an end and that we will have a new owner in place who actually cares about the club.

The gloom was lifted slightly when Wrexham reached the final of the LDV Trophy. It meant a day out to the Millennium Stadium in Cardiff for the final against Southend United. At least it gave all the fans something to feel good about, and it was made even better when we went on to lift the trophy with a 2-0 win. Juan Ugarte and Darren Ferguson scoring the goals. It was a memorable day for Denis Smith, the coaching staff, players and especially for the fans. Let's hope we have more days like it.

Despite what's happened at Wrexham, I'm still very much involved with the coaching side of things. I really do enjoy being involved in the day-to-day running of the club and being able to work with the promising youngsters there. Our School of Excellence is now very well run, showing how far we have come since the days of me and Cliff Sear taking the youngsters training on the club car park on wintry Monday nights; we used to play under a single light that was fixed to a telegraph pole in the car park, which I always thought was highly dangerous. When you ran away from the light, you could actually see in front of you, but when moving the other way, the glare blinded you. I always said to Mick Buxton and Cliff Sear, 'Someone's going to get seriously injured here one day,' but luckily they didn't. The facilities were absolutely terrible.

It is a credit to the coaching staff at the club that we've had so many lads make the step up into the first team. Time has moved on and Wrexham Football Club have moved on – certainly as regards the development of youngsters through our School of Excellence, which is expertly run by the likes of Steve Weaver and Steve Cooper – and long may it continue.

There's plenty more to come on the conveyor belt, which is exactly what a club like Wrexham needs, but looking back on those nights on the car park, the youngsters at this football club today don't know they were born!